FRENCH'S MEDICAL HALL
KIELYS
AFTON
AFTON

JFK
In Ireland

FOUR DAYS THAT CHANGED A PRESIDENT

RYAN TUBRIDY

LYONS PRESS
Guilford, Connecticut
An imprint of Globe Pequot Press

First published in 2010 by Collins
First Lyons Press edition, 2011

Lyons Press in an imprint of Globe Pequot Press.

Library of Congress Cataloging-in-Publication Data
Tubridy, Ryan.
JFK in Ireland : four days that changed a president / Ryan Tubridy.—1st Lyons Press ed.
p. cm.
Includes bibliographical references and index.
ISBN 978-0-7627-7257-5
1. Kennedy, John F. (John Fitzgerald), 1917-1963—Travel—Ireland. 2. Visits of state—Ireland. I. Title
E842.47.T83 2011
973.922092—dc22
2011016383

Printed in China

10 9 8 7 6 5 4 3 2 1

For Ella and Julia
My little dotes

MRS. JOHN F. KENNEDY

January 22 1964

Dear Mr. President

I do wish to thank you with all my heart - for coming to my husband's funeral - and for bringing with you the Irish Cadets - who had moved him so a few months before in Ireland - and who then moved the world at his grave.

I am only grateful for one thing in these sad days - that he did have the chance to return to Ireland as President of the United States last summer. That trip meant more to him than any other in his life - He called me every night of it and would tell me all that had passed in the day.

He would never have been President had he not been Irish. All the history of your people is a long one of overcoming obstacles. He felt that burden on him as a young Irishman in Boston - and he had so many obstacles in his path – his religion, his health, his youth. He fought against each from the time he was a boy, and by always striving, he ended as President –

He was so conscious of his heritage – and so proud of it – and Ireland can be proud that they gave the United States its greatest President. Now those words may sound the words of a bereaved wife – but in a generation that is what they will be teaching to school children.

I know your country mourned him as much as his own country did – and through you I thank them for that –

I will bring up my children to be as proud of being Irish as he was. Already our house is

3)

MRS. JOHN F. KENNEDY

named Wexford - and they play with those beautiful animals - the Connemara pony and the deer. Wherever they see anything beautiful or good they say "That must be Irish" - And when they are old enough I will bring them there.

Please thank Mrs de Valera for me for her most touching letter which you gave me. She taught him poetry - which he remembered and often said to me - and tried to teach his daughter -

All the most moving things I have read about his death have been Irish poetry - "Who to console us now, Sean of the Gael" - and so many others.

I send to you and to Mrs de Valera - two cards - One was how he looked during the campaign, the youngest one - and the other as President -

4) How it aged him in less than three years –

I know we were all so blessed to have him as long as we did – but I will never understand why God had to take him now –

I send you my deepest gratitude –

Sincerely

Jacqueline Kennedy

A letter from Jacqueline Kennedy to President de Valera, thanking him for attending her husband's funeral.

The Irish tricolour comes alive for JFK as children from local schools dressed in orange, white and green rainwear rush to greet him in Galway.

Contents

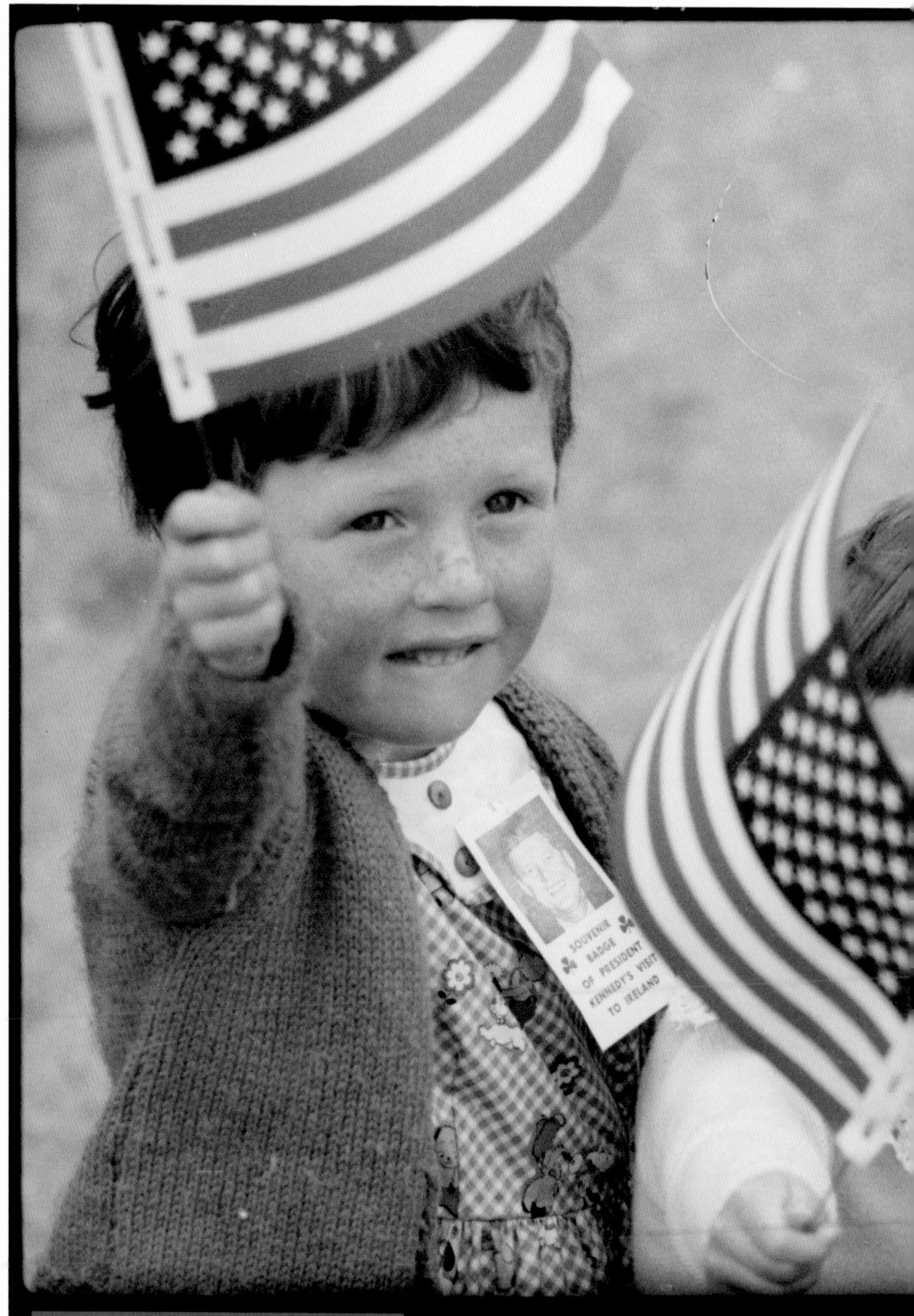

Badge of honour: three small children cheer JFK during his Irish visit.

PROLOGUE

Kenny O'Donnell, the President's right-hand man was flabbergasted. "Ireland?" he said. "Mr. President, may I say something? There's no reason for you to go to Ireland. It would be a waste of time. You've got all the Irish votes in this country that you'll ever get. If you go to Ireland, people will say it's just a pleasure trip."

Nobody thought it was a good idea. Not the American media, not the presidential advisers, nobody. But President Kennedy had made up his mind and when O'Donnell went back to the President the following day to relay this message, Kennedy looked up at him from his newspaper "with an air of exasperated impatience". "Kenny, let me remind you of something," he said with a distinct air of finality and authority. "I am the President of the United States, not you. When I say I want to go to Ireland, it means that I'm going to Ireland. Make the arrangements."[1]

It was meant to be a band-aid trip to key European allies, an attempt to show them that America cared as the Soviet beast breathed down their necks. Italy demanded a visit, Germany needed attention, England desired a distraction and France sulked. But there were bigger problems at play; Italy was between governments and there was an ailing Pope in the Vatican. In Germany, Chancellor Adenauer's government was in disarray after the *Der Spiegel* affair. In England, Harold Macmillan was suffering through the extraordinary Profumo Affair, which saw his War Minister caught lying about his affair with a call-girl who happened to be sharing a bed with Russian naval attaché Eugene Ivanov. The thought of America's glamorous young president popping over for tea was political manna for the electorally beleagured leaders of Europe.

June 1963 was as busy a month as any for President Kennedy. He had some significant dates in his diary and he had some housekeeping to attend to. In the latter category fell his appointment with Governor John Connolly of Texas. The two men needed to discuss the

President's visit to Dallas some five months later. In the former category, Kennedy delivered his "Peace Speech' in which he addressed nuclear weapons and atmospheric test bans and urged the world to "cherish our children's future". But there were domestic problems too as the Kennedy administration confronted one of the great seismic struggles of twentieth century American politics, that of civil rights.

At home, the media natives were getting restless; the *Washington Post* made the wry observation that "Ireland is the only country the President will visit that has what can be described as a firmly-established and durable Government" while in a reference to the race riots in the South, Senator Hugh Scott said "I'd rather see him go to Birmingham (Alabama) than Berlin just now".[2] The spring of 1963 saw Birmingham inflamed with racial tension as the civil rights movement, spearheaded by Dr Martin Luther King Jr, sought to overthrow the bastions of racial segregation.

"It would be difficult to dream up a more unjustified and time-wasting trip than the one on which President Kennedy is scheduled to embark", trumpeted an indignant *New York Herald*, before adding, "In Rome Mr. Kennedy will find neither a Pope nor an established Government; in London he will find a Prime Minister with other things on his mind. In Germany, too, he will find something in the nature of a 'lame duck' Government." This grave assessment of the international situation was capped by a side-swipe at the other "explanation of the trip – the sentimental call of Dublin and the Kennedy ancestral town of New Ross; but surely his Irish friends would understand that urgent Congressional and racial problems required his continued presence in Washington at the moment."[3]

And yet, the man who was always interested in history and global politics, the man who started life as a journalist and had visited Europe on the cusp and in the aftermath of World War II, wanted to go to. He not only wanted to go, he felt entitled to a little something for himself. John Fitzgerald Kennedy wanted to visit the land of his forebears. He wanted to go home.

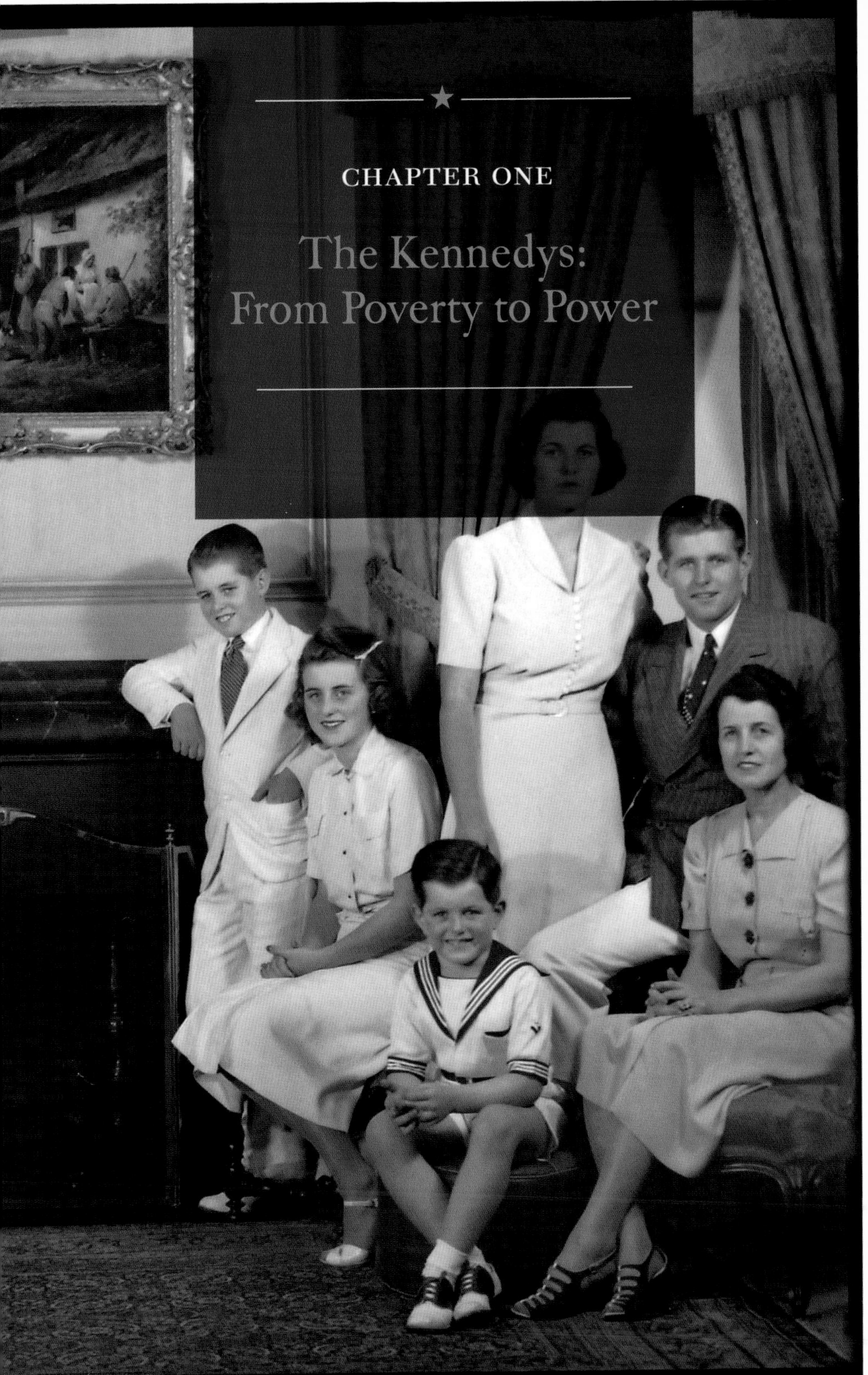

CHAPTER ONE

The Kennedys: From Poverty to Power

—★—

Ireland in the 1840s was a country on its knees. It was a time that robbed a nation of a generation. The exodus that took place saw the kernel of the Kennedy clan take hold on the shores of Boston. Here was a family forced together by the horrors of history. John F. Kennedy's great-grandparents fled the greatest disaster that this island ever witnessed – The Great Famine. Caused by the blight of the potato crop in 1845, this killed a million Irish men, women and children in the course of five years, an eighth of the island's total population, while another million fled the plights of starvation and disease.

It is hard to put this catastrophe into context as there is a distinct lack of contemporary reference, or indeed deference, to this tragic episode. Yet it was our Holocaust, it was the wind that sent our people like feathers from a pillow to all corners of the globe and particularly to Britain, Australia and the relatively youthful USA. Boston especially was a natural fit for the Irish. Like an exaggerated Dublin, the leafy city was as near to Ireland as a homesick peasant was going to get.

Among those who fled was John F. Kennedy's great-grandfather Patrick Kennedy, who left New Ross, County Wexford, in 1848 for Liverpool from where he sailed to Boston. The fact that the third son of a Wexford farmer managed to cobble together enough money to pay for his voyage was an achievement in itself. While most of those on board that boat to Boston were fleeing poverty and almost certain death, Patrick saw his move to America as a search for something better. Like so many others of his generation, he would never see his parents or his brother and sister again.[4]

Either during the voyage or more probably when he arrived in Boston, Patrick met a fellow Wexford woman, Bridget Murphy.

The two married in Boston, had four children and Patrick supported the family through his work as a cooper, making barrels and casks. It was in Boston that four families – the Fitzgeralds and the Kennedys, the Murphys and the Coxs – would mix, work and intermarry. It was here too that the upwardly mobile next generation would endeavour to shed their links with the old country. To this second generation, Ireland would represent a past without promise, a land of impoverished indignity and political impotence.

The Land of Opportunity was a harsh one for immigrants of all nationalities, but the Irish were on the lower rungs of society in 19th-century America and the attitude to them was ugly. Job adverts frequently read "No Irish need apply" and they could only find accommodation in ghettos, nicknamed "Paddyville" or "Mick Alley", despite the fact that by 1850, a third of the population of Boston was Irish. They were seen as filthy, hard-drinking Catholics, under the thumb of the Pope. They also spoke in an accent no one could understand but their own people. Most Irishmen found work as manual labourers, and the paltry salaries meant they had to live in slum conditions. The only way to survive was to work long, back-breaking hours, and although the shops stocked plenty of food, unlike those back in Ireland, the Irish couldn't afford to buy much of it. Like many of his fellow immigrants, Patrick Kennedy died prematurely after just ten years of this new life.

Alone, with four children to raise, Bridget embodied what would become the Kennedy work ethic. She worked as a shop assistant, took in lodgers and cleaned houses. When she had saved up enough money, Bridget bought the shop she worked in, expanded the business and started selling groceries and alcohol. She was going to raise her family's standard of living through sheer determination and grit, even if it killed her, as it had her husband.

Patrick Joseph Kennedy (John F. Kennedy's grandfather) was just one year old when his father died. Given that three in ten children living in American cities perished before the age of one in the mid-19th century, and the fatherless were more vulnerable than most,

O'Cinneidiġ, ċosnaṁ ga,
Ar Ġleann fairsing réid Omra,
Sliocht ar n-Duinnċuain, tré ċródacht,
Na fuinn fuair gan iarmóracht.

O'Cinneidigh, wh
Over the wide sm
The race of our D
Obtained the land

—from a poem by Giolla-na-

Lorcan, King of Munster

Kennedy, [son of Lorcan] had three brothers Cosgrach, Lonnargan and Congal from whom are many families . . . .

Brian Boru, son of Kennedy . . . King of Munster, then of Leath-Mogha and lastly Monarch of all Ireland . . . slain at the great and memorable battle of Clontarf . . from him his posterity took the surname of O'Brien . . .

Donnchuan, [brother of Brian] from whom are— O'Kennedy . . . . . .

— extracted from the Linea Antiqua of Roger O'Ferrall, 1709.

— from a seal used by Cornelius O'Kennedy in 1582.

Patrick Kenn
of the County of Wexf

Patrick J. Kennedy = Ma
of Boston in the
State of Massachusetts

Joseph Patrick Kennedy = Ros
Ambassador of the
United States of America
at the Court of St. James
1937 – 1940

Joseph

John Fitzgerald Kennedy = Jacqu
President of the United
States of America

John Fitzgerald Kennedy

s the javelin,
eann-Omra,
an, who through valour,
ıt dispute—

)'Huidhrin, d. 1420.

ckey

hter of
is Fitzgerald.
Boston, 1906,
– 1914.
ive in U.S.
395–1901, 1919.

e, Robert F. Edward Rosemary Kathleen Eunice Patricia Jean

e III

ne Bouvier

Genealogical Office, Dublin, Ireland.

The Kennedy coat of arms and family tree. Down the left side are the names of Kennedy ancestors, beginning with Lorcan, King of Munster. At the top of the chart is an excerpt of a poem by Giolla that dates back to 1420.

Patrick J. Kennedy, paternal grandfather of JFK.

it was a miracle that he survived at all. Known to all as PJ, he left school at fourteen and worked on the Boston docks. Like his mother, he was a good saver and with some financial help from Bridget, PJ bought his own saloon in East Boston. By the time he hit thirty, PJ owned three such saloons and ran a side business importing whiskey.

Around Boston, PJ Kennedy was seen as a fixer, somebody who could get things done, a good guy who was always ready to do a favour for you. He dispensed advice across the bar in his saloons, helping men to find jobs and mothers to get medical help for sick babies. He had an ability to listen, as well as an eloquence that won him friends wherever he went, so when he decided to run for public office in 1884, he had plenty of people willing to vote for him. He was a perfect fit for the offices he was about to win, first in the Massachusetts State Legislature and later in the State Senate. The brief generational journey from a devastated port in Wexford to the state political ladder was not typical – not unless you were a Kennedy – but he was setting a pattern for the generations to come.

With his professional and political situation in hand, PJ turned to the personal, and for this he set his sights on Mary Augusta Hickey. Always aiming slightly above his station, PJ didn't mind that Mary was from a "better" Irish-American family, wealthier than his own; he knew his mind. Opportunities for social advancement were limited in the notoriously snobbish world of Boston high society, particularly if you had Irish Catholic heritage, and Mary knew it. This was a society that was as anglicised as it was rarefied. The rulers of this pompous roost were the Boston Protestant élite – the so-called Boston Brahmins, made up of a select number of Boston families who celebrated each other at parties, in politics and in toasts:

And this is good old Boston,
The home of the bean and the cod,
Where the Lowells talk only to Cabots,
and the Cabots talk only to God.

Yet Mary Augusta Hickey was won over by PJ's affability and ambition and in 1887 she duly became Mrs Mary Kennedy, then gave birth to a son on 6 September, 1888. Rather than calling her first-born after his father, as was the norm, the class-conscious Mrs Kennedy christened the boy Joseph Patrick, and as he grew older, his mother always introduced him as Joseph.[5] His friends would call him Joe. The Irish name Patrick was a scar from an unwanted past that she preferred to remove.

Over the next decade, life improved for many Irish-Americans and none more so than for Mary and PJ. In 1901, the respectable couple sent young Joe to Boston Latin, a Protestant secondary school that boasted such alumni as Benjamin Franklin. Joe stood out from the start. Despite being one of a handful of Catholics in a Protestant school, the boy thrived and was so popular among his classmates that he was elected class president. He did well enough at school to be accepted as a student at Harvard University, where he played on the baseball team.

Harvard boasted a number of college clubs, which granted privileged access to the Old Boys' Network and should have given Joe a headstart in one of the big brokerage firms in Boston. However, despite his popularity and his many achievements at Harvard, to the well-groomed Wasps of Ivy League colleges, Joe was still a 'Mick'. He had two strikes against him: he was too Catholic and his family's money was too new, so he found himself blackballed from the most influential clubs. Kennedy would never forget this rejection.

History had different plans for Joseph Patrick Kennedy and all who would follow him. Left to blaze his own trail, Joe got a job as a bank examiner and in 1913, he made his first big deal when he borrowed enough money to take control of the Columbia Trust Company, the Boston-Irish bank his own father had helped to set up in 1892, while it was being threatened with takeover.[6] He had a genuine gift for business and over the next few years would make a fortune speculating on the stock market.

John F. Fitzgerald, JFK's maternal grandfather, and Rose, JFK's mother, at the Giant's Causeway in 1908.

his brother's achievements and made his way through Choate and then Harvard at his own pace, making lifelong friends, despite the occasional bout of racial prejudice. He was smartly groomed and well-spoken, but his sandy hair and blunt features gave him away as Irish before his surname was even mentioned, and the older, more puritanical Bostonian families still saw the Kennedys as nouveaux-riches upstarts.

As Joe Sr's stock rose (metaphorically and otherwise), newspaper and magazine articles were written about his film and business interests, but time and time again they referred to the Kennedys as "Irish", which was tiresome for both Rose and Joe Sr. On seeing the term used in a newpaper one morning, Joe is reported to have looked up and fumed "Goddam it! I was born in this country. My children were born in this country. What the hell does someone have to do to become an American?"[9]

Another family might have crumbled under such resentment and latent racism but it wasn't the house style for the Kennedys, who soldiered on. Realising that money per se was not enough to win society's acceptance, Joe Kennedy Sr pursued his career in politics, where respectability was attainable and money was always welcome. He pumped a fortune into Franklin D. Roosevelt's successful presidential campaign of 1932 and for this, he was rewarded with the post of first Chairman of the Securities and Exchange Commission, which Roosevelt established in 1934. For the 1936 campaign, Kennedy added to the small fortune he contributed by self-publishing a book entitled *I'm for Roosevelt*. All of this support was duly acknowledged and in 1937, as the world rumbled towards war, Joseph Patrick Kennedy, grandson of an immigrant cooper, was made American ambassador to the Court of St James. Kennedy was FDR's man in Britain. In the space of a generation a tragic Irish family was slowly embodying the American Dream. The journey from Famine to Boston and now, the heart of the British diplomatic establishment was very quick but it was also vintage Kennedy.

A model of Irish Catholic achievement in America: a family portrait of the prosperous Kennedys, taken in 1938.

The ambassadorship was an exceptionally prestigious diplomatic position but in reality such posts are in the gift of the President and, to this day, they are often given to party grandees and important donors to party political funds. This appointment would prove to be a turning point in the story of the Kennedys and Ireland, as it was a year later, in 1938, that the head of the Kennedy clan met the Irish Taoiseach, Éamon de Valera. From here on, Irish-American relations would be transformed and all roads would lead to O'Connell Street, June 1963.

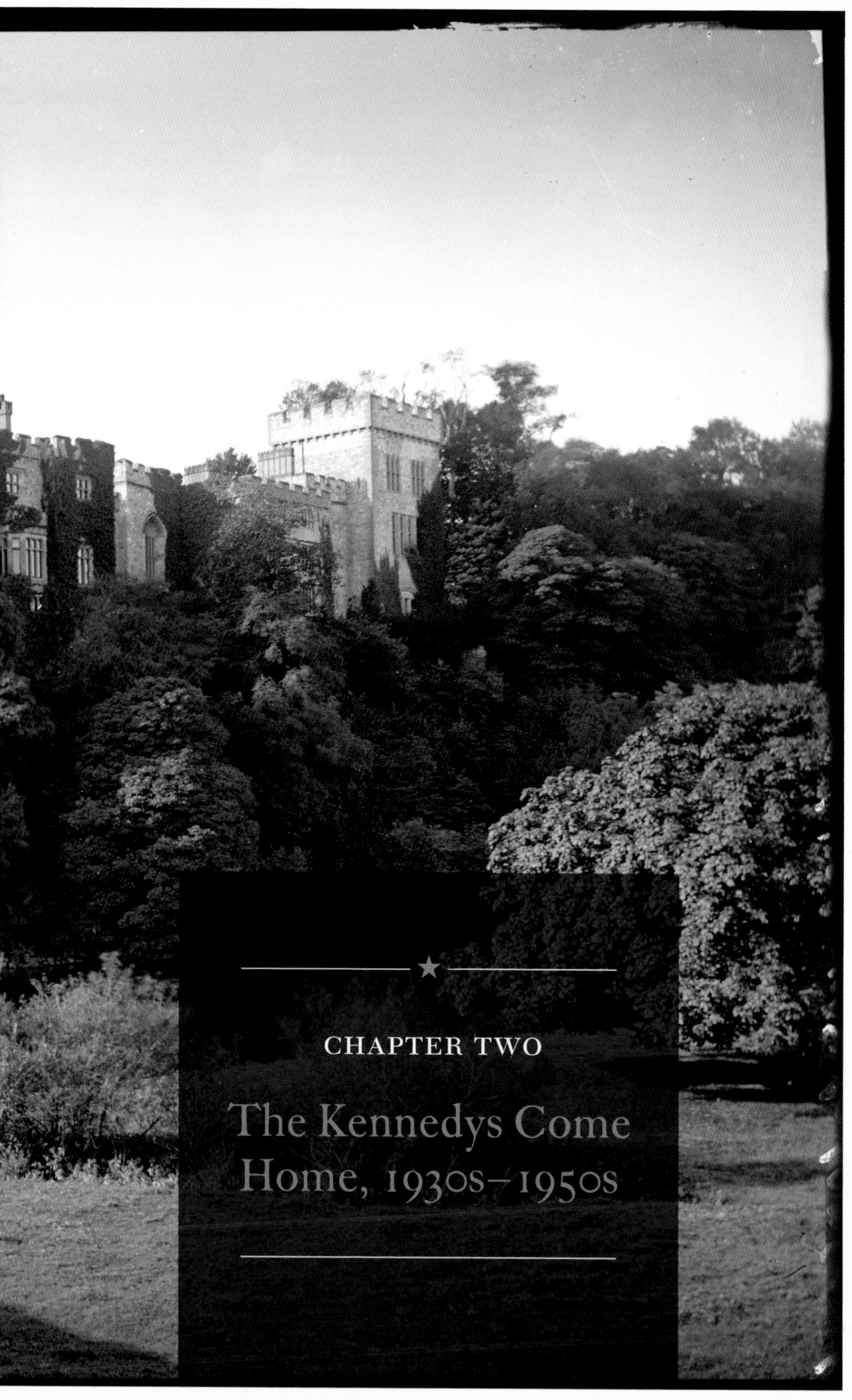

CHAPTER TWO

The Kennedys Come Home, 1930s–1950s

—★—

On 8 July 1938, Ambassador Joseph P. Kennedy flew back to the country his grandparents had left less than a century earlier. "My visit is not merely a sentimental one," he told waiting reporters, but he couldn't tell them the real reason for it: he'd been invited to receive an honorary doctorate from the National University of Ireland, which would be presented by Éamon de Valera, then Chancellor, but university rules forbade recipients of honorary degrees from disclosing the honour until the actual conferral. This was an honour that appealed to Joe Kennedy, as he had been snubbed recently for an honorary doctorate by Harvard University, his own Alma Mater.

The day was a wet one. In Dublin city, cinema-goers were flocking to the Metropole to see Robert Donat in *The Count of Monte Cristo* when the fourteen-seat de Havilland 86 touched down. Newspaper reports suggested that the Ambassador would be accompanied by his son John and his wife Mrs Rose Kennedy, and the day before the visit, *The Irish Press* published a front-page photo of Ambassador Kennedy flanked by Joe and John with the headline "US Ambassador Here Tomorrow" but that is the last suggestion of JFK's involvement, and photographs taken during the visit show only Joe Sr and his eldest son.[10] The Ambassador was accompanied by his long-time secretary, Edward Moore (after whom Ted Kennedy was named), Joe Jr and an embassy aide with the outrageously coincidental name of John Kennedy. It is probably here that the confusion arose about his son John's inclusion on the trip, but Joe Jr was the son being groomed for political greatness, not John. He is the one that Joe Sr would have been keen to introduce to the great and the good of Dublin.

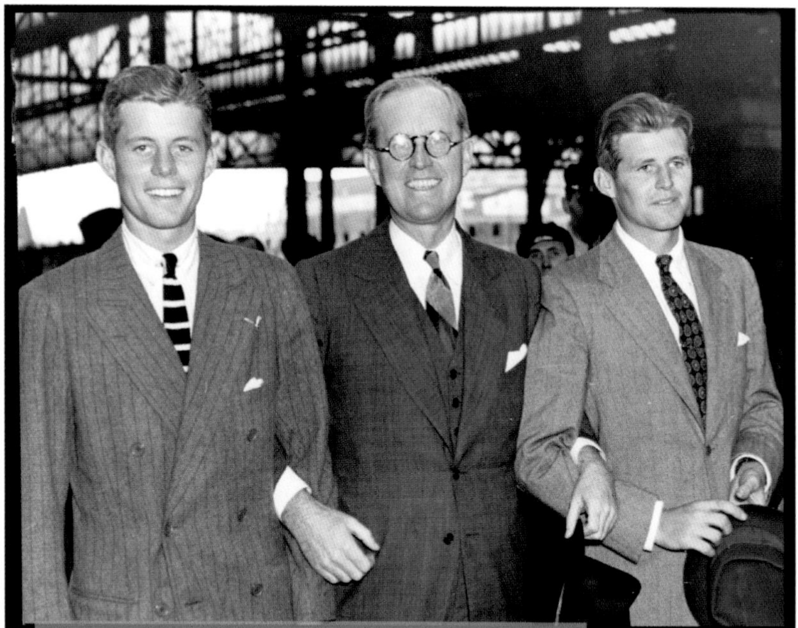

Joseph P. Kennedy, US Ambassador to Britain, is greeted by his sons Jack (left) and Joseph on his return to London after a visit to New York. Two days later, he flew into Dublin's Baldonnel airport.

The Ambassador's visit was given all the attention of a major occasion, just shy of an official state visit, and achieved front-page news for his two days in Ireland. With the real reason for the trip undisclosed, there was much speculation in the Irish media that Joe Kennedy was in town to discuss Anglo–Irish relationships, and the thorny issue of Partition in particular.[11]

The division of the island of Ireland had its origins in the British Government of Ireland Act of 1920 that had introduced separate parliaments in both north and south, based in Dublin and Belfast. With the end of the Anglo-Irish War and the Treaty of 1921 this arbitrary separation began to solidify into a more or less permanent divide, which provoked bitter splits in the newly founded Irish Free

State and led directly to the Civil War of 1922–23. A Boundary Commission set up to decide the final border largely followed the original line of 1920 and, in 1925, both the British Parliament and the Dáil ratified the final borders. The Partition of north and south was anathema to some and would remain a live political issue throughout the 20th century and beyond.

De Valera was behind one of the main groups campaigning against Partition and for the island of Ireland to be unified once more, but those who thought Joe Kennedy Sr would speak out on behalf of their cause would be sadly disappointed. Britain was on the brink of war and Kennedy was already in a tense diplomatic situation as the British government invoked their so-called "Special Relationship" with the US and sought American help to stop Hitler from dominating Europe. Kennedy was known to be an isolationist, but at the same time he couldn't risk upsetting his British hosts because losing their goodwill would make his position as Ambassador untenable. Speaking out about Partition at that time would have been a very bad idea, and that's why he was careful to describe his trip to the press at least in part as "sentimental"; not political – sentimental; a way of reconnecting with his roots.

In a private meeting at the Department of External Affairs, he said he didn't want to discuss the progress of negotiations between the British and the Irish but he passed on President Roosevelt's views that it was important for Anglo-American relations that a settlement was reached. Even this is considered so sensitive that the document was marked "secret".

The mercurial Kennedy patriarch kept to a busy and full schedule while in Dublin. From the airport, he was driven to the American Legation, which would later become the American Embassy in Ireland. Over lunch he caught up with John Cudahy, the United States Minister in Ireland (effectively, Ambassador). The two were old friends and the meeting served as a useful scene-setter for the esteemed guest. From there it was off to the main business at hand, the conferral at the university's offices in Dublin's Merrion Square.

On arrival at the National University headquarters, Ambassador Kennedy was met by Éamon de Valera, who was dressed in black and gold robes. The Ambassador, dressed in the scarlet and purple gown of the law faculty, was watched by, among others, Joe Jr. Afterwards, photographs showed father and son mingling with guests, of which Rose Kennedy would write twenty-four years later to de Valera: "Joe often speaks of his visit to Dublin when he was Ambassador in London, and there is a place of honour in our home reserved for your photograph with the former President of Eire [Douglas Hyde] and our eldest son, Joe, drinking tea together."[12]

Kennedy and de Valera made their way separately across the city to the Dáil, where the latter welcomed the former in his official capacity as Taoiseach, or "Prime Minister", then the Ambassador was driven to Áras an Uachtarain, the President's official residence, where he met President Douglas Hyde and the President's secretary, Michael McDunphy.

The following day, the Ambassador had an appointment with Ireland's Papal Nuncio, which was followed by a visit to Trinity College for a look at the Book of Kells and a trip to the National Museum for a tour guided by the director, Adolf Mahr. There was a courtesy call to Dublin's Lord Mayor, Alfie Byrne, who expressed the hope that the Ambassador's visit would help to end Partition. The Ambassador wished happiness to the people of Ireland, Britain and America but told him firmly that he couldn't interfere in matters such as the Irish border. He wasn't about to break his diplomatic silence on the subject.

That night the Ambassador was guest of honour at a state banquet in Dublin Castle. A beautiful building commissioned by England's King John in 1204, this was the physical seat of former British rule in Ireland and the target for revolutionaries like Silken Thomas (1534), Robert Emmet (1803) and the leaders of the 1916 Rising against British rule. Dublin Castle had only been handed over by the British to the Irish Free State sixteen years before the Ambassador crossed its threshold.

HIGH COMMISSIONER
FOR IRELAND

ÉIRE

33-37 REGENT ST.
LONDON, S.W.1.

15th March, 1938

S E C R E T

No.10

The Secretary
Department of External Affairs
DUBLIN

On the day of his arrival in London I left a card on Mr.Kennedy, the recently appointed American Ambassador, informing his Secretary that I would make a call later when he had settled in to his new duties. Accordingly an appointment was arranged for today when I called at the American Embassy.

Mr.Kennedy began by speaking of his close and sustained interest in Ireland and the Irish. He did not wish to ask questions about the progress of the negotiations between the Irish and the British Governments but he would like to be allowed to say how much he hoped that they might reach fruition.

Speaking in the strictest confidence he said that President Roosevelt's opinion was that a settlement between the Irish and British Governments was a matter of importance in regard to the question of Anglo-American relations. Whilst that was the President's opinion it could not be regarded as the opinion of the American Government since the subject had not been through or fully considered by the State Department. Nevertheless he had himself spoken to Mr.Chamberlain - a good friend of Eire, the Ambassador thought, - acquainting him with President Roosevelt's opinion. He emphasised the very secret character of what he was saying and entreated me to communicate his remarks to no one but An Taoiseach himself.

J. W. Dulanty.

High Commissioner.

Sizing up America's new man in London: a report by John W. Dulanty, Irish High Commissioner in London, following his meeting with the new US Ambassador, Joseph P. Kennedy, 15 March 1938.

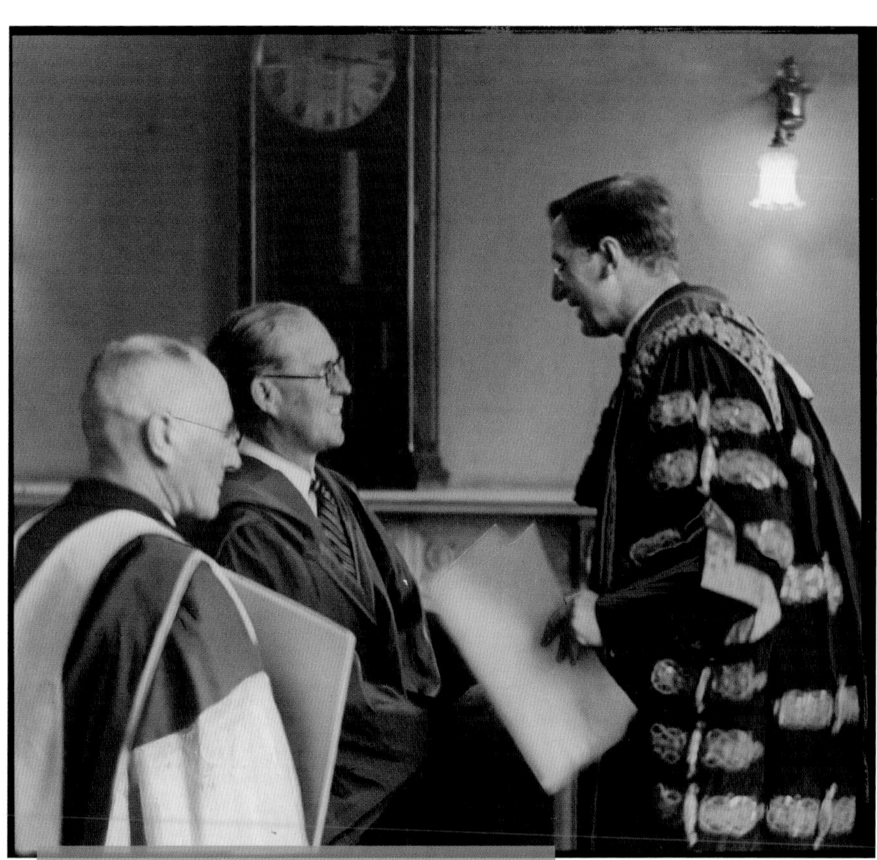

Joseph P. Kennedy receives his honorary doctorate from the Chancellor of the National University of Ireland, Éamon de Valera, 7 July 1938.

At the state banquet, de Valera was effusive: "We welcome you for yourself and for your race. We are proud that men like you not merely do honour for your country, but honour to our race."[13] These words must have meant a lot to a man coming from the East Coast of America, where his Irish nationality had always been held against him. To be told that the Taoiseach of the country of his ancestors respected his achievements must have been welcome praise indeed.

Writing to Senator Edward Kennedy in 1964, President de Valera recalled: "The impression your father made on me … was that he was brisk in thought and action, very forceful and decisive in opinion. I looked upon him as a stout American who had served his country in important offices in critical times and believed that the United States was the leading nation of the world and deserved recognition as such."[14]

There was some talk about the Kennedys' Irish heritage during the visit, with *The Irish Times* speculating that "if there are any relations left, they probably reside in the Clonakilty district or Wexford Field".[15] At a press conference at the American Legation in Dublin, while fielding questions from journalists, the Ambassador had trouble understanding a particularly strong Cork accent. "I am sorry, I can't quite understand you," he remarked. And the Corkman answered: "Well, I come from near Clonakilty, where your people came from." The Ambassador laughed. "Yes. But I haven't managed to keep the accent through a generation and a half."

Before he left, Ambassador Kennedy was asked two questions that would have resonance in the future. The first, "Will you be a candidate for the Presidency of the United States in 1940?" went unanswered. When asked whether the rest of the Kennedy children would visit Ireland, the Ambassador smiled and said "by instalments".[16]

JFK's first visit to Ireland, 1945

The Kennedys were a competitive family. On the sports field, at war or in the political arena, they were in it to win it. In what was a traditionally patriarchal set-up, the first-born son was the Chosen One and so it was that from a young age, Joe Jr was groomed to be America's first Catholic president. He made no secret of his ambitions, and in 1940 he took the first steps by attending the Democratic Convention as a delegate. But then America entered World War II and like so many young men of their generation, the Kennedy brothers volunteered to fight.

John F. Kennedy took to the seas of the South Pacific, and earned himself a reputation as a war hero after he saved his crew members on a patrol boat, *PT-109*, which was rammed and sunk by a Japanese destroyer. Joe Jr took the fateful decision to fight in the skies over Europe and in 1944, his plane exploded in the air over Southern England. After the shocking news had been absorbed at the Kennedy homestead, all eyes and expectations turned to the slight twenty-seven-year-old with his head stuck in books. Joe Sr explained: "I told him [John F. Kennedy] Joe was dead and that it was therefore his responsibility to run for Congress."[17] The baton was being handed on.

At college, John F. Kennedy's thesis, "Why England Slept", had explored the reasons behind Britain's lack of preparedness for World War II. Thanks to the help and influence of his father this was published as a book, giving an academic lustre to the man on whom Joe Sr now placed such great expectations. Within a year, John F. Kennedy went from being the second son with a potential career in academia to war hero, author and the first son in a fiercely ambitious family.

In the summer of 1945, when John Kennedy was twenty-eight years old, he was keen to see more of the world before embarking on his political career. A history fanatic, he secured a job as a cub reporter with the Hearst newspaper group, which saw him head for post-war Europe. The trip took the young reporter to England, France, Germany and, most intriguingly, Ireland, where he arrived on 24 July 1945. He had a clear interest in the country of his ancestors and a curiosity to see what it was like, so he persuaded his bosses to let him go over and write an article about it.

In a brief but busy visit, Kennedy found time to visit the American Minister to Ireland at the United States Legation, Mr David Gray, and, more interestingly, he called on and interviewed then Taoiseach

Three generations: JFK with father Joseph P. Kennedy Sr. (standing) and grandfather John F. "Honey Fitz" Fitzgerald.

Éamon de Valera. Gray, a first cousin of Franklin D. Roosevelt, wasn't a fan of de Valera, whom he referred to as a "paranoiac and a lunatic". Gray ascribed the cause of the Irish Civil War to the "pride of de Valera", because of his role as one of the leaders of the Easter Rising, for which he was imprisoned and very nearly executed.

De Valera had commanded the 3rd Battalion of Irish Volunteers during the rising, launched on 24 April 1916, Easter Monday, and had gone into captivity following its collapse on 29 April with much of central Dublin in flames. The leaders of the rising were tried by British military courts martial under military law, sentenced to death and executed with indecent haste. De Valera was only spared because of ths issues arising out of his American birth.

Gray's opinion reflected an Anglocentric view, the cub reporter with the Hibernian background was much more impressed.

On 25 July, John Kennedy and de Valera talked about the state of the Irish nation in 1945. Ireland had remained neutral during World War II, which the Irish government referred to as "The Emergency", and when the two men got down to business, the Taoiseach defended neutrality "at some length" according to Kennedy's diary at the time.

Reflecting on de Valera's career, Kennedy wrote that "as a Parliament and political boss he is unique". The young Irish-American was also impressed by de Valera's "mystic hold on the hearts of the people".

Incorrectly referring to "The" Fianna Fáil as the Soldiers of Ireland (they were and are the Soldiers of Destiny), the rookie hack also slipped up when he reported in his diary that Fianna Fáil came to power in 1930 (rather than1932). He referred to W.T. Cosgrave, the man who had led the Irish Free State of the 1920s, as "President Cosgrave" (he was no such thing) and called James Dillon, a future minister for agriculture and leader of the Fine Gael party, "Michael Dillon". Perhaps it was as well that Kennedy's career in journalism was short-lived.[18]

The primary upshot of his 1945 visit was a first-hand encounter with Ireland, in which it is obvious that his feeling of affection for the country was sparked. Some reports suggest he spoke with other political leaders such as Richard Mulcahy of Fine Gael and Frank Gallagher, ex-director of the Government Information Bureau,[19] and that he may have sat in on a session of the Dáil (a joint sitting of which he would address eighteen years later). What we do have are his diary entries and a full article written on the subject of Partition for the *New York Journal American*, part of the Hearst newspaper group.

The article shows a keen, if prosaic, grasp of the Irish situation in July 1945. A straightforward take on the political parties of the time is peppered with a romanticised Irish-American vocabulary. On the subject of de Valera's response in the Dáil to James Dillon's question on the subject of Ireland's status within the British Commonwealth, Kennedy writes sentimentally: "De Valera's elaboration of his remarks left the situation to many observers as misty as the island on an early winter's morning." Later within the same article, he talks about the military background of some Government members, saying they "have been in both English and Irish prisons, and many have wounds which still ache when the cold rains come in from the west." He tries to take a balanced, neutral line on Partition, but his respect for de Valera and his comrades shines through: "The only settlement they will accept is a free and independent Ireland, free to go where it will be the master of its own destiny." However, he said he couldn't see a solution to the problem in sight, because Britain would never accept "a neutral and weakly armed power on the vulnerable western flank".[20] It is interesting that he was prepared to tackle the subject his father was unwilling to comment on, knowing that his own political career lay ahead. Perhaps he was not yet fully aware of the censorship that political office can impose on your own opinions.

Scattered among his diaries from the year 1945 are a series of scrawled book titles and catalogue numbers. *Irish American History* by John O'Hanlon, *Ireland the World Over* by Edward Fergus and *Ireland's Contribution to the Law* by Hugh Carney[21] are just some of the titles that featured on Kennedy's reading list, which also boasted the Irish Constitution for good measure. This is not the bedside reading of a man with no interest in his heritage. The old country was getting under his skin. While his parents and grandparents had tried to move away from their Irishness, there had been a generational shift and JFK obviously no longer felt it was a badge of shame. Perhaps his change in attitude reflects the fact that so many Irish Americans were making a success of their lives in the mid 20th century, reaching the top of every profession. Far from trying to hide his background, John Kennedy was intrigued by it.

The Congressman in Dunganstown, 1947

Back in the US once more, it was time to start fulfilling the family's political ambitions with a precocious run for Congress in 1946. When John F. Kennedy announced his intention to run for office in a working-class, Irish-Italian district of Boston, the reaction was rather sniffy. One newspaper described the candidate as "ever so British", a jibe that would be levelled at him throughout his life, in an ironic turn of events after the childhood taunts that he was "too Irish".

Kennedy was at an ethnic crossroads of sorts. Irish-Americans felt he wasn't quite one of them, complaining that "He never even went to a wake unless he knew the deceased personally."[22] Most candidates with Irish roots attended wakes whenever there was one to attend because it was a good way to canvas for votes while showing yourself as a caring member of the community, but Kennedy was cut from a different cloth and would have felt it inappropriate to attend a stranger's wake. His East Coast American sensitivity was more dominant than his Irish showmanship.

Equally, Kennedy wasn't as inclined to glad-hand as his grandfather, the über-Irish American politico Honey Fitz, had been. An early biographer noted that Kennedy "disliked the blarney, the exuberant backslapping and handshaking".[23] He came from a new breed of Irish-Americans, an emerging middle class who didn't see the need to get drunk every night and moan about the Brits, but who also had no problem embracing their ethnicity. JFK wasn't scared of his roots, they didn't embarrass him and he certainly wasn't going to let them get in his way as he stood on the first rung of the political ladder.

Despite the negative reactions, Kennedy's eloquence and charm were such that he won easily, getting nearly double the votes of his Republican opponent, and this victory put him on the road to political greatness, although you wouldn't have known it to look at him. Nearly every commentator at the time passed some class of remark on his boyish demeanour, his slight appearance and gaunt features. He was taking steroids for his spastic colon at a dose that caused osteoporosis in his lower back, and a back injury sustained during the war meant he was in constant pain. The steroids also triggered Addison's disease, a disorder of the adrenal gland, which had caused him to lose weight. The extent of his health problems was kept hidden from the public, on his father's advice, because it was felt that they might have hesitated to vote for an invalid.[24]

During JFK's successful race for Congress in 1946 there had been several campaign parties at which Kennedy's favourite Irish songs were sung: songs such as "Macushla", "Danny Boy" and "When Irish Eyes Are Smiling".[25] His sense of Irishness was emerging strongly at this point, as evidenced by a holiday he took in the old country in September 1947 with the purpose of exploring his roots.

Before leaving America, the young Congressman made calls to track down some of his family connections in Ireland. One of these was to his aunt Loretta Kennedy Connelly, who happily obliged with directions for New Ross in County Wexford, a short trip away from where Kennedy would be staying. He went on to get a guidebook which came with a map, and that map is peppered with the letter 'X' beside places that interested him.[26] He was eager to get to know the old country and investigate his family's history there.

On 1 September 1947, thirty-year-old Congressman Kennedy arrived at Shannon airport for a three-week stay with his sister Kathleen. She had married the eldest son of the Duke of Devonshire and, despite being widowed after only four months, was still given the use of Lismore Castle in County Waterford, an extravagant holiday home owned by her late husband's parents.

The guest list was like something out of an Agatha Christie novel, including Pamela Churchill and Anthony Eden (former British foreign secretary and future prime minister), Sir Shane Leslie (a writer and first cousin of Winston Churchill) and William Douglas-Home (a playwright). Kennedy stayed in the Queen's Room, which afforded him river views; he would have been accustomed to such luxury, with the splendid homes his family occupied back in the USA.

One morning the future president went searching for his roots, taking Pamela Churchill with him. She must have been bemused. Until 1945, Ms Churchill had been married to Randolph Churchill, son of Winston, and had been linked with some of the more exotic men of the time, including the American broadcaster Edward R. Murrow and the Italian car magnate Gianni Agnelli. But on this particular morning, she was accompanying a skinny Congressman down the narrow, winding roads of New Ross. It didn't take Kennedy long to find Dunganstown and, once there, he was directed along a rough track to a thatched-roof cottage, the home of Mary Ryan, a third cousin on his father's side.

Their house was a far cry from the luxury of Lismore Castle, with sparse comforts, an outdoor toilet and chickens and pigs wandering in the yard, but John F. Kennedy was delighted to sit down and listen to Mary Ryan's stories of his grandfather, Patrick, who had visited there thirty years previously, and other family members who had stayed behind in County Wexford during the Famine. Kennedy produced a camera and took some photographs, which continue to grace photo albums in the Dunganstown homestead.

Alas, in the time he spent there, Kennedy failed to make a significant impression as years later, the only recollections Mary Ryan and James Kennedy, another third cousin, had were physical. Respectively, they commented "He didn't look well at all" and "Begod, and he was shook looking!" However, hospitality was forthcoming and tea was duly served to the young American and his aristocratic companion. Sixteen years later, the eyes of the world would focus on Mrs Ryan when she once more served her distant relative tea and cake but by then the circumstances would be utterly changed.

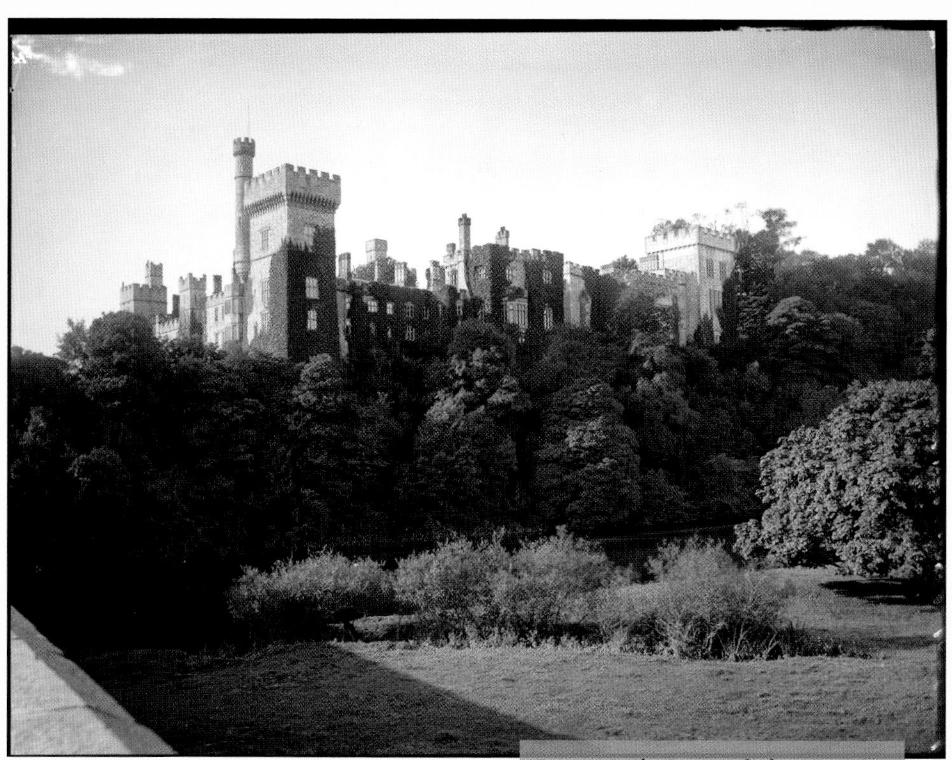

Lismore Castle, Co. Waterford, as it was in the early 20th century. It was here in 1947 that Congressman Kennedy came to stay.

Though Kennedy may not have made much impact, the time he spent with Mrs Ryan had profound resonance for him. As they drove away down the dirt track that afternoon, a wistful Kennedy claimed later that he "left in a flow of nostalgia and sentiment". He turned to Lady Churchill for her thoughts on the visit and she offered pithily "That was just like Tobacco Road!" (a novel set amongst farmers struggling in the Great Depression of the 1930s). Flying towards Ireland on Air Force One sixteen years later, Kennedy would remember this moment: "I felt like kicking her out of the car. For me, the visit to that cottage was filled with magic sentiment. That night at the castle … I looked around the table and thought about the cottage where my cousins lived, and I said to myself, 'What a contrast!'"[27]

One of the photographs taken by JFK when he visited the ancestral homestead in Dunganstown, Co. Wexford, in 1947.

Further evidence that he was beginning to feel his own Irishness more strongly comes from his support for a 1947 bill in Congress, proposing that post-war aid for the British should be contingent on their government ending Partition in Ireland. Rhode Island Congressman John Fogarty had introduced this resolution on a number of previous occasions, and would do so again later. The bill was never going to become law but it was an easy way for Kennedy to underline his Irishness with his Irish-American base and may well have reflected his own views on Partition at the time. It was defeated in Congress by 206 votes to 139, with 83 abstaining but JFK had laid his cards on the table. As far as the Irish nationalists were concerned, he was on their side.

The Senator in Dublin, 1955

Kennedy's years as a Congressman gave him a good training in how to be a grafting politician, complete with all the requisite wheeling and dealing, and in 1952 he decided to make a run for Senate. His most important decisions at this stage lay in the people with whom he surrounded himself. Top of the list was his brother Bobby, who ran the Senate campaign. Another three key players formed the group commonly known to all as the Irish Mafia. Bobby's Harvard roommate, Kenny O'Donnell, became a key adviser and organiser while Dave Powers, a first-generation Irish-American, was a political fixer who aided in morale maintenance, acted as court jester[28] and kept secrets. Larry O'Brien completed the unholy trinity that formed Kennedy's inner circle. With parents hailing from Cork, O'Brien was described by Kennedy as "the best election man in the business", who could read elections and their results like no other. He helped run the two Senate campaigns, the Presidential race and acted as Kennedy's man on Capitol Hill for the duration of the Kennedy Administration.

The other two men whom Kennedy kept close were the non-Irish Ted Sorensen, who joined the Senator in 1952 and remained by his side until 1963, and the thirty-three-year-old Pierre Salinger. Kennedy described Sorensen, who wrote most of the President's key speeches, as his "intellectual blood bank". Salinger became press officer for the Presidential campaign and, later, White House Press Secretary.

In order to win the Senate seat in 1952, Kennedy first had to eliminate the biggest beast in the Boston jungle, Henry Cabot-Lodge. Cabot-Lodge was a member of one of the most esteemed Boston Brahmin families, who had run the state for generations. This didn't daunt the young Congressman who felt that as a war hero and author, and armed with a bottomless financial well, he was ideally placed to take the seat – and he did. By the end of 1952, Senator Kennedy was ready to take his place among the men of power on Capitol Hill.

During his early years as a Senator, Kennedy focussed on his personal rather than his political affairs. In 1953 he married Jacqueline Bouvier, a highly glamorous union in a business not noted for beauty, and in late September 1955, he and his wife paid a visit to Ireland, at her instigation. It wasn't a nostalgic meet-the-relatives trip this time, but a piece of calculated meeting and greeting designed to enhance Kennedy's image with Irish-American voters at home. They would be staying in Dublin's luxurious Shelbourne Hotel rather than driving down muddy back lanes looking for distant cousins.

They were en route back from a European tour during which Kennedy had spoken in Poland on the Catholic Church's successful fight against Communism.[29] (This fight would spur on a young Karol Wojtyla to keep writing his religious treatises, despite opposition from the Communist government. He would later become John Paul II, the first non-Italian pope in 450 years, a man who in 1979 commanded the biggest-ever turnout for any visiting dignitary to the island of Ireland.) On a previous visit to Dublin, Jackie Kennedy had befriended a Vincentian priest by the name of Father Joseph Leonard, and he now arranged for Kennedy to address students at All Hallows College, which he duly did, happily answering questions on Catholicism and American issues.

John F. Kennedy wasn't yet being talked of as a candidate for the presidency but the thirty-eight-year-old politician's status and importance had grown between each of his flights over the Atlantic and his wife was keen that he should appear presidential wherever they stopped off. It might have been unusual for a politician to engage in religious questions, but he had never made a secret of his religion, even though it could have proved a liability in electoral terms.

Irish Minister for External Affairs Liam Cosgrave hosted a lunch for the visiting Kennedys. Protocol dictated that such a lunch should have been held at the Department of External Affairs in Iveagh House but JFK had recently had an operation on his back and "was at that time moving around on crutches, [so] instead of giving him lunch anywhere else, we arranged that it be given in the Shelbourne," the Minister recalls. Among the guests that afternoon were Father Leonard and Mrs Kennedy. With illness-related problems proving a theme, the Taoiseach John Costello's wife took over as hostess because Mrs Cosgrave was unwell.

Liam Cosgrave's memories of Kennedy in 1955 tally with the man who would return eight years later as US President: "He was very friendly, matter of fact, devoid of pretence of any sort, good sense of humour, clear grasp of the essentials, the current international political situation, was reasonably familiar with conditions here. He was overcoming or just shortly before had his serious illness [Addison's disease]." And yet, the Minister for External Affairs was struck by Kennedy's physical appearance, which Cosgrave had assumed would be particularly youthful. "Those who didn't know [him] were always struck by his boyish appearance. When you were nearer to him he didn't look quite so young. In fact, his face showed certain signs of the suffering he'd undergone."[30]

During their stay at the Shelbourne, Mrs Kennedy called a few journalists to tell them that her Senator husband was in town and that he would be available for interviews if they were so inclined. It was a Sunday morning when the chief reporter of *The Irish Independent*, Michael Rooney, picked up his phone on the way out to a game of golf. At the other end of the line was Jacqueline Kennedy. She wanted to know if Mr Rooney would care to come to the Shelbourne Hotel to meet her husband, the Junior Senator for Massachusetts. Rooney didn't care to go, he had other things on his mind. As he would later recall: "Three fellows were waiting for me on the golf course and I was in serious trouble already for being late." Instead, he scratched down some notes and submitted his copy. The fruits of Mrs Kennedy's efforts resulted in a tiny, four-paragraph story buried away inside the *Irish Independent*.[31] Clearly, nobody could tell that they were dealing with future greatness.

Winning the White House

Kennedy's book *Profiles in Courage*, published in 1956, bagged him the esteemed Pulitzer Prize, and in the same year he made a bid for the Vice-Presidential nomination. While unsuccessful it was well received and saw him in demand at Democratic functions as soon as the Convention was over. It also saved him from being politically redundant as "the other guy" in the 1957 race to the White House, which was always going to be won by the incumbent President Eisenhower. The fates were kind to Kennedy in that respect at least.

A year later, his own dynasty began with the arrival of a baby girl, Caroline, and so the boy became a man and the Presidential whispers began in earnest.

But what about the American people? How would they feel about an Irish-American President? The omens were quite good in that respect. President Andrew Jackson's parents were born in Ireland, making him the first politician of Irish blood to occupy the White House. The fathers of both Presidents James Buchanan and Chester A. Arthur were Irish-born. Kennedy had never tried to hide his ethnic background. He marched in the St Patrick's Day parades in Boston and he gave speeches with Irish reference points throughout his career. But there was a problem. Those other Irish Presidents had been Protestant, while he was a Catholic.

Kennedy's religion was a more difficult nut to crack in the eyes of the national electorate, and there was form. In 1928, New York Democratic Governor Al Smith ran against Herbert Hoover. Throughout the campaign Smith, a Catholic, repeatedly had to deny

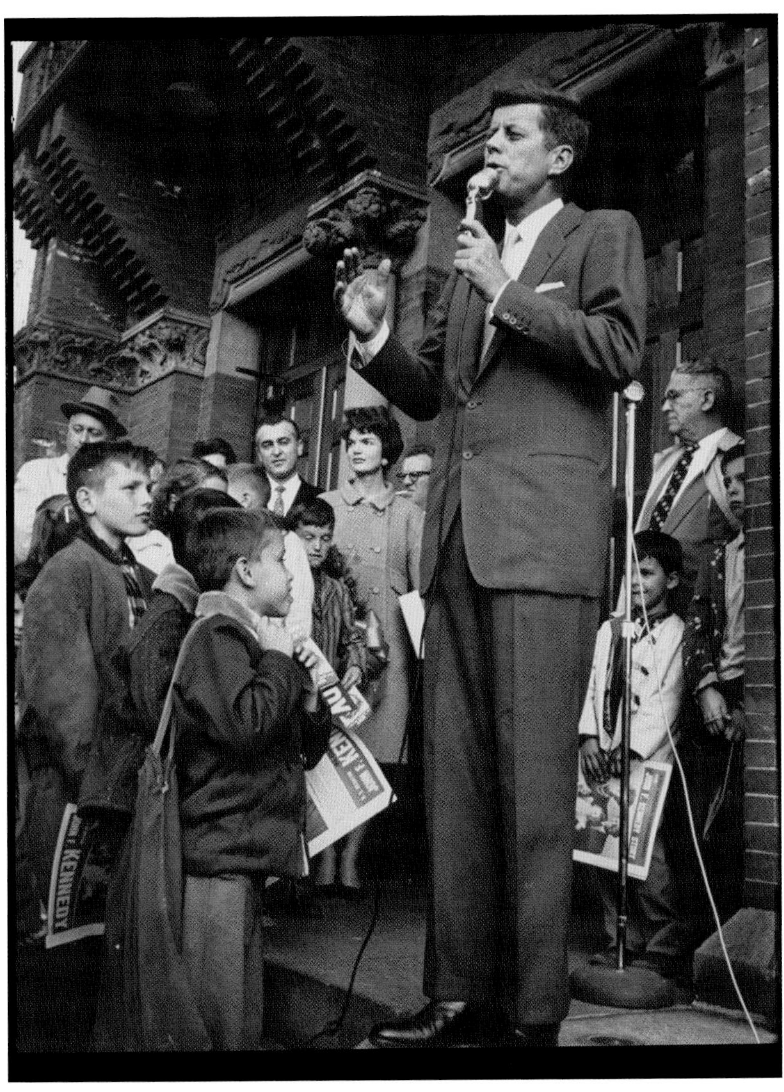

On the campaign trail: Senator John Kennedy tries to sway voters as he seeks re-election in October 1958. In the background, Jacqueline watches on.

that his religion would influence his judgement as President. It was no use; he lost heavily to Hoover. Now, just thirty-five years later, was America prepared to hand over the reins of power to a Catholic? Had times changed enough?

Kennedy's speechwriter Ted Sorensen later observed: "American voters didn't mind an Irish Catholic as a mayor or a legislator or certainly not as a county chairman, but President? Al Smith's smashing defeat in 1928 had made it clear that an Irish Catholic, or any other kind of Catholic in all likelihood, was not acceptable in the White House because they feared the Catholic hierarchy, led by the Pope, would influence decisions that under the Constitution should be based only on America's interest and American public policy."[32]

This resistance from within and without Catholic Irish America led many local politicians to urge caution on the ambitious Senator. He was too young, too Irish, too Catholic and they thought he should take it slowly, bit by bit. But Kennedy felt his time had come and threw the dice. Knowing that his Catholicism was an issue for voters, he chose a meeting of Protestant ministers in Houston, Texas, to address concerns about his religion. In the speech, which many felt helped Kennedy over the finishing line, the candidate announced: "I am not the Catholic candidate for President. I am the Democratic Party's candidate for President who happens to be a Catholic." This speech helped to answer a lot of questions and also to silence many critics.

On 8 November 1960, Kennedy beat Richard Nixon in one of the most closely fought Presidential elections of the twentieth century. He knew the wall was high but he was brought up to take on challenges and duly win – which, by a not uncontroversial whisker, he did, while his Republican opponents muttered about stolen votes skewing the result against them.

Kennedy actually only received 113,000 votes more than Nixon out of the 68 million cast, which translated into a victory by a margin of 303 to 219 in the electoral college. The controversy over this election has largely focused on two states, Illinois and Texas, where

Republicans have alleged – and Nixon himself clearly believed – that fraud enabled Kennedy to win. Had Nixon won those two states he would have obtained enough votes in the Electoral College to take the presidency.

In Texas Kennedy had won by a margin of 46,000 votes, but in Illinois it was much closer, with only 9,000 votes in it. Perhaps more suspicious was the fact that despite a heavy Republican vote throughout the State, Kennedy won Cook County, which included the city of Chicago, by a massive 450,000 votes – heavily aided by the impressive vote-winning machine run by the Democratic Mayor Richard J. Daley. Despite repeated legal challenges in both these states, and elsewhere, the Republicans failed to overturn the deficits – though evidence of some voter fraud was discovered – and Kennedy went to the White House.

The significance of a forty-something Irish-American Catholic reaching the White House was extraordinary, an event that historian Robert Dallek says "breached this wall that America would only have White Protestant males as President."[33] It was ground-breaking and exhilarating, and the American people expected great things from this dynamic, young man with the glamorous wife and the heroic war record.

Those early years in the White House were strewn with difficulties, though. The botched Bay of Pigs invasion in April 1961 rattled the entire Administration. This attempt to oust Fidel Castro from power in Cuba had been planned by the previous administration but was supported by Kennedy and the invasion went ahead on 17 April. It was defeated emphatically by the Cuban military providing an embarrassing setback right at the start of Kennedy's presidency.

Domestically, Kennedy's handling of the civil rights issue won him detractors from both sides of the argument; he was moving towards the end of state-sanctioned racial discrimination but too slowly for civil rights campaigners, while white Southerners were appalled. The ruling of the Supreme Court in 1954 that segregated schooling was unconstitutional had unleashed a wave of protests against other aspects of segregation, and the issue of civil rights had proved key in

the 1960 election, with Kennedy's support for Dr Martin Luther King Jr winning him some 70 per cent of the Black vote. However, his narrow victory coupled with the Democrats' shaky control of Congress gave him little room for dramatic gestures.

Kennedy was also a Cold War leader and knew he had to take on the Russians during the Cuban Missile Crisis. Sparked by the discovery of Soviet nuclear missiles in Cuba on 18 October 1962, just 100 miles from American soil, this crisis lasted 13 days and brought the world to the brink of nuclear war before its eventual resolution.

Now, attention shifted to the battleground of Europe. Could the former Allies hold the fort against Russia? Would the Iron Curtain extend its coverage from the East into the West? Europe was weak and in need of leadership. Kennedy was the unofficial Leader of the Free World. His presence was required in Europe, where there were important matters to confront. He was also exhausted, drained by the demands of life in the White House. Shouldn't he be entitled to a little diversion? Shouldn't he be allowed a quick visit to the old country? These were the questions that played on the President's mind in the early months of 1963. In the diplomatic offices of Irish officials from Dublin to Paris and on to Washington, a plan was being hatched that would swing the argument.

OPPOSITE Crossing the threshold: the Kennedys take up residence at the White House, 4 February 1961.

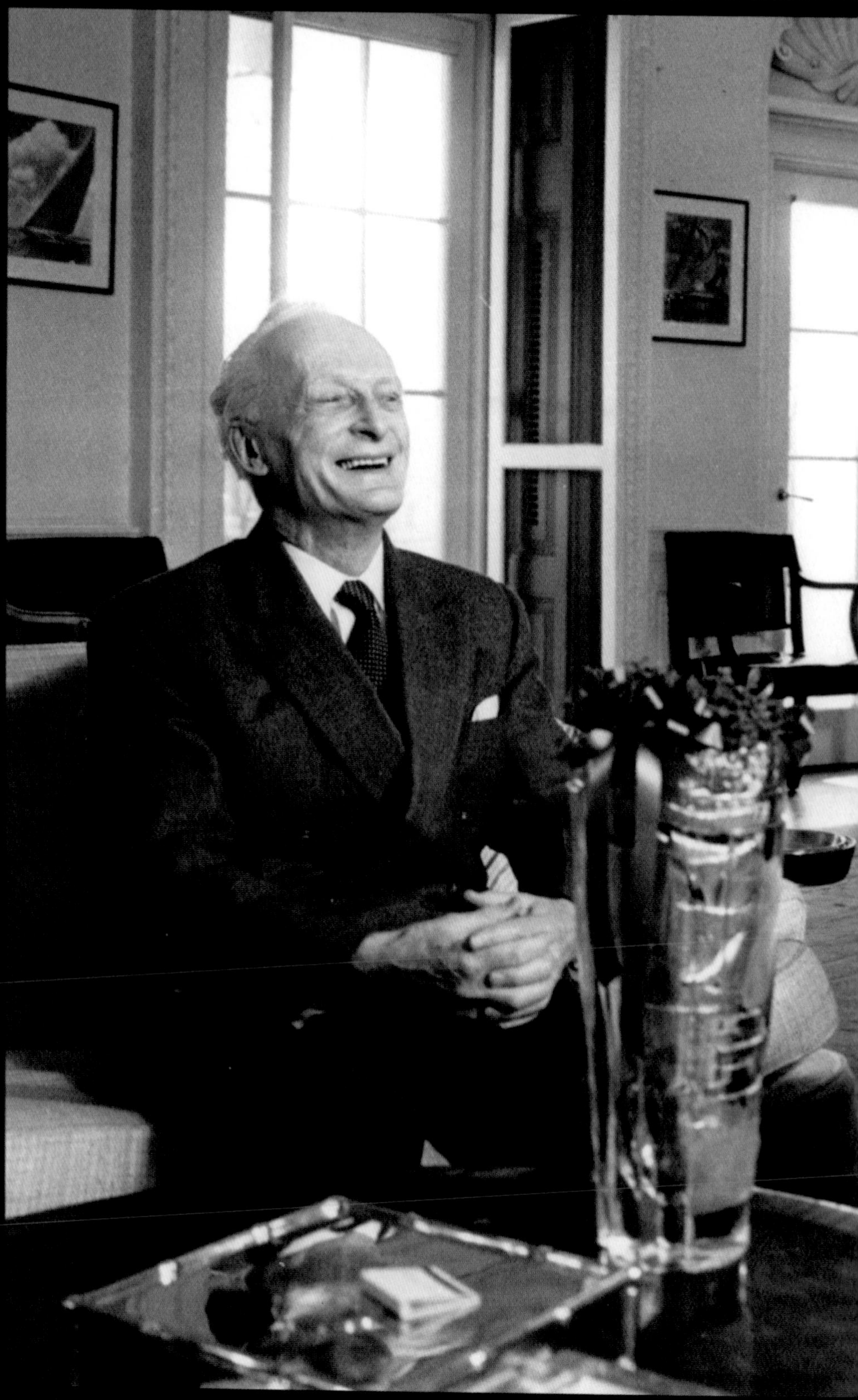

CHAPTER THREE

Wooing the President

—★—

For many years, Ireland had been effectively ruled by co-regents: the sorcerer, President Éamon de Valera, and the apprentice, Taoiseach Seán Lemass. Both men were products of Ireland's Civil War but by the early 1960s it was apparent that the two were looking in different directions. De Valera was looking over his shoulder, obsessed with freeing Ireland from the last vestiges of British influence, while Lemass was looking at the road ahead, wondering about the possibilities beyond the stone walls and green fields of Ireland. The world was changing at an unprecedented pace and Ireland was faced with stark choices. It could sit back and let the opportunities pass by, or it could sit up and keep up.

Lemass had always had the more modern attitude of the two men. Less than two decades previously, as Minister for Industry and Commerce, he'd been behind a high-profile campaign to supply electricity to those living in the Irish countryside for the first time by building electrical poles across the country. He expressed his sense of hope and optimism through the prism of domestic bliss: "I hope to see the day that when a girl gets a proposal from a farmer she will enquire, not so much about the number of cows, but rather concerning the electrical appliances she will require before she gives her consent, including not merely electric light but a water heater, an electric clothes boiler, a vacuum cleaner and even a refrigerator." Within ten years, a million electrical poles had sprung up and villagers and townspeople across the land held switching-on celebrations. Ireland was literally emerging from the Dark Ages.

Lemass was also concerned to try and halt the mass exodus of young people from the island. Economically, it was important for the country to start exporting products rather than people. In the early 1960s, there only 2.9 million citizens left, while a million people born in Ireland had taken up residence in England.[34] Stroll along any platform on the London Underground and you can be sure that the hands of Irishmen built the walls. Look up at the magnificent buildings of the capital, or at some of the mundane housing estates scattered all around England, and you'll find that in all likelihood, they were built by Irishmen who populated ghettos in North London suburbs such as Camden, Kilburn and Cricklewood.

There were as many Irish women as men in Britain, searching for a way to raise their family's standard of living. Most of these emigrants ended up changing beds and preparing tea for middle-class English homeowners. The problem for the Irish government was that they

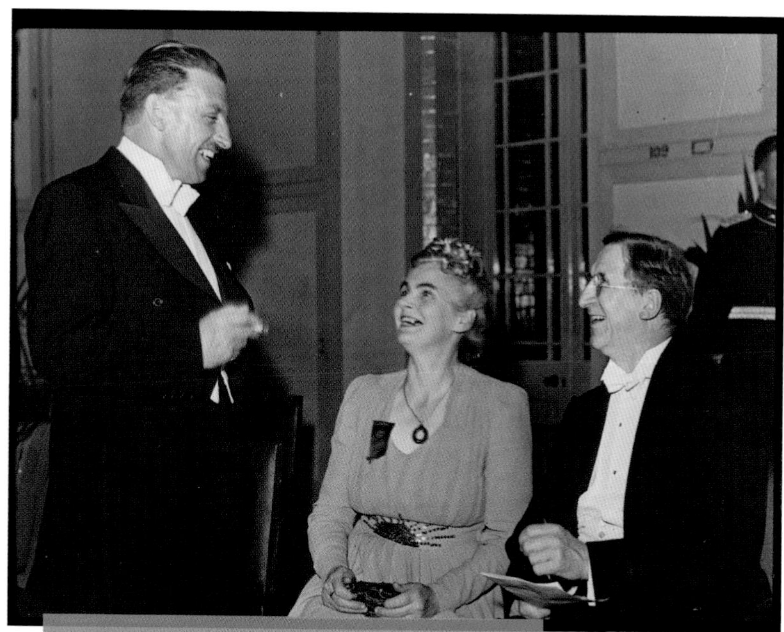

The sorcerer and the apprentice: Éamon de Valera (seated) and Seán Lemass at the 'Military Tattoo Dance' in Dublin, August 1945. Mrs Kathleen Lemass, Seán's wife, sits beside de Valera.

didn't have a lot to offer the next generation and something needed to be done to keep the nation alive.

In order to make Ireland breathe again, some of the repressive elements in daily life would have to be relaxed. The Church-State anschluss throttled cultural awakening, and the country's ludicrous censorship laws had worsened in the middle years of the 20th century. In the early days of the Irish State, nearly a hundred books a year were banned from curious eyes, but by the early 1950s, the number of books being kept from the shelves numbered six hundred annually. When Irish book-lovers went to a bookshop or library and sought certain books by John Steinbeck, Graham Greene or Ernest Hemingway, they would find an empty space on the shelf. Thankfully, by the late 1950s there was a small but important shift as the number of books being censored began to drop and the fog of cultural repression slowly started to dissipate.

The proliferation of television aerials on chimneys from Dublin to Drogheda and the 1961 launch of State broadcaster RTÉ had a direct influence on Irish politics. Now people could see the faces of their politicians and make up their own minds about who they trusted and who made them suspicious. The days of the grey-suited older generation were coming to an end. Television would soon topple governments and lose wars and in Ireland, it would allow viewers to watch an Irish-American President address the Dáil, the first foreign head of state to visit since the attainment of independence.

The 1959 handover of the reins of power, when Lemass became Taoiseach, or Prime Minister, and de Valera took the symbolic role of President, was easily the most significant and important of the guard-changing exercises of the time. It signalled a real transition from the Old Guard to the New, mirroring the feeling in Washington, DC, that Kennedy's election to the White House would inspire at the end of the following year. Also in 1959, James Dillon ascended to the top of the Fine Gael party while a year later, William Norton handed over to Brendan Corish in the Labour Party.

Within Lemass's party, Fianna Fáil, there was major change too as a younger set assumed new positions that would lead to high office in the future. Young bucks like Patrick Hillery, Donogh O'Malley, Brian Lenihan and, of course, Charles Haughey jockeyed for attention, knowing full well that their time was coming.

But Lemass was the key figure of the era and modern historians are quick to recognise the Dubliner as the architect of modern Ireland.[35] Lemass was perfectly placed to lead Ireland out of the rather gloomy period that marked the country's nascent independence. Working alongside a visionary civil servant called T.K. Whitaker, a Secretary at the Department of Finance, Lemass drew up the Programme for Economic Expansion, a critical blueprint that dragged Ireland into the 1960s. Foreign investment became a keystone for the future. Agricultural pursuits shifted to massive exporting of beef and cattle. It became easier to access loans and invest in industry. Ireland was open for business. Having had the slowest rate of growth in Europe throughout the 1950s, Ireland surpassed itself by reaching annual growth of 4 per cent between 1958 and 1963 – higher than Britain and as good as most other countries in Europe. While Whitaker and his team should take much of the credit for this turnaround, his boss, Seán Lemass should share the plaudits as a gambler who wasn't afraid to take risks.

As Irish writer and broadcaster Tim Pat Coogan wrote of Lemass: "He helped to solder past and present together, and suddenly to make politics something which gave a future meaning to the present."[36] Eighteen years older than the American President, Lemass was by no means the Kennedy of his time but in a weary Ireland, it was probably enough that he wasn't de Valera and at least his cabinet reflected the fact that there were people in Ireland under the age of sixty.

Making the first moves

The idea of any American president coming to Ireland was beyond the pale for people at the time. The very thought of an Irish-American Catholic becoming leader of the Free World had been unimaginable right up to election day in 1960. Here was Ireland, struggling to break free of the historical stranglehold that had gripped it for so long, an Ireland keen to move on from the de Valera years. It would bring glory by association for the country to welcome the man from the White House, a dynamic young politician from an Irish family who had reached the pinnacle of world power. For the Irish people, a visit from him would provide a shot of much-needed confidence on the world stage.

For all these reasons, from the moment John Fitzgerald Kennedy stepped through the pillared portico of the White House in January 1961, Lemass was keen to entice him over to Ireland, and he entrusted the job of achieving this to Ireland's man in Washington, Dr Thomas J. Kiernan.

What began was effectively a dating game involving two interested parties who weren't quite sure how to move things along despite a mutual attraction and a determination to make it work.

The job of Irish Ambassador to Washington has always been perceived as a plum post and has usually been manned by the brightest and best that the Irish diplomatic service has to offer. Such was the case with Thomas Kiernan, whose dispatches from the American capital are smart, wry and always perceptive. Born in the Dublin suburb of Rathmines, Kiernan was a career civil servant who in 1935 had been seconded to be director of Radio Éireann. He was married to the singer Delia Murphy, and while Kiernan was posted to the Vatican (1941–46) their semi-bohemian lifestyle in wartime Rome made them something of a talking point. Although strongly rumoured to become Ambassador to Britain, Kiernan in fact ended up running the embassies in Australia and Canada before being given the top job in Washington, a post he held from 1961 until 1964.[37]

The first time Kiernan met Kennedy was on 8 February 1961 at a function the President was hosting for upper echeclons of the diplomatic corps. It was an early evening affair, starting at 5pm and attended by Mrs Kennedy. The First Couple formally met and shook hands with all the heads of mission, Kiernan included. As was the way on these occasions, the guests sipped wine and made small talk while keeping one eye on what was happening in every other part of the room. In the diplomatic corps, everything, no matter how mundane, is an incident, real or imagined. Kiernan was doing just this when the President approached him. The two men chatted briefly but it was enough for them to make a connection. After those few minutes, Kiernan commented: "I realised that we were on the same wavelength, the same communication between us which was very important … he had Irish reactions and the Irish reactions helped me in understanding."[38]

And with that, the diplomatic manoeuvres in the dark began. The plan? Get Kennedy, "our" other president, an Irishman, a Catholic, to Ireland. Things are never straightforward in the world of diplomacy, though. You can't just issue an invitation when there's a possibility that the other party might not be able to accept. Everything has to be handled slowly, step by step.

Despite Kennedy's "Irish reactions", the way he understood a wink and a nod without everything being stated openly, Kiernan felt let down by the quality of Ambassador the President decided to send to Ireland. At that diplomatic gathering, Kennedy had asked Kiernan who the current American Ambassador was. When Kiernan told him that it was Scott McLeod, Kennedy responded "Oh, he's no good", before adding "I'm going to send you a really good ambassador, an ambassador that will really represent America."

Despite this statement, the next ambassador, Edward G. Stockdale, was of the same mould and dismissed by Kiernan as "a very, very poor type … [who had] very little intelligence … His I.Q. wasn't very high. And that's all we got." Kiernan was disappointed and felt that "it showed President Kennedy's lack of interest in Ireland at the time … He certainly had no intention of sending a good ambassador." The truth is probably that the President's choice of Stockdale was rooted in his contribution to party coffers, as was the normal practice, but it was a setback for Kiernan. Having a US ambassador in Dublin with whom he could work closely, in confidence, would have been a huge help, but Stockdale was not going to be that person.

The Irishman decided to play the long game. The Kiernan approach involved putting away the sledgehammer and going the softly, softly route. First things first for the Ambassador was not to play the Green Card, "There was no question of attempting to take advantage of the fact that his ancestors had come from Ireland ... we bent backwards to avoid any kind of what I would regard as an intrusion." Despite this, the Irish card made a natural apearance anyway. On 17 March, St Patrick's Day, an Irish delegation gets annual access to the White House for what's called the Shamrock Ceremony, during which the President is given a bowl of the famous Irish greenery. In recent years, the Taoiseach has made the trip but in 1961, the Ambassador did the honours and so, just a month after their first encounter, Dr Kiernan found himself back in the White House. In preparation for the ceremony, the wily diplomat made a call to the Office of Heraldry in Dublin and arranged for them to create a coat of arms that would bring together the O'Kennedy and the Fitzgerald clans. The two men met and Kiernan presented the bowl of shamrock and the coat of arms to the President, who was very appreciative. A rapport was slowly building beween them. It was a critical relationship in the story that was about to unfold.

Just three weeks later, on 11 April, the secretary at the Irish Department of External Affairs, C.C. Cremin, wrote to Kiernan noting that Kennedy was due to visit President de Gaulle in Paris at the end of May and adding "If the President and Mrs Kennedy should desire to come to Dublin they would, of course, be heartily welcome." He went on to express his desire not to take advantage of Kennedy's heritage or what the secretary described as the President's "friendly sentiments for Ireland". Cremin was at pains to stress that the Irish Government didn't wish to embarrass Kennedy by issuing a formal invitation which he might in the circumstances feel it difficult to refuse and he urged Kiernan to take a discreet approach. Cremin finished this missive by mentioning a series of dates that wouldn't be suitable because ministers would be otherwise occupied; these included early June (there was to be a visit from the German foreign minister), mid-June (Princess Grace of Monaco was bringing her husband to town) and late June (when there was to be a week of ceremonies, prayer and pageantry marking 1,500 years since the death of St Patrick).[39]

Kiernan decided not to force the issue. On 15 April the US army began the ill-fated Bay of Pigs invasion and it was obvious that President Kennedy's thoughts would be elsewhere, so he didn't issue an invitation on that occasion. Kiernan's strategy was still, like Augustus', *festina lente*, and in order to make haste slowly, the diplomat had to take advantage of every opportunity, no matter how tiny, to turn the President's attention to things Irish. He didn't have long to wait before another opportunity arose.

Courting Kennedy: Dr Thomas J. Kiernan, Irish Ambassador to the United States, with JFK after presenting him with a vase of shamrock for St Patrick's Day. This photograph was taken in the Oval Office on 15 March 1963.

The people of Wexford, home to the original Kennedys, decided through their local political representatives that they would like to present the President and his wife with a christening cup for their baby son, John Jr, who had been born in November 1960. The seventeenth-century cup made its way across the Atlantic and into the hands of Dr Kiernan, who gave it to his wife, who in turn arranged to hand the gift to Jacqueline Kennedy at a small ceremony in the White House. President Kennedy had sent his apologies, citing meetings that day, but just as they were leaving home, the Kiernans' phone rang. It was the White House. Kiernan was informed that the President would leave the meeting he was attending, so keen was he to attend the christening cup ceremony.

This was a most welcome diplomatic development. The Kiernans made their way briskly to Pennsylvania Avenue. Kiernan's main concern that morning was that he hadn't written a speech and couldn't decide what to say. When he got to the podium, facing a battery of cameras and pressmen, he had to think on his feet. With Mrs Kennedy to his left and the President to his right, Kiernan had a lightbulb moment. He turned to Kennedy: "I asked him if, instead of a speech, I might recite a poem which had been [written] for my son the day he was born." The President nodded and Kiernan proceeded.

… When the storms break for him
May the trees shake for him
Their blossoms down;
And in the night that he is troubled
May a friend wake for him
So that his time is doubled;
And at the end of all loving and love
May the Man above
Give him a crown.[40]

The President was moved. He whispered to Kiernan "I wish that was for me," before making his way up to the microphone. As a reciprocal gift, the President presented to the people of Wexford a piece of the podium at which he had been inaugurated, to be delivered by Dr Kiernan.

It was little ceremonies like this one, and the increasingly relaxed nature of the President's encounters with the Irish Ambassador, that helped build the bridge to Ireland.

Finding a reason to visit

The dispatches from the embassy in Washington back to the Department of External Affairs in Dublin suggest that Kiernan and Kennedy were discussing the possibility of a visit to Ireland by early 1962. Writing to C.C. Cremin in May 1962, Kiernan explained that Kennedy had expressed an interest in making a special visit to Ireland and not just one that was tacked on to some other journey (which is exactly what would happen). The problem for the President was that he needed what Kiernan called an "occasion". Kennedy said he would visit without such an event but that a justifiable reason for the trip would be preferable.

Kiernan wracked his brains. De Valera had visited America before, so he wondered whether they could present this as a return visit: "I had thought of President de Valera's eightieth birthday next October, which would be an occasion for the timing of a return visit by Kennedy; but there is no visit of President de Valera to return … I wonder if I [should] throw out the idea of reciprocity, for the visit of our President, as justification for a return visit?"[41] The arguments didn't stack up, though, since it was some time since de Valera's last visit.

Kiernan would go on to suggest the unveiling of a plaque at the Kennedy homestead in Dunganstown, County Wexford, or the naming of the Agricultural Institute after the President as a thank-you for the American aid which had helped in its establishment.[42] The Ambassador was adamant in his dispatches that the conferring of an honorary university degree would not constitute enough of an occasion. He described them as "small change in the United States" and added "the President has picked up twenty-three in his first year". He felt the President wanted "all the works" when he did arrive officially in Dublin and felt that they needed to devise a carefully planned, worthwhile occasion.

Still Kiernan hung back, sending a note to the State Department in May 1962 suggesting that a formal invitation should only be made as soon as the President was able to accept. The move was on, the interest was intensifying but there was just one more big push required to set the wheels in motion.

Before that could happen, in June 1962, the President had a diplomatic appointment to make. The American Ambassador to Ireland, Edward Stockdale, was going home and Kennedy decided to appoint Matt McCloskey, a Philadelphia businessman and major Democratic Party fundraiser to the job. McCloskey threw himself a party and gave a speech that instantly rubbed Kiernan up the wrong way with an emphasis that he considered anti-Irish. He wrote later that the new man was "not in the least Irish or interested in Ireland; that he had never attended anything Irish in his life; that on St Patrick's Day he went about his business as usual; that he resented very much this nonsense in America of Irish-American; and that he was 100 per cent American."

Kiernan was livid as he sat watching his diplomatic counterpart rubbishing the country and the culture he had been appointed to. Worse was to come when McCloskey quoted an Irish expression in the national tongue. "I'll go to Ireland as 'Mr America' and I'll say when I get there *Fág an Bealach*."

Kiernan, a published scholar and fluent native speaker knew immediately what the round, ruddy Ambassador was saying. The expression was an old Irish war cry that translated roughly as "Get out of my way!" Kiernan noted wryly: "You say it when you're going to cut a fellow's head off."

It was a dreadful start to the new appointee's term of office. McCloskey was obviously another Ambassador chosen for his wallet rather than his diplomatic skills, but Kiernan had been around the block and knew how to circumvent such people. "He showed himself to me, 'Mr Bad Mannered American' and he lived up to that reputation right up to the end."

They never got on but Kiernan still kept nurturing the President, waiting for the right moment to strike, watching for the tipping point.

A game of diplomacy

Kiernan continued his campaign of dropping little suggestions and reminders to the President whenever they met and in February 1963 he casually mentioned at an informal function that the Irish government would be prepared to offer Kennedy honorary Irish citizenship. The President's ears pricked up. It was obviously a suggestion that appealed to him, and he asked for some time to consider it.

The next move came on 15 March 1963. The President wasn't free to celebrate St Patrick's Day on the 17th because he was taking a break in Miami before a working trip to Costa Rica, so the ceremony was held two days early. Kiernan had requested some "face time" with the President, away from the clutch of Congressmen who usually attended the event. He reported that "in former years, this has been an embarrassment, putting a damper on conversation."[43] The President agreed to a private chat.

After the shamrock had been presented and the media had got the pictures and quotes they required, Kiernan, the President and the White House Chief of Protocol, Angier Biddle Duke, sat down in the President's study for an informal conversation. Before long, the President got up from his rocking chair and invited Kiernan to step outside with him. The two men walked out onto the White House veranda and the President shut the doors behind them. Duke was not invited.

Kennedy turned to a baffled Kiernan and set out his stall: "I'm glad to say that I can go to Ireland and I'd like you to find out if that's agreeable with your government."

Kiernan was delighted but the President was still worried that he had no compelling reason to go to Ireland and he knew he would get a lot of grief from Congress and the media if he was seen to be heading over to indulge himself on a sentimental journey. "Ireland is not a nuisance in international affairs or is not, one way or the other, in the picture very much," Kennedy told Kiernan, "so there's no justification to Congress to go. For that reason I'll have to make the visit in association with another visit." He then suggested a stopover in Ireland after a visit to Germany and Italy that was planned for June

1963 and asked if Kiernan thought that might be possible.

Kiernan could hardly believe his ears. The President of the United States was asking him for permission to visit Ireland and what's more, he was taking the initiative himself. Kennedy obviously meant business now.

Kiernan didn't hesitate. "The dates, you may take it straight away without referring to the government, will be agreeable and you can come and have a comfortable rest."

Kennedy's eyes widened. "I don't want to rest in Ireland. I want to go around and meet people. I want to meet plenty of people. I don't want to stay in Dublin. I don't want too many official receptions. I don't want any of the stuffed shirt arrangement, if you can avoid it. But it certainly won't be a rest. The more I can cover, the better it will be. That's what I call a rest."

Kiernan asked if there was anything he could do to make the trip relevant rather than whimsical and reminded Kennedy of his government's offer of honorary Irish citizenship.

The President was keen but unsure of the legal implications: "You know – there are all kinds of procedures and it probably will need legislation. The Senate would have to approve. In any case, it's gone to my brother [Robert Kennedy, then Attorney General]. He's the main fellow and he may turn me down. I'd love it, but we'll see what he says."

With a spring in his step, Kiernan went to meet the assembled members of the press. As was the norm by now, he was asked about the possibility of a Presidential visit to Ireland. Without batting an eyelid, the diplomat responded "There's a standing invitation, and he knows he needs no special invitation to visit his other home. We don't press him … he knows he's welcome."[44]

After the St Patrick's Day event, Kiernan moved fast. The next step in the delicate diplomatic game was for President de Valera to send a friendly yet formal note to President Kennedy, extending an invitation to Ireland. The letter is dated 27 March 1963, just twelve days after the veranda rendezvous at the White House. De Valera wrote:

27 March, 1963.

Dear Mr. President,

I am very happy to learn from our Ambassador in Washington that you hope to find it possible to come to Dublin in the course of your forthcoming visit to Europe in June next.

I have the honour, therefore, to extend to you and Mrs. Kennedy, on my own behalf and on behalf of the Government and the people of Ireland, a most cordial invitation to be our guests and to pass with us such time as is available to you on a State visit to our country.

It will be a source of joy and pleasure to me to learn that you will be able to accept this invitation, and I hasten to assure you, Mr. President, that the warmest of welcomes will await you and Mrs. Kennedy from my wife and myself and from the Government and the people of Ireland.

Yours very sincerely,

Eamon de Valera

His Excellency John F. Kennedy,
President of the United States of America,
The White House,
WASHINGTON, D.C.

The formal invitation: Éamon de Valera promises JFK "the warmest of welcomes" should he decide to visit Ireland in 1963.

Within a fortnight, a cream envelope with the words "White House" printed discreetly on the top left-hand corner dropped into the letterbox at Áras an Uachtarain, President de Valera's official residence. It was Kennedy's response to de Valera's invitation. He wrote that he was "delighted" to receive the "warm and generous invitation" but he feared that his schedule would not allow "a very long stop in Ireland, but there is no country and no city I would rather visit." He explained that the dates for his visit to Italy (and by now, Germany) had yet to be fixed but he expected to be in Ireland "for a day or so either on June twenty-sixth or June twenty-seventh".

As if writing to a distant relative or an old friend, Kennedy added: "If these dates are in any way inconvenient for you, I hope you will let me know."[45] His old-school manners never left him, even in high office.

The news breaks

Word got back to Kiernan that the President wanted to firm up details of the trip later in the month of April and to keep it under wraps until then. Work still had to be done on the politically sensitive Italian and German legs of the Presidential odyssey before he could focus on the Irish dimension.[46]

All the while, the diplomatic pouches criss-crossed over the Atlantic as senior diplomats endeavoured to smooth the path, but they were never going to succeed in keeping the news out of the media for long. As rumours spread and the press started to speculate, it was decided to bring forward the announcement of the visit to 18 April, and arrangements were made for the news to be confirmed simultaneously in Washington, DC, and Dublin.

Time magazine was one of the few publications that could find something positive to say: "In all three countries the President plans to visit, more people want to meet him than time or space can accommodate.The problem is especially acute in Ireland: just about every ambulatory person in the country, it seems, wants to shake the hand of the first US President of 100 per cent Irish descent. … Yet White House staffers unanimously predict that the trip is going to be a splendid success. When Kennedy's way with crowds gets working, they argue, the trip will turn into a popular triumph. A staffer's recent comment on the visit to Ireland sums up the White House expectations about the entire trip. 'It will be a mess,' he said, thinking of the eager, jostling crowds. 'You can't even imagine how terrible it will be. But it will be just wonderful.'"[47]

WN-9FS-AC&R
REV (9-51)

American Cable & Radio System

"Via All America" "Via Commercial" "Via Mackay Radio"

To Telephone a Message or Call a Messenger
ADams 9000 or DEcatur 4300
Teletypewriter Exchange: WA-332
WASHINGTON OFFICE
8 DUPONT CIRCLE, N. W. 6

A.C.&R. SERVES THE WORLD BY CABLE AND RADIO
An IT&T Associate

NO.
TIME
MM
CHECK

SENDER SHOULD INDICATE (MARK "X") CLASS OF SERVICE DESIRED; OTHERWISE ORDINARY RATES AND SERVICE APPLY

ORDINARY ☐ LETTER TELEGRAM (LT) ☐

AN ORDINARY MESSAGE IS SENT AT THE UNREPEATED MESSAGE RATE, UNLESS OTHERWISE SPECIFIED

SENDER'S NAME ______ ADDRESS APRIL 18, 1963

SENDER MUST FILL IN ROUTING HERE "Via ______"

ESTERO DUBLIN (IRELAND)

IN VIEW OF PERSISTENT LEAKS WHITE HOUSE HAS REQUESTED TODAY THAT ANNOUNCEMENT BE BROUGHT FORWARD AND SUGGESTS SIMULTANEOUS RELEASE WASHINGTON DUBLIN AT NINE A.M. WASHINGTON TIME FIVE P.M. DUBLIN TIME SATURDAY TWENTIETH IN FOLLOWING TERMS QUOTE THE PRESIDENT HAS ACCEPTED A CORDIAL INVITATION FROM THE PRESIDENT OF IRELAND TO VISIT IRELAND FOLLOWING THE VISIT TO ITALY AND GERMANY IN JUNE STOP DETAILS OF THE VISIT ARE BEING ARRANGED BY THE AMBASSADORS OF BOTH COUNTRIES AND WILL BE ANNOUNCED AT A LATER DATE UNQUOTE PARAGRAPH PLEASE CONFIRM BY RETURN THAT THESE ARRANGEMENTS AND THE TEXT ARE ACCEPTABLE SO THAT WHITE HOUSE MAY BE INFORMED ACCORDINGLY

HIBERNIA

SEND THIS MESSAGE SUBJECT TO RULES AND REGULATIONS SET FORTH IN THE COMPANY'S TARIFF BOOK ON FILE WITH THE FEDERAL COMMUNICATIONS COMMISSION.

A telegram confirms JFK's acceptance of the invitation to visit Ireland, April 1963.

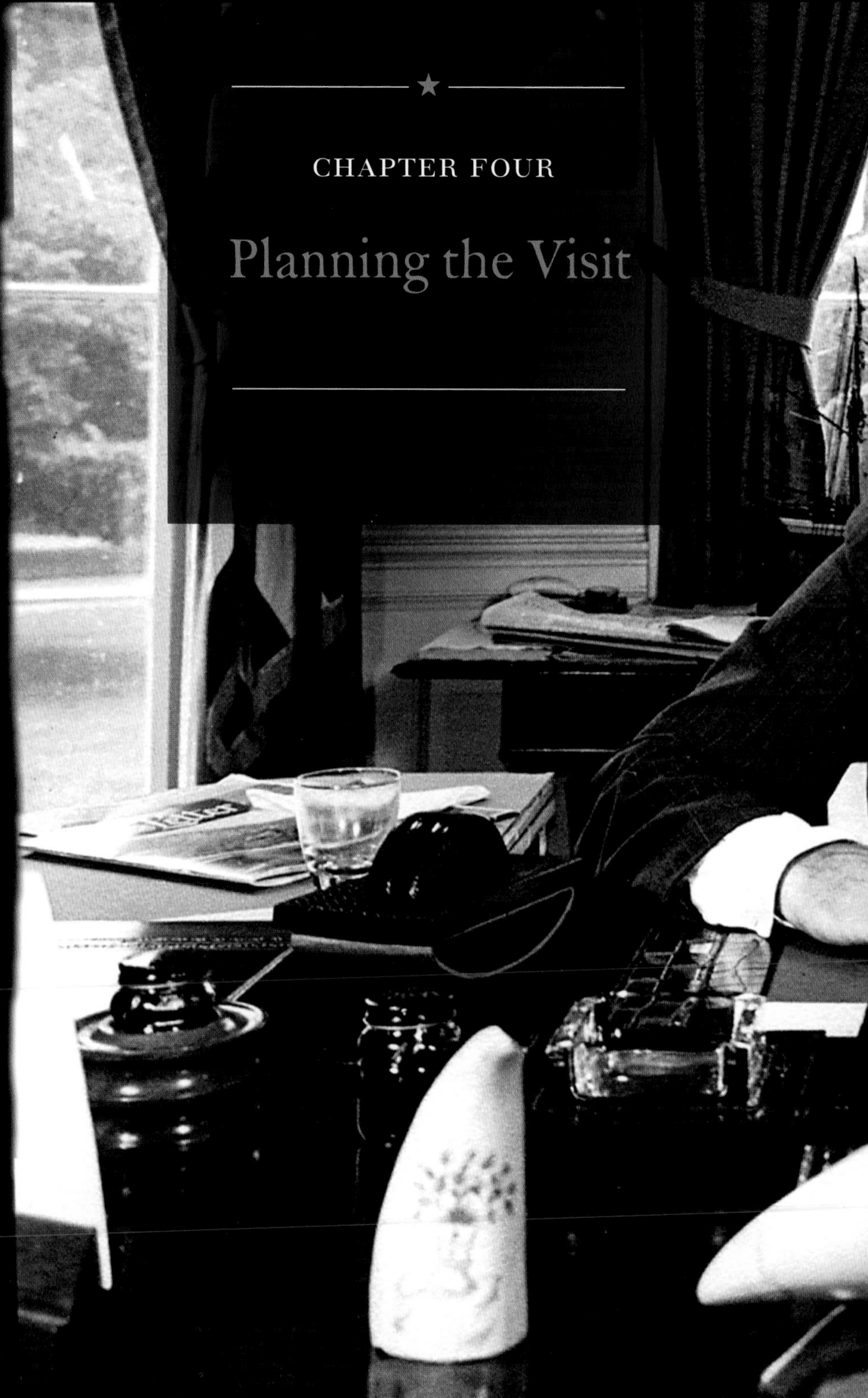

CHAPTER FOUR

Planning the Visit

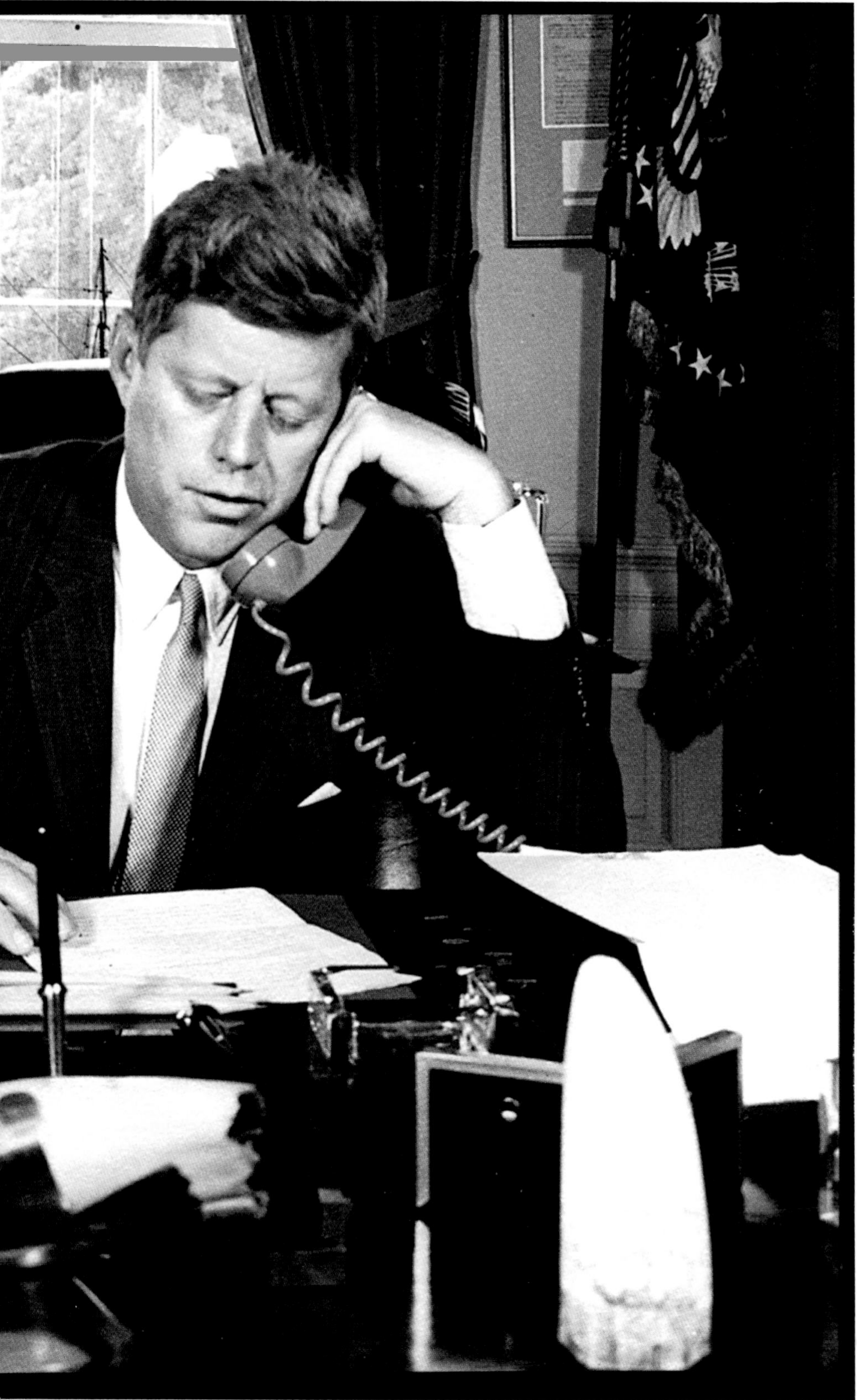

—★—

Throughout April and May 1963, there was a flurry of activity as plans were drawn up, locations inspected and itineraries compiled. Thomas Kiernan knew he had to tread carefully on the subject of the proposal to offer the President Irish citizenship. The government were especially keen that it shouldn't be made public only to be rejected. In Washington, where there was to be a reception for the Grand Duchess of Luxembourg, Kiernan was nervous. The Lord Mayor of Dublin was due at the White House and the Ambassador was concerned that a slip of the tongue might cause problems. In his experience, local politicians had their own agendas and could easily interfere in his delicate negotiations. His chief worry was that Kennedy might raise the issue of honorary citizenship when he met the Mayor, and that the Mayor might then talk to the press. With this in mind, Kiernan approached Angier Biddle Duke, the White House Chief of Protocol, and suggested that it would be prudent for the President not to talk about the general arrangements for the forthcoming visit. A nod was as good as a wink.

The next morning, Kiernan spoke with the Mayor, who told him that he intended to bring up the idea of Kennedy being conferred with the Freedom of the City of Dublin. Kiernan explained that the aim was to confer that and other honours at a garden party that was being planned at Áras an Uachtarain. "The Lord Mayor said this was a good idea and seemed to approve of it."

Later that day, in the White House, Kennedy met the Mayor, who asked his host how long he intended staying in Ireland. Eavesdropping from a discreet distance, Kiernan was happy to report that the President fudged his answer. The Mayor tried again later in the conversation and again, Kennedy delivered a vague answer. Some small talk followed concerning the conferral of degrees with the President singling out the proposed degree from the National University of Ireland, an honour, Kennedy pointed out, that his father had received in 1938.

This encounter with Dublin's Mayor proved to both Kiernan and Kennedy that they could rely on each other not to risk scuppering the delicate arrangements that were being put in place with a misplaced comment. The level of trust between them increased.

On 14 May, the idea of offering President Kennedy honorary citizenship was abandoned, however, when Kiernan received a letter from National Security Advisor McGeorge Bundy. In it, Bundy explained to Kiernan that he had been sent a fifteen-page opinion from the Attorney General's office which referred to "peculiar and antiquated [US] laws and tradition which hedge the President from accepting any honour from a foreign government".

Kiernan wrote to Hugh McCann, Secretary at the Irish Department of External Affairs, explaining that Kennedy "takes very kindly indeed the offer suggested and the spirit which inspired it, and hopes that we will not be disappointed to know of the difficulties which incline him to ask us not to proceed with the matter."[48]

Taoiseach Seán Lemass wrote in confidence to the leaders of the opposition, explaining why the President had turned down the offer. He requested their discretion on the matter, writing: "It might embarrass President Kennedy if any publicity were given to the foregoing, and I should accordingly be glad if you would keep a knowledge of it within as narrow a circle of your immediate Party colleagues as possible."[49]

The people of Ireland were never told about the offer, but it wouldn't have made a dent in their fevered excitement if they had been. They would, of course, have loved to welcome the President's wife Jackie, who was already making a name for herself as an accomplished First Lady, well capable of charming foreign heads of state. Magazines around the globe were always focussing on her

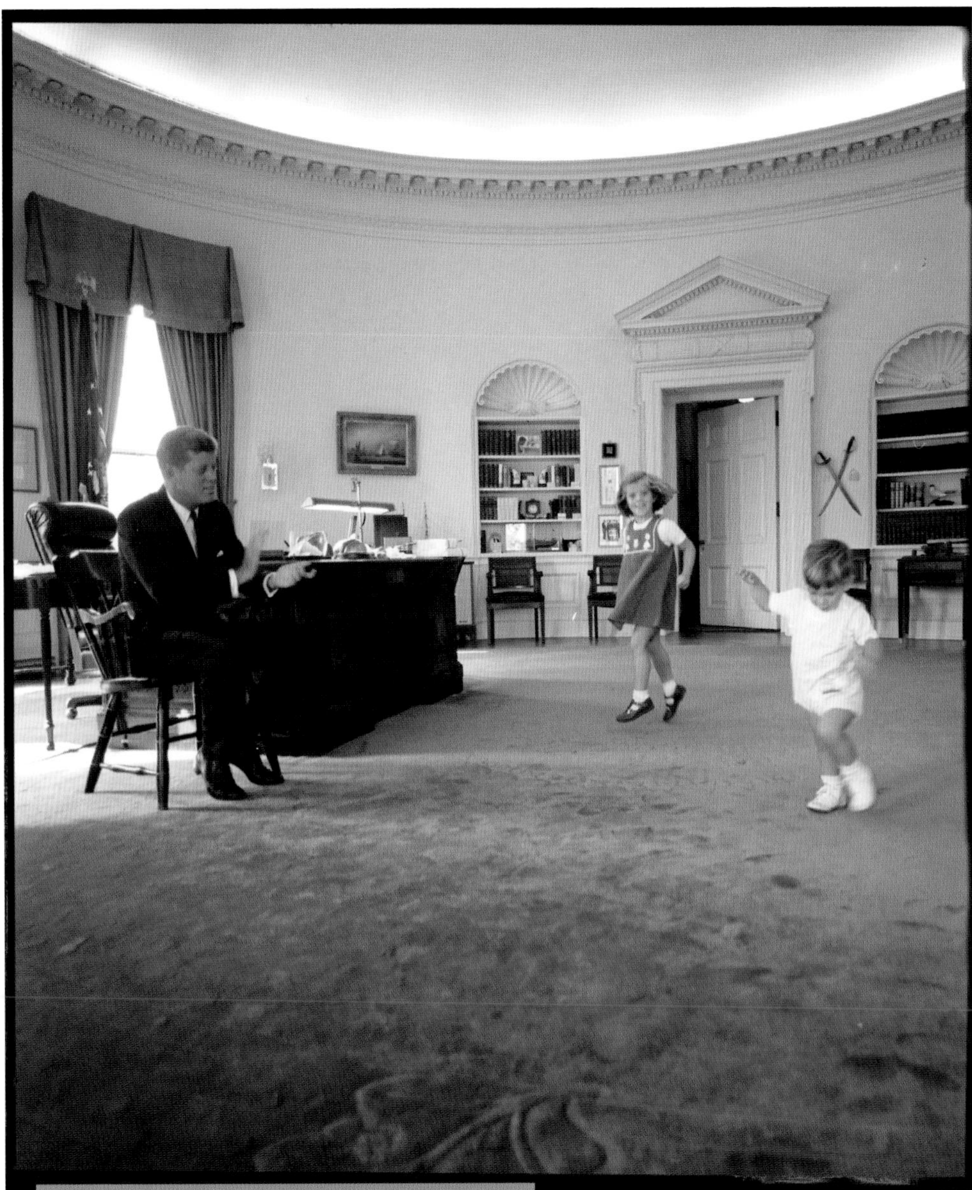

Dancing for Dad: JFK takes a break from work to play with his children, Caroline and John Jr, in the Oval Office, 10 October 1962.

stylish outfits and her much-admired renovation of the White House. Early in 1963, however, it had been announced that Mrs Kennedy was pregnant and would not be undertaking any official engagements that year. President Kennedy would have to go to Ireland without her.

He was not to be devoid of female company, though, as his sisters, Eunice Kennedy Shriver and Jean Kennedy Smith (who would later be Ambassador to Ireland under President Clinton) decided they would like to come along to see the old country and meet their distant relatives in New Ross. Mrs Kennedy's sister Princess Lee Bouvier Radziwill, married to a Polish prince, would also join the party. Between them, these women would up the glamour quotient of the trip. They wouldn't follow the President on every single leg of his tour, but would have an itinerary of their own, that would include visiting schools for handicapped children and charity projects.

The Irish Mafia contingent (nicknamed "the Murphia" by Jackie Kennedy) would also be coming along to oversee the smooth progress of the visit. Ted Sorensen was set to work on all the big speeches the President would deliver, particularly an address that he was to give to the Dáil in Leinster House. Sorensen would be on hand throughout to advise on any last-minute adjustments to prepared speeches. Dave Powers, Kenny O'Donnell and Larry O'Brien would be there as general "fixers" and Pierre Salinger, White House Press Secretary, would arrange liaison with the media. As White House Chief of Protocol, Angier Biddle Duke would remind the President who needed to be thanked and when, which suits should be worn for what occasion, and all the other little matters of etiquette that arose. Ambassador Kiernan would accompany the Presidential party, making introductions and overseeing the careful arrangments he had helped to put in place. And there was a further list of people with Irish-sounding names: Larry O'Brien, Dick Donahue, Louise Donnelly, Jack McNally, Dorothy McCann, Mary Durkin, Pat Burke and Richard McGuire.

Jim Rowley, Head of the US Secret Service, was in charge of security for the tour – a crucial role. Before the Presidential party landed on Irish soil, the authorities knew of three separate death threats. Two came via anonymous phone calls to the police and a third came through a call made to the *Irish Independent* newspaper. A *New York Times* article in 2006 reported that one threat suggested a sniper would take up position above the motorcade while the president travelled from Dublin airport to Áras an Uachtarain. Another said a bomb would be planted on a plane at Shannon airport as the President was about to leave, and a third said the President's life would be in danger when he landed at Dublin airport.

Garda commissioner Daniel Costigan wrote to his staff: "While any attempt on the life of the President is most unlikely, we cannot overlook the possibility of some lunatic, fanatical, Communist, Puerto Rican or some other such like person coming here to try to assassinate the president." He added: "This is the most important visit to this country since the establishment of the state, with worldwide publicity. British journalists are likely to be ready to criticise any fault in arrangements."[50]

Angier Biddle Duke flew to Ireland on a reconnaissance trip to look at the places where the President would stay and consult with his Irish equivalents about the protocols that would be observed along the way. It was decided that the Presidential party would stay at the American Embassy, much to Éamon de Valera's disappointment. "We regretted very much that he didn't stay with us here [at Áras an Uachtarain]. He … pointed out that he wanted to be in very close contact with Washington and that meant that the installation of a great deal of equipment and tone of equipment *[sic]* were necessary to keep that contact."[51]

Not only would the President need a special communications centre in the Embassy, but he would also need a "hot phone" in every port of call. The leader of the Free World couldn't be out of contact for any length of time, given the volatile international situation and all the crises he faced at home. On 20 June 1963, just before the trip started, Kennedy signed an agreement with the Russian government to establish a direct line between the United States President and the

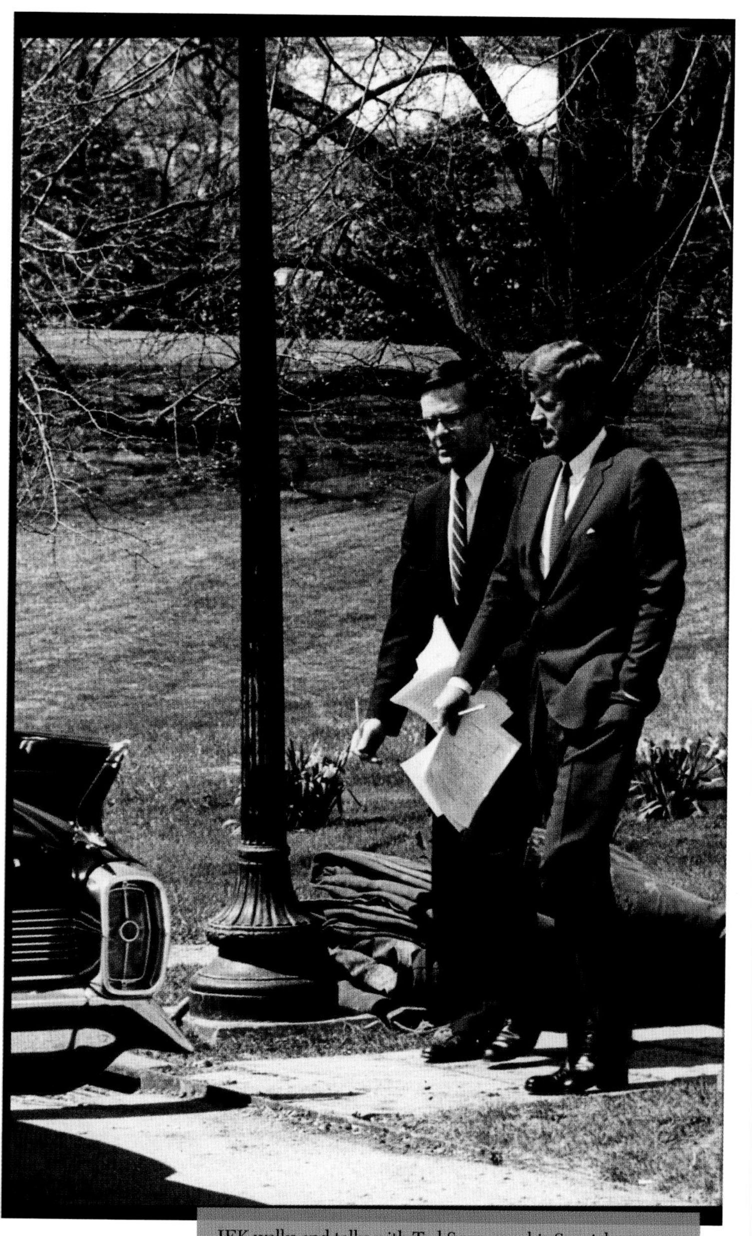

JFK walks and talks with Ted Sorensen, his Special Counsel and speechwriter, 12 March 1963.

The Murphia: JFK and Dave Powers (left), one of his key Irish American advisors, on the steps of the White House, September 1961.

Soviet leader in the hope that nuclear war could be averted by speedy communications. In fact, he would never use it – the first time the "hot line" came into operation was in 1967 during the Six Day War between Israel and Egypt – but it was vital that he remained easily accessible throughout his European tour.

The issue of Partition

One of the great tests of Kennedy's level of loyalty to and interest in Ireland was always going to be the question of Partition and right from the moment he first announced he wanted to visit Ireland as President, his aides were aware that this would be a tricky diplomatic issue. Ireland had only declared itself a republic fourteen years earlier, on Easter Monday 1949, and that's when the border with the North was formally acknowledged. Partition was now a very real problem and became the foremost Irish foreign policy issue throughout this period before crystallising into the bloody Troubles of the 1970s, 80s and much of the 90s. This was an issue in which few American politicians wanted their President to become embroiled, but how could he avoid it if he visited?

JFK's visit in June 1963 would be the first by a head of state to this young nation, laden down with the weight of Anglo-Irish history, and Partition was always going to be up for discussion. And when that first Head of State was a Catholic man called Kennedy whose interest in and knowledge of Irish history was well known, Partition was surely going to be on the table. The question for the Irish government was how far they could go, how far they *should* go and how the President would react to any requests on Partition. They knew that back in 1951, Congressman Kennedy had supported the resolution prepared by Rhode Island Congressman John Fogarty calling for the reunification of Ireland. But what would his position be now that he was a President visiting his home country? It was time to find out just how Irish Kennedy was and how far he was prepared to go.

As the visit drew closer, Kiernan decided to broach the subject of Partition with the President. It was rare for T.J. Kiernan to get his timing wrong but Monday morning, 17 June 1963, less than ten days before Kennedy would touch down in Dublin airport, was going to be one of those times. Kiernan arrived at the White House for his 10am appointment but he knew from the moment he stepped into the Oval Office that something was wrong. The usually jovial Kennedy had a pained expression on his face and this time it wasn't just his back that was annoying him. All around him, Kennedy was being bombarded by matters of critical international and national importance. Way above his head, a female Russian astronaut, Valentina Vladimirovna Tereshkova, was floating around, completing a successful mission. It gave the impression that the Russians were pulling ahead in the Space Race. Back on earth, racial tensions in the deep South threatened civil society itself after the Alabama Governor, George Wallace, tried to stop two African-American students enrolling at the university. These were just two of the matters on Kennedy's mind when Kiernan came through the door of the most famous office on the planet that morning.

The Ambassador, as always, was quick to grasp the mood: "Whether it was the Monday morning feeling or the weekend news of the Russian woman astronaut or the rapidly growing racial disturbances, he was in an unusual state of irritation and nervousness." According to Kiernan, it wasn't just the President who was in a bad mood: "I think every American was in one. I mean it was a tiresome thing that a woman was circling round about."

Kennedy opened proceedings, asking how things were in Ireland. Kiernan told the President that there was great excitement about the forthcoming visit that was "working up towards hysteria". Kennedy wasn't in the mood for flattery and growled back that there was a different sort of hysteria building up in opposition to the whole European trip. But he added that he was determined to go ahead with the tour "and hope that by the time I am in Italy, there will be a new Pope and a settled Government".

It was onto business then as the two men discussed elements of

A new Irish hero: the satirical magazine, *Dublin Opinion*, anticipates JFK's reception in Ireland.

Three years after this White House encounter, Kiernan looked back on the conversation and observed that Kennedy had only been prepared to travel so far down the Irish boreen and was probably more comfortable heading down the British road. When it came to the Partition question, Kiernan was in no doubt that Kennedy "was very cold about it. That is, he was looking at it with a cold attitude. You see, Kennedy was in his blood reactions … Irish in his speed of communication, in his wit, in his debunking – self-debunking, which is part of the Irish attitude … Behind that was something that wasn't Irish; the cold summing up, the logical follow up … When it came to any kind of practical business … the cold man would take control."[54]

In some respects, the issue here concerns Kennedy's level of interest in Ireland. Sure, he was happy to wear green and walk in parades during March but was that the limit of it? He would later describe Ireland as a "misty" island, the sort of Irish-American language reserved for Bing Crosby dressed up as a priest in some movie. With the exception of a few semi-political speeches when he was a younger politician and that bill he'd supported as a Senator, Kennedy was not interested in taking his Irishness any further.

It's true to say that he had a tightrope to walk in terms of Anglo-Irish relations. There was an invitation to visit the North during his trip, to open the new National Trust visitor centre at the Giant's Causeway. The reply came that the President wouldn't have time in his busy schedule, and many in the North took this as a snub. Kennedy must have been aware that a visit to the North would have made the South uncomfortable, as it would have looked like a validation of Partition. He wouldn't go that far – but he wouldn't speak out against Partition either.

Kiernan later noted: "President Kennedy was … more British than Irish … It's the New England attitude in him, I suppose it's the Harvard attitude … Kennedy's first reaction, if there were any even minor dispute between Britain and Ireland, would be to side with Britain."[55] His brothers were Edward and Robert, his sisters included Eunice and Rosemary, not quite Sheamus and Aine. However, it's hard to fight your ethnicity despite the march of time and the shifting generational sands. For Kennedy, his sense of Irishness was always there but it was latent. What becomes apparent is that with every day he spent in that big house on Pennsylvania Avenue he was being drawn back to Ireland, back to the home of his ancestors. Once he got there, it was going to be an emotional homecoming for him, not a political one.

PRESS POOL

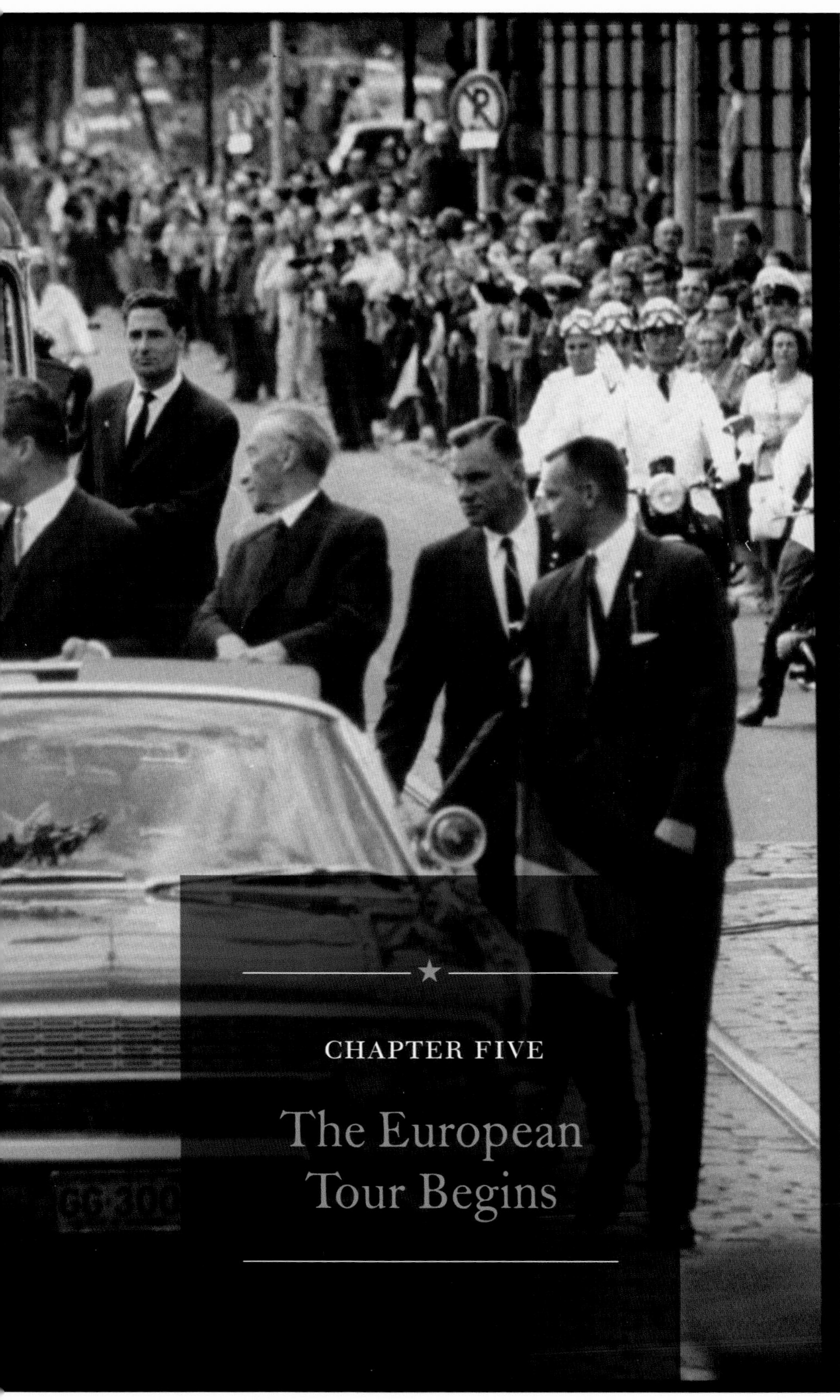

CHAPTER FIVE

The European Tour Begins

—★—

Emotions were running high in June 1963. On his own doorstep, Kennedy was fire-fighting increasingly incendiary civil rights battles. In Congress, he was accused by New York Republican John Lindsay of cynically abandoning the civil rights issue "on the eve of a possible explosion this country has not seen in decades".[56] The media were generally hostile to the trip, seeing it as a waste of time – "Ireland is the only country the President will visit that has what can be described as a firmly-established and durable Government," sniped *The Washington Times* – but he was helped by some unlikely voices, including that of Richard Nixon, who felt that America's image abroad needed a lift and the President was right to pack his bags and head for Europe.[57]

Across the Atlantic, in the debating chambers and official residences of Popes, Presidents and Prime Ministers, there were great expectations of this young leader whom they felt could act as a political salve to innumerable wounds. First and foremost, the Soviet shadow was long and menacing and everyone was keen to get President Kennedy over for a show of strength.

On 10 June, he raised eyebrows with a landmark speech that stressed his desire to develop a peaceful co-existence with the Soviet Union. "Both the United States and its allies, and the Soviet Union and its allies, have a mutually deep interest in a just and genuine peace and in halting the arms race." He announced that he would soon be meeting Soviet leader Nikita Khrushchev and British leader Harold Macmillan to try and reach early agreement on a nuclear test ban treaty, and said that the US would not continue with atmospheric testing as long as other states didn't do so either. He urged the world to "cherish our children's future" and to re-examine their attitudes towards the Communist bloc, looking at what they had in common with the Soviets rather than their differences.

Of all the European countries to shudder at this so-called "Peace Speech", it was Germany that feared the most. With the Berlin Wall providing all-too-tangible evidence of the Soviet threat, West Germans were frightened that Kennedy's talk of "co-existence" might be a precursor to the withdrawal of American troops from Europe. Just a week before he was due to arrive in Berlin, thousands of West Berliners marched to the Wall and demanded that it be torn down, in a protest marking the anniversary of the 1953 anti-Communist revolt in the city. The very night before Kennedy touched down on German soil, Chancellor Konrad Adenauer addressed the nation on television and told his people: "Only the leadership of the United States can protect the free world, and therewith us, from slavery."[58]

The truth was that while Kennedy wanted to make overtures towards the Soviets in the interests of world security, to prevent a repeat of any incident like the Cuban Missile Crisis escalating into full-scale nuclear war, he still saw Europe as a key Cold War ally. He needed to reassure the leaders and the people of Europe that America was not about to abandon them, and felt that the only meaningful way he could do this was to show up. The problem was, who would be there to greet him?

Europe in June 1963 was a mess. In fact, the whole itinerary had to be reorganised at the last minute and the Italian visit moved from first to last after the death of the Pope on 3 June, and the hasty resignation of the head of government, Amintore Fanfani, on the 21st. In Germany, the Chancellor was about to change, so while Kennedy was greeted on 23 June by Chancellor Adenauer, power had already shifted to incoming Chancellor Ludwig Erhard. The most lurid complications occurred in Britain. When it was eventually announced that Kennedy and Prime Minister Harold Macmillan would meet in London, *The Washington Post* described it as a "master stroke of miscalculation" given that it came at the height of the sex scandal involving War Minister John Profumo and a call girl called Christine Keeler.[59]

A letter in *The New York Times* read: "A short while ago the President announced that he would visit Italy, Germany and Britain. In rapid succession shortly thereafter Premier Fanfani of Italy received a resounding rebuff and submitted his resignation, Chancellor Adenauer of Germany was compelled to relinquish control of his party ahead of time, and a sex scandal has so upset the Macmillan Government that even if the party survives the test, Prime Minister Macmillan is certain to resign." And with tongue firmly in cheek, the correspondent concludes: "Conceivably, scheduling visits to Khrushchev, Castro and Mao would do more to advance our interests than any other diplomatic move."[60]

The broad consensus within the American media can be summed up in *The Washington Post*'s pithy headline: "Europe: A Tour of Political Ruins."[61]

One of those ruins was the President's homestead and mother country. New Ross in County Wexford, like so much of Ireland, was beside itself in anticipation of the President's visit but in the American press, it scarcely figured. In fact, just two weeks before the visit, *The New York Times* reported that Kennedy was "scheduled to visit Ireland and his ancestral home, New Rex [*sic*]",[62] while a later editorial sniffily dismissed the entire Irish leg of the European tour by saying "The jovial Irish phase needs no comment."[63]

The whole "sentimental journey" tag trailed the Irish visit wherever the President went. Eventually, White House Press Secretary Pierre Salinger felt it necessary to point out that the President would be having "discussions with Prime Minister Seán Lemass … Trade questions, United Nations affairs and the President's view of the world situation head the agenda."[64]

The truth was that all eyes were on Berlin and what the President would say there. A pacifist with a military past, John F. Kennedy was a war hero whose country had helped win a war against Germany. Here he was, just eighteen years since the war had ended, visiting the country that had wreaked havoc on several continents. As leader of the Free World, he needed Germany; but on Sunday, 23 June 1963, Germany needed John Fitzgerald Kennedy more.

The city of Berlin had been a flashpoint for Soviet and Western confrontation throughout the Cold War. The division of Berlin into Western and Soviet zones reflected the division of the rest of Germany and provided a front line between the two opposing sides. The flooding of some 4 million East Germans into the west through Berlin caused the Soviet authorities to build the Berlin Wall in August 1961 to cut off this escape route.

It was 9.30 in the morning of 23 June when the President's plane touched down at Wahn airport, just outside the cathedral city of Cologne. So began an extraordinary ten-day trip that saw Kennedy spend three nights in Germany, three in Ireland, just two nights in Italy and only one in Britain.

The Germans were well prepared for the President's arrival. A commemorative stamp had already been issued by the post office, a medal with Kennedy's face on one side and a German coat of arms on the other had been struck, as had a double-sided pin with Kennedy on one side and Adenauer on the other. Commuters were told to leave their cars at home (they did) and the countless young women of West Berlin persecuted their hairdressers for Jackie Kennedy hairstyles.[65] The only big surprise for host and guest alike was the sheer number of people who showed up to catch a glimpse of the President. Close to one million Rhinelanders were there to see the five-hour motorcade make its way from the airport near Cologne and on to Bonn and Bad Godesberg.

Wherever they went there was a huge turnout of people desperate to catch a glimpse of the charismatic American leader, and crowd control gave the German police and Kennedy's security officers a bit of a headache. When the President's sister Eunice took a boat trip on the Rhine, there was some relief when the President decided not to accompany her because German authorities feared someone might drown in the crush. As it turned out, the only emergency reported that

—★—

The roar of German cheers ringing in his ears, President Kennedy boarded Air Force One with a sense of relief and anticipation. His visit to Berlin was not only a success – it made history. He wasn't to know that the speech he gave that day was to become one of the most iconic ever delivered by an American president, but the cheers and sheer size of the crowd must have afforded him a few quiet moments of self-congratulation.

His speechwriter and advisor Ted Sorensen remembers that in Berlin "he received the most vociferous welcome he had ever received anywhere, US or abroad, in his life. And not just after his speech, but as he went through the streets, everything … He climbed into Air Force One, I was already on board, he sat down across from me and said, 'We'll never have another day like this as long as we live.'"[69]

It was a Wednesday evening, 26 June 1963. Next stop: Ireland.

The country had been in a frenzy of excitement about this visit since it had first been announced to the public on 18 April. Every minute of the President's stay in Ireland had been analysed and people planned to show up at whatever point they felt might afford them the slightest glimpse of him, even if they weren't close enough to hear what he had to say. On the flight across Europe and on towards the Irish Sea, the President was nostalgic and reminisced with some of his advisors about his previous visits to Ireland. He told them about the trip he had made to the Kennedy homestead as a young Congressman in 1947, along with Pamela Churchill, and asked Kenny O'Donnell, "How soon will we be going back to see my cousins in Dunganstown?"

O'Donnell replied "Tomorrow ... They'll all be there waiting for you with a big spread of salmon and tea." He added, "This time in Ireland you won't be mixed up with any members of the British nobility."

The President was happy about this. "Good," he said.[70]

Dublin airport had never seen anything like it. The total hardware involved in transporting the Leader of the Free World to Ireland included Air Force One, a chartered 707 for media, a DC-7, four jet-propelled helicopters and six smaller helicopters that were flown in from US military units in Europe.[71] Dozens more members of the party who hadn't been on the German leg of the trip had already arrived. According to the *Washington Post*: "Everybody with an ' O' or a 'mc' on his name took a big Air Force jet to Ireland from Andrews Air Force Base on Tuesday, June 25, at 8:10pm. All of the

The press pack line up at Dublin airport for a first glimpse of JFK on Irish soil.

Excited crowds salute the new arrival at Dublin airport.

A military salute: Irish defence forces provide a guard of honour for the visiting President.

so-called 'Irish Mafia' who had not left with the President earlier were aboard."[72] Jean Kennedy Smith was on this flight, which had arrived earlier on the 26th.

It was 8pm when Air Force One touched down. There was a nervous hum of excitement among those gathered to welcome home "their" President. President Éamon de Valera was waiting patiently at the end of a strip of red carpet, accompanied by an aide to guide him because he was by now half-blind. The atmosphere was tense. The Irish people had never experienced such a visit before and when that plane landed in all its glory, the physical presence of the world's foremost superpower had quite an effect – so much so that when President Kennedy emerged from Air Force One, he thought there must have been a mistake because it was so quiet.

Ted Sorensen recalls: "We got off the plane at Dublin, it's almost silence. There are people there, there are people on the balcony, there are people at a very safe, respectful distance, and there's a smattering of applause, but no cheers, no shouts."

The authorities had decided that the President's first moments in Ireland should be a solemn affair, dominated by military procedures and formal handshakes. The silence was a mystery to the President, who later commented to Sorensen: "I thought maybe we [had] just left Ireland with that wonderful applause and welcome and flown and landed in West Berlin" (where the Germanic population was normally known for its coolness).[73]

It wasn't until the motorcade left the confines of Dublin airport that the full force of an Irish welcome would become apparent. Once the Irish decided it was appropriate to applaud, he met with nothing but cheers every day thereafter.

Cold and civil: two wars collide

Before the cheers came the formalities, and so it came to pass that the New York-born Irish Civil Warrior shook hands with the youthful Cold Warrior, whose unquestionable Irish heritage he would wear proudly on his sleeve for the next three days.

Emerging from his aircraft, clutching a hat to his chest and dressed in a smart, dark suit, white shirt and skinny tie, Kennedy was greeted by the army's brass and percussion section before the Presidential party faced the Irish Tricolour and the American Stars and Stripes and their respective anthems echoed around the runway of Dublin airport. A 21-gun salute was fired before Colonel P.J. Halley, the officer in charge of Eastern Command, accompanied the 35th President of America on an inspection of the Captain's Guard of Honour.

The two Presidents then made short speeches that were weighted heavily with history: the history that had brought them to this moment and the history that was being made with every utterance.

De Valera, the light breeze blowing wisps of hair across his face, true to form, delivered a magisterial performance that mixed the past, patriotism and pride. Speaking without notes and with the perfect

JFK is introduced to a line-up of Irish dignitaries at Dublin airport by Taoiseach Seán Lemass.

diction of a schoolteacher, he went back nine and a half centuries to recall the "Cinnéide clans of the Dál gCais" who defeated Norse invaders at the time. (Cinnéide is Gaelic for Kennedy and the Dál gCais were an ancient tribe based in Munster.)

In a speech that lasted less than four minutes, he welcomed Kennedy on three counts: first, as President of America; second, as representative of the land "in which our people sought refuge when driven by the tyrant's laws from their Motherland" (a weighted reference to the fact that the policies of the British occupiers contributed significantly to the suffering during the Great Famine); and third, as "a distinguished son of our race, who has won first place among his countrymen in a nation of 180 million people". This wasn't any ordinary State visit; this was the return home of the son of a lost generation and in his short message of welcome, President de Valera made that very clear. "We are proud of you, Mr President, we admire you for the leadership you are giving … We wish God's blessing upon you, and upon your work. God save you."

As de Valera spoke, Kennedy stood, poker straight, his gaze fixed, eyes front. Here were two giants among men, both born in the United States, one sentenced to death for taking part in the 1916 Easter Rising a year before the other was born, and yet it would be the older President who would soon mourn the younger. For those watching, it was a mesmerising moment. The physical contrast between them was stark. De Valera cut a waxen figure, almost bald, nearly blind, his old-world elegance out of place beside this confident creature who had just emerged from the mighty Air Force One. Tanned, smiling and immaculately groomed, with a full head of sandy-coloured hair, President Kennedy approached the microphone and addressed his counterpart.

"Mr President, there are many reasons why I was anxious to accept your generous invitation, to come to this country … Eight of my grandparents left these shores in the space of almost months, and came to the United States. No country in the world, in the history of the world, has endured the haemorrhage which this island endured." In a short but sharp speech, Kennedy matched de Valera in tone

THE KENNEDY VISIT

AN EASY-TO-FOLLOW GUIDE TO RE A

MEN BEHIND THE MIKES

● MICHEAL O'HEHIR and GAY BYRNE will handle TE's commentary. They are listed here with RE's commentators.

BRIAN FARRELL

● Broadcaster, television interviewer and university administrator. Studied at Harvard and is expert in U.S. affairs. Frequent contributor to Irish newspapers and periodicals. (No. 1).

SEAN Mac REAMOINN

● Radio Eireann scriptwriter, interviewer and commentator. A bilingual and ebullient conversationalist who abandoned diplomacy for broadcasting. An expert on Church Liturgy. (No. 2).

MICHAEL O'HEHIR

● Famous sports commentator who has covered major events in Ireland, Britain and the United States. Became Head of Sport when Telefis Eireann opened. (No's 3, 8, 11 and 13).

KARL JONES

● Radio Eireann scriptwriter and commentator. Presents 'Doorway,' a weekly radio magazine. (No. 4).

GAY BYRNE

● Radio and television compere and commentator. Presided over T.E.'s 'Jackpot' and 'The Late Late Show.' News reader and current affairs interviewer for Granada TV, Manchester. (No. 5).

TERRY O'SULLIVAN

● Well-known columnist for Dublin evening newspaper. Army officer during World War II. Presents musical programmes on Radio Eireann. (No. 6).

KEVIN O'KELLY

● Will travel in the Presidential procession through Dublin. Now a television reporter with 'Newsview,' he was formerly on R.E.'s news staff. (No. 7).

JOHN BOWMAN

● One of Radio Eireann's youngest interviewers. Spent time in U.S. and has interviewed many famous personalities at home and abroad. (No. 9).

DENIS MEEHAN

● Radio Eireann Station Supervisor. Formerly Chief Announcer. Has commentated on many important occasions. (No. 10).

TERRY WOGAN

● RE and TE newsreader. Presents musical programmes on RE and is an amateur singer (No. 12).

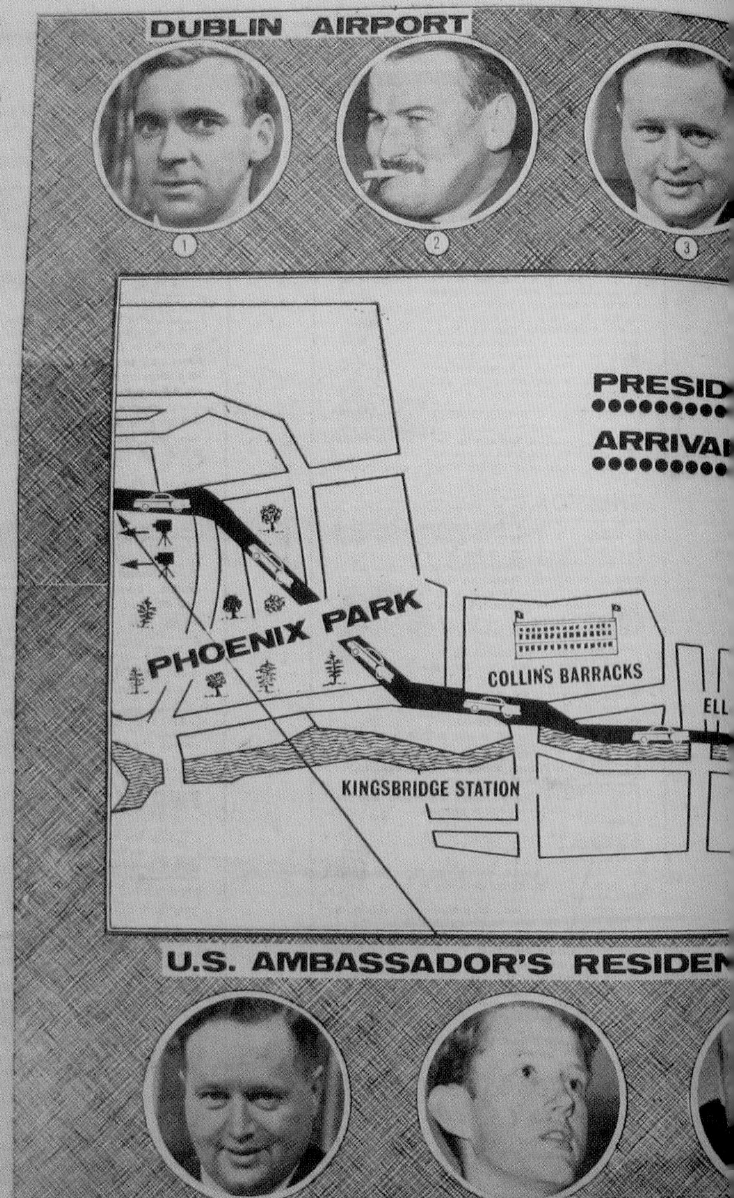

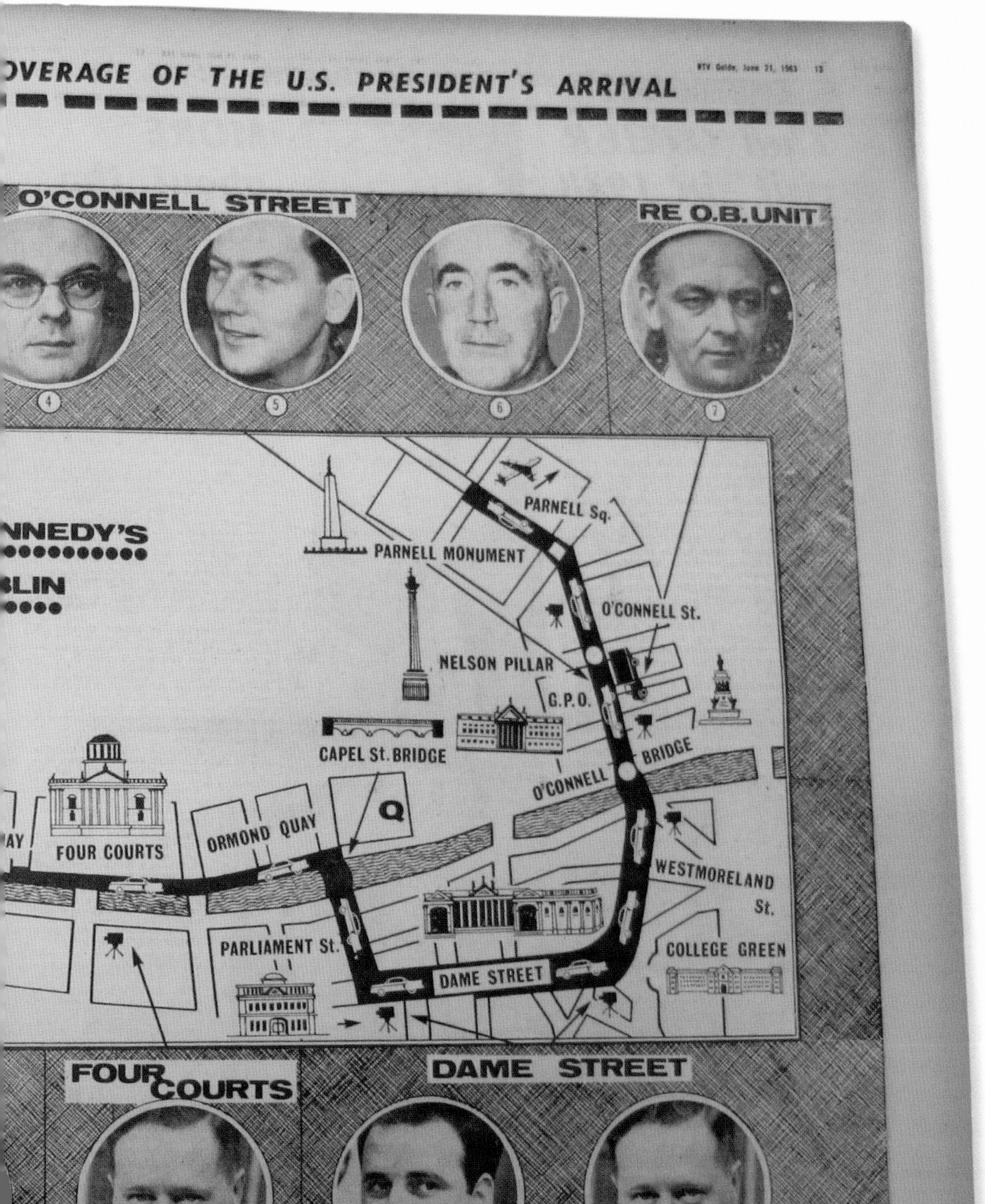

OVERAGE OF THE U.S. PRESIDENT'S ARRIVAL

RTV Guide, June 21, 1963 13

O'CONNELL STREET

RE O.B. UNIT

4 5 6 7

NNEDY'S

BLIN

PARNELL Sq.

PARNELL MONUMENT

O'CONNELL St.

NELSON PILLAR

G.P.O.

CAPEL St. BRIDGE

O'CONNELL BRIDGE

Q

AY

FOUR COURTS

ORMOND QUAY

WESTMORELAND St.

PARLIAMENT St.

COLLEGE GREEN

DAME STREET

FOUR COURTS

DAME STREET

11 12 13

The *RTV Guide*, a forerunner of the *RTE Guide*, provides readers with a map of JFK's route through the streets of Dublin, and a guide to the "men behind the mikes," many of them legendary broadcasters in the making.

DUBLIN OPINION
ONE SHILLING
July, 1963
The National Humorous Journal of Ireland
" What a candidate ! He'd have got in in Dublin North-East, turnover tax and all ! "

Wishful thinking: a satirical cartoon from *Dublin Opinion* makes reference to a by-election in the Dublin North-East constituency, held in May 1963, where the government party was defeated by Fine Gael. The election was caused by the death of Fine Gael TD, Jack Belton, and the seat was won by his son, Paddy Belton.

and message. What he called "Haemorrhage" we call "Diaspora", the former being hard-hitting and cruel, the latter, a modern and anodyne word that is stripped of its impact. He praised de Valera for expressing "in his own life and the things that he stood for, the very best of Western thought, and equally important, Western action".

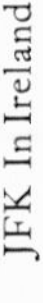

His only lapse into sentimentality came when he referred to "this green and misty island".

After the brief but eloquent speeches, the official party made their way to the airport's VIP lounge, along a path lined by army personnel. When he got there, President Kennedy was introduced to civic dignitaries, members of the Diplomatic Corps and the Cabinet, a giddy row of besuited men standing side by side and looking for all the world like a line of schoolboys waiting to be christened by the archbishop.

The waiting ministers had more reason to be happy than just the arrival of Kennedy. On the previous evening, the Irish government had narrowly survived a vote of "no confidence" over a controversial sales tax. As he approached the relieved ministers, a well-informed Kennedy joked aloud to the Taoiseach, Seán Lemass: "Are these the guys that kept you in office last night?"[74]

Kennedy shook hands with a Cabinet of young bucks, many of whom would soon be running the country. Jack Lynch from Cork would be Taoiseach, Patrick Hillery from County Clare would be President, and Charles Haughey from Dublin would become one of the most controversial political figures of his generation, serving three terms as Taoiseach. And then there was young Brian Lenihan, who would try and spectacularly fail to become President but whose son, a generation later, became Minister for Finance. Commenting many years later, Lenihan remembered that handshake on the runway.

"I was then thirty-two years of age. I was the youngest member in the government, the last man on the team to meet him. My first impact was of a man of extraordinary personality. The minute he shook hands with you, you knew you were in the presence of somebody who meant something. He had it."[75]

Such was the effect President Kennedy had on politicians and public alike. From this point onwards, the "Kennedy Effect" would be felt by all, from postman to president. Within minutes, free from the confines of the airport, the love affair between Ireland and Kennedy would begin.

In the President's Wake: crowds on O'Connell Street, Dublin's main thoroughfare, linger for a while after the Presidential cavalcade had swept past them.

METROPOLE
CINEMA
RESTAURANT

A Dublin city welcome

The two Presidents made their way towards an open-topped car for the brief journey from Dublin airport across the city to Phoenix Park, home of both the Irish President and the American Ambassador to Ireland.

Dubliners were well prepared for this drive. Maps of the route had been printed in the papers and every conceivable vantage point was utilised. Flags and banners of welcome festooned shop fronts and bridges. Flowerbeds had been re-planted and private houses freshly painted. What the airport lacked in atmosphere, the people and streets of Dublin made up for with their enthusiasm. A twenty-six-man motorcycle escort slowly guided the lengthy motorcade out of the airport towards the city.

The crowds were enormous and excited. On the capital city's main thoroughfare, O'Connell Street, between 60,000 and 80,000 people showed up to welcome the President. The motorcade made its way past the historically loaded General Post Office, headquarters for the leaders of the 1916 Rising, which had not yet celebrated half a century as the birthplace of Irish Independence. It was a wistful and sadly prescient de Valera who would later note of his guest, "when he was coming in with me from the airport, he was standing up, and it did pass through my mind, curiously enough, what an easy target he would have been."[76]

Kitchen staff in white caps, waitresses in aprons and civil servants leaned out windows and cheered from rooftops as thousands threw ticker tape onto the motorcade. A young broadcaster working for RTÉ, one Terry Wogan, wryly observed that the falling shreds of paper looked more like CIE bus tickets than ticker tape.[77]

The White House Chief of Protocol, Angier Biddle Duke, was struck by the reaction of Taoiseach Seán Lemass, noting that he "was so proud of the turnout and really so delighted to see his countrymen". He continued "It would be unfair to compare the hysterical passion of the Berlin multitudes to the jolly, friendly, hand-waving crowds on the streets of Dublin. It's a different population, different size, different motivation, and everything else, but it was

Travelling light? The bags of the Presidential entourage at Gresham Hotel.

almost touching to hear the Prime Minister being so proud."[78]

Seán Lemass was struck by the numbers that showed up but he was also intrigued by his guest's reaction to the proceedings: "I think he [Kennedy] was very, very, very deeply moved by the warmth of the reception he got here. It wasn't so much the enthusiasm of the crowd, the cheers, the general outpouring of welcome to him as what he sensed in them, meaning that there was no political significance in this. They weren't beseeching anything from him; they weren't asking for anything; it was just enthusiasm for himself as a person. He broached it with me on one occasion when we were out in the streets. He said that he had addressed many large meetings in the United States, he was very well received and welcomed by enormous crowds in many United States cities, but that he always realised that half of those who were there were Republicans and had qualifications about him. But he sensed in the reception in Ireland that there was no such qualification."[79]

Although seated throughout the journey across Dublin, de Valera was keenly aware of the welcome Kennedy was lapping up: "It was a triumphal procession from the airport," he remarked. Such was the magnitude and enthusiasm of the turn-out, Kennedy staffer and Irish Mafioso Dave Powers remarked to his boss, "You'd beat de Valera in his own precinct"[80], a point that was echoed in a number of satirical cartoons at the time.

Much of the crowd that showed up that evening in Dublin was composed of women, and their reactions were of the type that would later be reserved for rock stars and Hollywood legends. Despite the fact that the car kept moving so he only caught fleeting glimpses of individual faces, Kennedy was able to make a curious comparison between Irish women and the German women he had passed by in Berlin the previous day. He told Ted Sorensen later that "in Berlin, the girls along the street, along the curb in the motorcade, were different from the pretty girls along the streets in Dublin". He said that "in Dublin he could see them mouth the words as he went by, 'God love you!'. In Berlin, he felt they were mouthing something much more earthy which I won't repeat!"

There was a sharp contrast between the crowd reactions in Berlin and Dublin. Here were two very different cities, one scarred by the wounds of a bloody war, now threatened by the menace of Cold War, the other a city still echoing with the whispers of civil war, of internecine feuds, brother against brother and neighbour versus neighbour. Both cities wanted and needed validation. Berlin took strength and hope from Kennedy's visit, while Dublin took a bow.

The motorcade turned into Phoenix Park and made a swift courtesy call at Áras an Uachtarain, which was standard practice when a head of state arrived in the country. This was followed by a short drive across the road to the white-painted iron gates of the American Ambassador's residence.

It had been a long week and an exceptionally draining day. A tired but elated Kennedy was clearly enjoying himself, having arrived "home" for only the fourth time in his life. He was very impressed by the comfort of the Ambassador's residence and remarked to his representative in Ireland, Matt McCloskey, "This is a much better place than the White House." President Kennedy was later heard to say that he was willing to support any American Presidential candidate who promised to make him United States Ambassador to Ireland in 1968 at the end of his second term.

It was time for the President to sleep, before what promised to be a gruelling but unstressful tour. Angier Biddle Duke summed up the exceptional day they'd had: "You could hardly believe all of this happened in one day. It was hard to realise that you had awakened in Wiesbaden in the morning, had been … through a lifetime of experiences all through Berlin, and had gone through a full-scale tumultuous welcome in the capital of Ireland and thence to bed in the American Embassy in Dublin, as he [Kennedy] did that night. Books will be written of the events of that day alone!"[81]

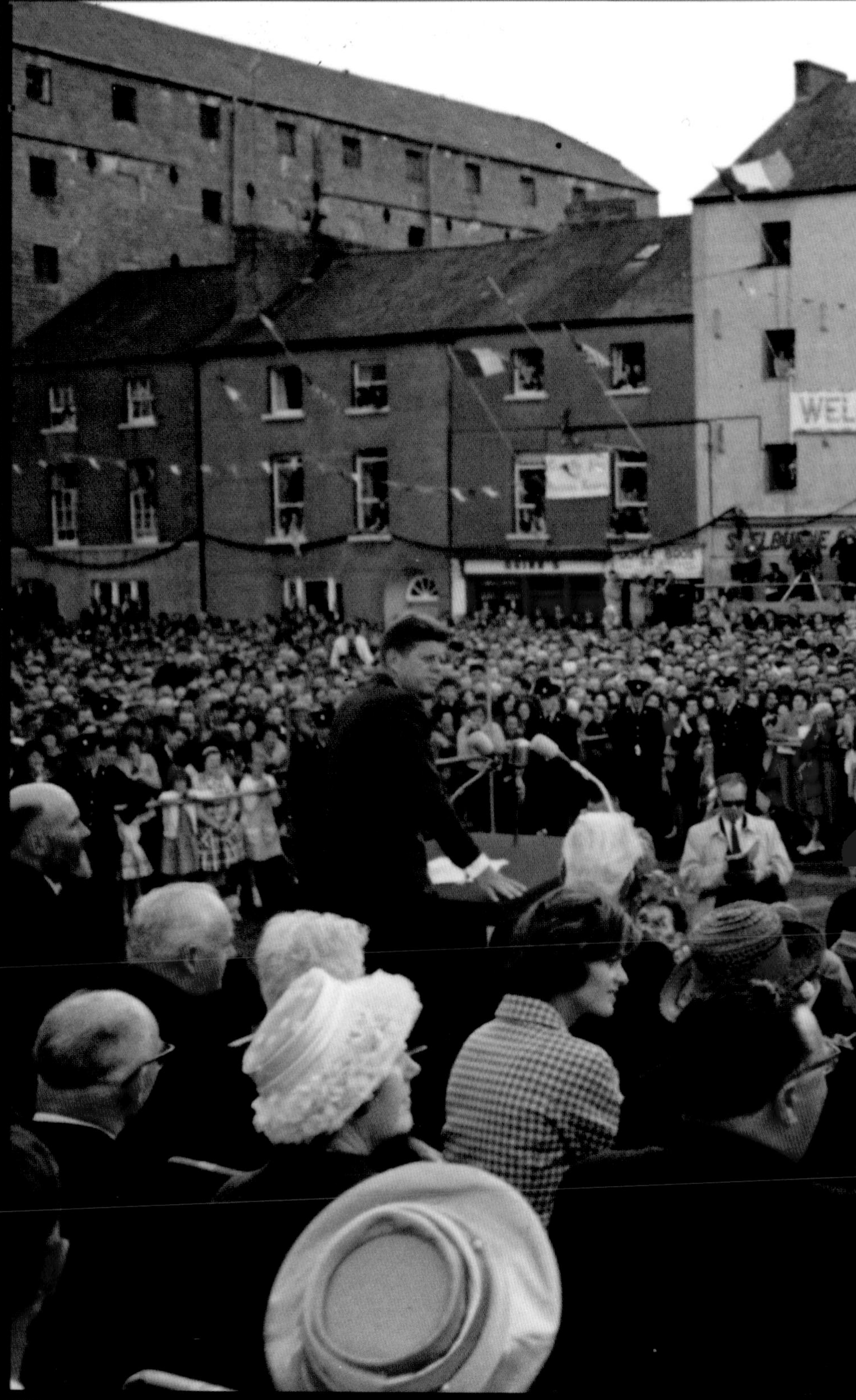

CHAPTER SEVEN

New Ross

—★—

On Thursday, 27 June 1963 JFK woke up in Ireland for the first time as President. After breakfast in the Ambassador's residence, he faced the first of seven engagements that had been arranged for him that day.

If any of the days he spent in Ireland were to be of heritage-related significance, this was it. This was the day when he would see Ireland's recent history come full circle. Here was the day when the Famine Generation of the 1840s met the Swinging Generation of the 1960s. One left in rags on a coffin ship, the other returned in bespoke suits and limousines. This was the day when President Kennedy could cut loose and enjoy himself. If any of the days were to emphasise the sentimental aspect of the visit, this was it.

Seán Lemass made his way over to Phoenix Park for an early forty-five-minute meeting with the young President, which would prove extremely useful if only because, despite the eighteen-year age gap, they found they spoke a similar economic language. Both men understood modern business and international trade, and were keen to find mutually beneficial opportunities.

As he waited at the bottom of the stairs in the residence, Lemass was struck by his host's physical discomfort as he moved: "When I went up to see him in the American Embassy early in the morning for formal talks … as he came down the stairs, I noticed … his feet came fairly heavily on the steps … as if he had some difficulty in walking down, whereas normally he liked to give the appearance of being agile and lighftfooted."[82]

The two men sat down and spoke for the allotted time and Lemass realised that Kennedy was up to speed on the political sensitivities on the island, particularly in the area of Partition, which otherwise remained the great "unspoken" throughout the visit. The two men discussed it that morning during their private chat, but Kennedy kept his stance neutral and, as agreed with Ambassador Kiernan, made it clear that he would make no public pronouncement on the issue. They discussed the nuclear test ban treaty Kennedy was pursuing with the Soviets and Lemass gave it his full support, but one other subject arose over coffee that morning on which they were not to reach agreement. At the time only 27.2 per cent of the population were able to speak Irish and far fewer than that actually used it, but the place of the national tongue was paramount for both President de Valera and for Lemass. President Kennedy was not persuaded of the case, though. Lemass later remembered his vocal opposition to the ongoing efforts to resuscitate and promote the language: "He was, I'd say, in complete disagreement … with our efforts here to revive the Irish language … He thought this was such a waste of national effort, and various efforts which we made to convince him that it was an important question of national revival involved in this which had its economic implication … did not convince him altogether."[83]

There was, however, one very positive development to come out of this meeting. Lemass had plans to visit America later in the year but only in a low-key way, to spend some time reaching out to Irish Americans. That all changed in the course of forty-five minutes and a cup of coffee. Later that afternoon, the *Evening Herald* reported: "Following the very cordial meeting between President Kennedy and the Taoiseach, my information is that Mr Lemass's visit [to the US] will be broadened enormously, and may become a formal visit as Head of Government, rather than a regional, social occasion."[84]

Such was the power of face-to-face negotiation and behind-the-scenes diplomatic activity. Within four months, in October 1963 Kennedy and Lemass would be driving through the streets of Washington in the Presidential motorcade, smiling and waving to crowds of Irish-Americans lining the streets from Pennsylvania Avenue to Capitol Hill.

After their meeting in Dublin that June morning, Kennedy and Lemass emerged to a battery of cameras and journalists. The President looked rested and smart, dressed in a light grey suit. "I'd like to introduce you to some of our White House pressmen," he said to the Taoiseach before introducing them all by name. Lemass shook hands with the men of the American press, then got into his car and made his way down the sylvan driveway of the US Embassy. As he did so, four enormous US helicopters warmed up on the rear lawn. Trees were bent and leaves scattered as the choppers prepared for lift-off.

For the time being, Lemass's notes on the content of their brief meeting would remain for the eyes of senior civil servants only but when they were released into the State archives thirty years later, they showed how little real substance there was to the visit. The President wasn't there to make major pronouncements on Anglo-Irish relations or to interfere in Irish domestic politics. He had other things on his mind and when his forty-five minutes with Lemass were up, Kennedy made his way to the helicopter that was going to take him home to New Ross, County Wexford, for his first visit since 1947.

Landing in O'Kennedy Park

John F. Kennedy had driven through New Ross as a young Congressman in 1947 and felt he had a connection with the place. In January 1961, on the night of his inauguration, the newly elected President of the United States had found time to send a telegram to the people of this small Wexford town. In it, he wrote:

"Fourteen years ago this summer I visited New Ross and saw the hall where over 110 years ago my great-grandfather had journeyed on his long voyage from Ireland to America. Three generations have passed since then, but across this long time and across the sea, I send to you all my very best wishes. New Ross and Washington DC are tied together today. My wife and I send you our very best wishes. We hope we will have a chance in the next months or years to visit New Ross and see again the people of Wexford county. I send to you all, our

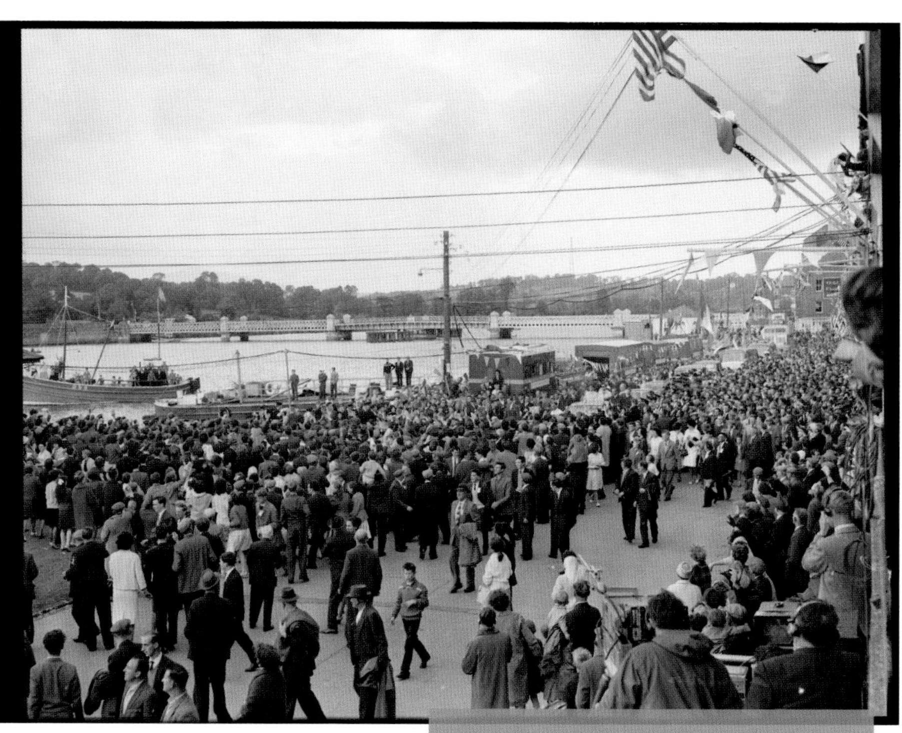

Crowds on the New Ross quayside prepare for JFK's arrival. Andrew Minihan, chairman of the New Ross UDC, summed up the local fervour when he declared, "It was a greater affair to us in New Ross than if the Pope had decided to come".

thanks. I pray the Lord's blessings on Ireland, on America and upon all those who believe in freedom."[85]

His warm memories of Wexford are obvious from the fact that he made time on such an important occasion to send a telegram to the people of a small town on the southeast coast of Ireland. They obviously mattered to him.

A lot of work had been put into the planning of the Wexford leg of the 1963 Kennedy visit. Early in May, an advance party had made its way to Wexford town, New Ross and Dunganstown with a view to checking the area for security risks and points of interest. When the party, consisting of White House Press Secretary Pierre Salinger, Appointments Secretary Kenny O'Donnell, America's Ambassador to Ireland Matt McCloskey, White House Secret Serviceman Gerard Behan and Secretary of the Department of External Affairs Hugh McCann, began a search for a suitable field on which the President's helicopter could land, they struck gold. The local golf course was considered, as was a quayside option, but it was the Gaelic Athletic Association field that caught the imagination of the delegation. The field was known as O'Kennedy Park and the officials were curious to know if it had been named after their boss. They were quickly informed that it was named after Seán O'Kennedy, one of Wexford's greatest-ever Gaelic football players. Salinger promptly took out his notebook and noted down his observations, including this detail about the origin of the name. Everyone felt it was the ideal place for the Presidential helicopter to land – and so it was.

The first sign of activity in the skies above O'Kennedy Park on 27 June came at 10.47 that morning. A huge cheer erupted from the crowd as two specks in the distance became enormous helicopters. They landed on the grass, and members of the White House press corps and a clutch of Irish journalists emerged. It wasn't the President yet but it meant that the wait would soon be over. At 11.05, with excitement and tension mounting, a low hum overhead signalled the approach of four more helicopters. Three of them landed and the crowd saw more journalists, some secret servicemen and several members of the Presidential party. But still, no sign of the President.

At 11.11am, President Kennedy's green and white helicopter emerged from the clouds above O'Kennedy Park. From his seat, the President could make out six huge letters that appeared to be swaying slightly on the ground beneath him. The word *fáilte* (welcome) was spelled out by the shapes of children from the local Christian Brothers School, dressed in black and white and standing as patiently as they could in their careful arrangement. They tried to stay still as the enormous flying machine came in to land, but given the size and power of the helicopter, all sorts of debris lying around the field was scattered in the wind. White House staffer Malcolm Kilduff noted that the unfortunate children even found themselves splattered with cow pats that had not been removed in advance of the helicopter's arrival.

Bounding down the steps of his chopper, smiling and waving, an eager Kennedy was greeted by the Artane Boys' Band and a group of schoolchildren who sang "The Boys of Wexford", known to be a favourite of the President's. When they had finished serenading their guest, the nun in charge of the children asked the President if he'd like to hear anything else. Kennedy didn't skip a beat before replying "Another verse of 'The Boys of Wexford' would be just fine." The nun handed him a sheet with the lyrics on it so that he could join in, which he duly did. When the song ended, the President asked if he could keep the lyric sheet. The nun agreed and he put it in his pocket before moving on to shake hands and chat with the children.[86]

Those with the unenviable task of minding the President could only watch helplessly as all security arrangements went out the window. Kennedy wanted to meet the children and shake hands with everyone, and that's what he did. When an American official allowed some photographers from his own country to get up close to the President, their British counterparts were fuming. Soon afterwards, the official returned and let the British photographers through. It was a chaotic pattern that would follow the President around the streets of Ireland wherever he went. Careful planning disintegrated in the wake of the universal enthusiasm to get close to the great man.

Hotline to the White House: a specially designated phone is set aside for JFK during his visit to New Ross.

A tap on the shoulder alerted the President to the fact that it was time to move on to New Ross, the nearest town to the Kennedy homestead, and at last he turned and headed for his car.

On the quay at New Ross

Ever since the Presidential campaign, win and inauguration, New Ross had spent two years getting ready for this day, this forty-five minutes, this moment. The chairman of New Ross Urban District Council (effectively, Mayor) Andrew Minihan was the local dignitary in charge. When he heard about the President's aspiration to visit, Minihan felt "it was a greater affair to us really in New Ross than if the Pope had decided to come". He wanted to be in personal control of the visit, and didn't relish the prospect of interference from outside. Representatives from the Department of External Affairs (whom Minihan described as "typical civil servants talking to me [as if I were]… the bogman down the country") and from the American Embassy started to make their presence felt in the area, but Minihan was determined that this would be a purely New Ross affair. Years later, he remembered telling the local organising committee: "The best thing we can do now is that we will agree to everything they say. If they say 'Turn left' we'll say, 'Yes, that's alright. We'll turn left.' But what we'll actually do is we'll do it our own way and … the day the President arrives he'll have a New Ross welcome not an American welcome, not an External Affairs welcome, but a pure New Ross one."

In his effort to keep things local, Minihan insisted that a local electrician be given the job of erecting the public address system. "Some people thought [he] wasn't good enough," recalled Minihan. "They wanted to get a Dublin firm to do it. Some of us said, 'Not on your life.' It was his day out as well as ours so he should have the job of putting up the public address system."[87]

And so it came to pass that on that Thursday morning, a local electrician went about his business while Andrew Minihan warmed up the expectant crowd, who could hear the approach in the distance of the 35th President of the United States.

Across town, the excitement was intense. Local dignitaries began to take their seats on a podium that had been erected by the riverside for the occasion. At the foot of the podium stood a lone chair and a table on which sat a telephone. This was the "hot line" that had been linked up with Washington, DC, so that the President would be just a phone call away from his generals and, if need be, from the Russian President Nikita Khrushchev.

With the Presidential motorcade just minutes away, led by the local An Fórsa Cosanta Áitúil (Reserve Defence Force) band, so the approach could be measured by the volume of the music, American secret servicemen carried out last-minute checks around the podium. Reporting for *The Irish Times*, Cathal O'Shannon observed: "Secret service men examined installations, asked photographers to empty out the contents of their bags, poked at a plastic bucket containing plants which was placed just beneath the best of the microphones. Not a bomb in sight."[88]

Anyone who was there on that bright Thursday morning remembers Andrew Minihan rushing around frantically, trying to be on top of every detail, right down to that public address system, which was troublesome from the start. With the advance band fast approaching, Minihan tapped the microphone before asking the assembled crowd, "Can you all hear me?" – to which one section of the crowd protested that they couldn't hear a thing. "Well, all I can say is that I'm sorry," he responded.

It was shortly after 11.30 when the New Ross Holy Rosary Confraternity struck up "The Star-Spangled Banner". On the makeshift podium, elegant heads craned to catch a glimpse of the star attraction. Ladies in elaborate hats, older men in chains of office and countless priests in clerical garb dominated the distinguished gallery.

Brian Farrell, a young journalist at RTÉ with a distinguished career ahead of him, observed that "the local politicians all looked so much older [than JFK], they all belonged to a quite different generation … and they were watching this young man with extraordinary intensity because they knew he had magic. They wanted to know, 'What was the key?' How could they discover how to turn people on?"[89]

With a mixture of benign envy and admiration, the local politicans gazed at this phenomenon and the effect he was having on the people of their town.

Unsurprisingly, the first person the President met in New Ross was Andrew Minihan. "He jumped out of the car and went straight forward to me and he said, 'Mayor Minihan, my brother Ted sent you his kindest regards and he said he had a whale of a time with you here in New Ross.' [Ted had been there the previous year on a private visit.] And I knew from that minute that I was speaking to a man. He was no longer the real President of America or anything formal. He was a human being and naturally I fell for him and so did everybody else. He gave you the feeling that you were the only one that counted while he was talking to you."[90]

Approaching the podium, a smiling and relaxed Kennedy was followed by his sisters, Eunice Kennedy Shriver and Jean Kennedy Smith, and by his sister-in-law, Princess Radziwill. Dorothy Tubridy, a close friend of the Kennedy family who worked as a representative of Waterford glass, and who is a cousin of the present author, accompanied the Kennedy women on every leg of the trip. As they ascended onto the podium at New Ross, she introduced them in turn to the wives of all the dignitaries on stage and they shook hands and exchanged pleasantries.

Within minutes, Andrew Minihan was back on stage with the faulty microphone. Once again, he asked no one in particular, "Can you hear me?" The crowd roared "No!" and one man added, "We hear too damn much of you!" Looking increasingly agitated, Minihan muttered loudly, "Oh, we're in trouble now. Some of the pressmen have walked on the cables. This will be a terrible anti-climax."

As this amusing sideshow was taking place, President Kennedy smiled throughout. Minihan turned back to the crowd: "I'll have to shout, but you'll be able to hear President Kennedy, he has a fine, loud voice."

As technicians tried desperately to fix the cable, Minihan ploughed on with his speech of welcome. This was a proud day for New Ross, Wexford and the people of Ireland, North and South, he said, before presenting his guest with some gifts. The President was given an Irish Georgian silver goblet for himself and a lace handkerchief for Mrs Kennedy, which had been made at Mount Carmel Convent School in New Ross, where they had also made a crochet bag for five-year-old Caroline, who Minihan described as "the boss of the family". In a reminder of the touchy Northern question, Minihan presented the President with what he described as "a little gift from me". He announced: "If Mohammad cannot come to the mountain, the mountain must come to Mohammad. I have here a piece of rock from the Giant's Causeway, which I would like you to accept."

By the time President Kennedy stood up to speak, it was clear that he was having a ball. Having chuckled his way through Minihan's

Dancing days: local entertainment is laid on for the Presidential party along the quays at New Ross.

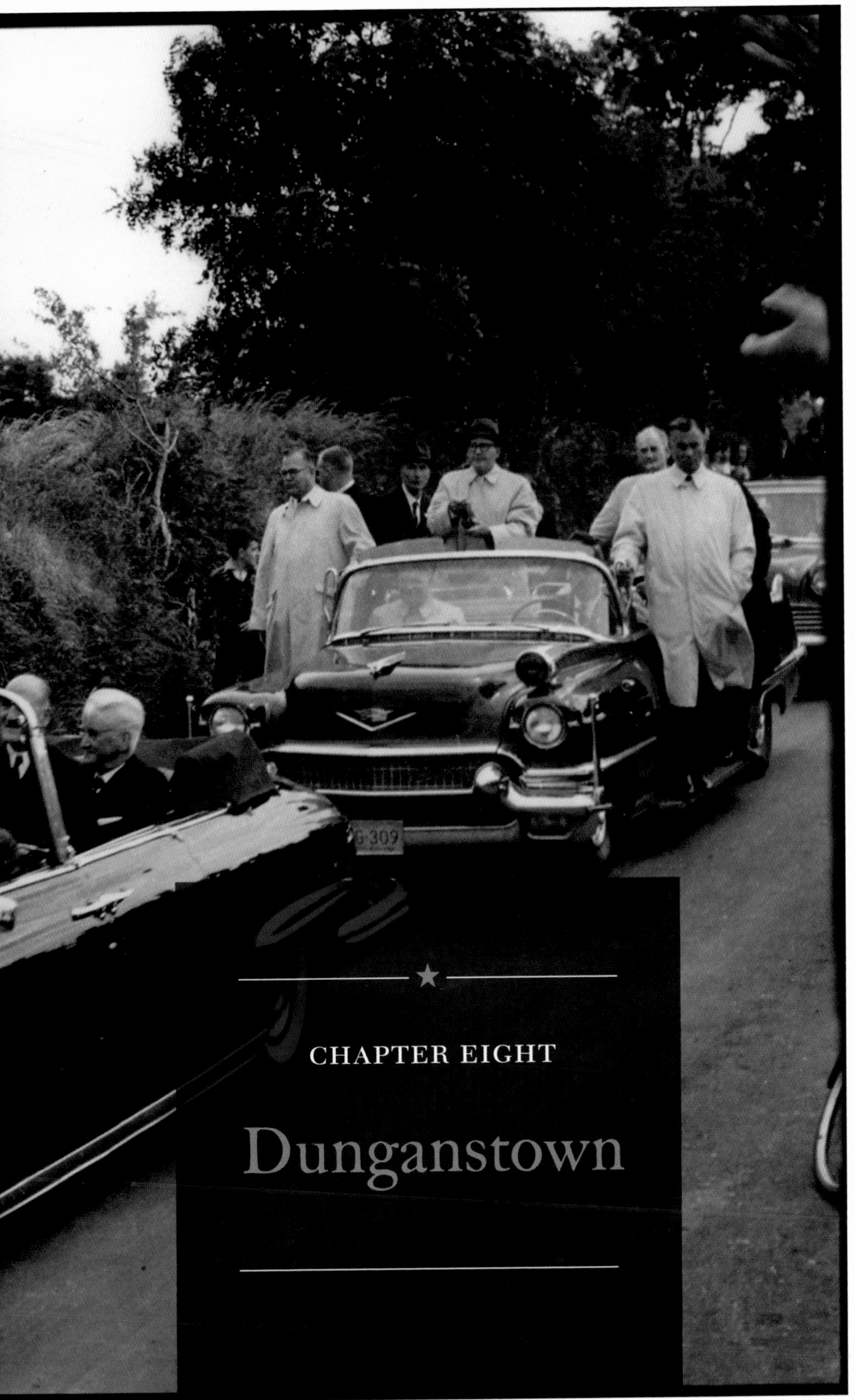

CHAPTER EIGHT

Dunganstown

—★—

It was only a short drive from New Ross to Dunganstown. The motorcade made its way slowly up a leafy, winding road and from his car, the President spotted a man he recognised in the crowd. Dave Powers recalled later, "He's looking out and he says, 'Dave, do you see that fellow there? He's run all the way from New Ross, side by side! We oughta take him back to America and put him in the marathon!'"[93]

When the car stopped, the President got out and turned towards a group of farmers and their families who were being kept at a close but respectful distance. Kennedy beckoned them over but they hesitated and glanced at each other as if to say "What do we do now?" A bemused Kennedy had to call them a second time, gesturing with his hand. A couple of the braver farmers broke from the group with arms outstretched, the others quickly followed and within minutes, Kennedy was mixing it like he was running for local office.

The media were all in position to witness the family reunion, and cameras began to flash. John Bowman, who was commentating on the visit for RTÉ radio, was struck by Kennedy's hair which, he told listeners, was auburn, not the sandy-brown seen in photographs "and the familiar quiff there, very neatly in place".[94]

Mrs Ryan, the strongest connection between the White House and the homestead, was waiting by her gate and President Kennedy greeted her with a wide smile and a warm handshake. She reciprocated by kissing her distant cousin on the cheek. This became the "money shot" that appeared on the front of every paper the next morning. The President stopped and shook hands with everyone within arm's reach. He introduced his sisters and sister-in-law to Mary

OPPOSITE Local children hoist the Stars and Stripes in anticipation of JFK's arrival at his ancestral home in Dunganstown, Co. Wexford.

JFK is kissed by his Irish cousin Mary Ryan during his visit to Dunganstown, 27 June 1963. The Kennedy sisters, Jean and Eunice, look on.

Ryan then greeted more relations, including James Ryan, who the President questioned about the photographs he [JFK] had taken of the family on his 1947 visit. "It was the very first thing he asked."[95] Of course, they still had them and were able to produce them for his scrutiny.

Mrs Ryan's daughter, Josephine, chatted with her cousin and was struck that the President remembered the name of Robert Burrell, the man who gave him directions when he got lost on the road there in 1947. She said that the President "remembered passing by our house and going down to Jimmy Kennedy's before returning to the ancestral home. From the photograph he took on that occasion, he recognised everyone in it."[96]

Josephine introduced her esteemed cousin to fourteen further members of his extended family – Ryans and Kennedys – before entering the house itself where he was presented with gifts, including a set of Belleek china for his wife, a handkerchief for Caroline and a boat for little John-John from his cousins. James Ryan gave the President a blackthorn walking stick cut on the Kennedy lands in Dunganstown. Other gifts included an Aran sweater from the Maudlins Guild of the Irish Countrywomen's Association.

As the family reunion continued, James Kennedy poured a large glass of whiskey and said, "Here cousin, that'll make you feel better." The President accepted the glass but quickly and discreetly passed it to Dave Powers, who drank the contents so that he could hand back an empty glass to his boss. The President later explained, "I had to give him [James] an empty glass, I couldn't lose face among my cousins!"[97]

For fifteen minutes the President chatted amiably with his cousins and sat beside the fire on a chair that had previously been the back seat of a car. He asked Mary Anne Ryan, a nurse at Dublin's Rotunda Hospital at the time, if she would be interested in nursing over in America, and he invited Josephine and her family to Washington. "We may go next year," she suggested at the time. There were a couple of major differences at the Ryans' house from when he had

JFK with Mary Anne Ryan and cousins inside the ancestral home at Dunganstown.

PREVIOUS PAGES The Irish connection: JFK's relatives, the only living direct descendants of John Kennedy (great-grand uncle of President Kennedy), stand for a picture outside the Kennedy family homestead in Dunganstown. Left to right: Mary Anne Ryan, Josie Ryan, Mrs Mary Ryan and Jim Kennedy.

visited it sixteen years earlier. According to *Time* magazine: "Their little farm had been transformed only a few days before: the dirt yard had been laid with concrete, and plumbers had installed an indoor bathroom (wags dubbed it 'John's john')."[98] Nobody went on record as to whether or not he used the new plumbing during his visit.

When he emerged into the concreted-over garden, the President was animated, making jokes and admiring the feast that had been prepared for him. On seeing a salmon on the table, he turned to James Kennedy and asked "Did you poach this salmon, Jimmy?" Scones, Swiss rolls, sandwiches and tea had been laid on. The President spotted a large cake with his image on the icing.

"Should I cut this, Mrs Ryan?" he asked his older cousin.

"Yes, yes, cut your…" she replied, her voice tailing off.

The President smiled at this and plunged the knife into the cake, exclaiming "Cut yourself!" and he burst out laughing. He appeared to be momentarily oblivious to where he was and the office he held. He was relaxed and behaving like a long-lost cousin rather than a visiting head of state.

He cut himself a slice of cake and then Mrs Ryan asked him to cut one for her too. The whole atmosphere was extraordinarily informal, despite the press photographers clicking away all around them and a cameraman filming throughout.

In a few off-the-cuff words to the assembled company, Kennedy announced "We promise we'll only come every ten years … We want to drink a cup of tea to all the Kennedys who went and all the Kennedys who stayed."

Among the pressmen, there was a slice of cynicism from Sterling Slappey of the *Los Angeles Times* who wrote: "President Kennedy probably launched his campaign for re-election Thursday at Dunganstown near Wexford … (he) has been photographed with many distant cousins, has drunk tea and had homemade cookies." But his article ends on a note that would be more prescient than he probably realised: "The President has placed the Kennedy hut alongside Abraham Lincoln's log cabin in American political folklore."[99]

PRESS
O'CONNELL
PRESIDENT KENNEDY'S EUROPEAN TOUR
NBC NEWS
GERMANY
IRELAND · ITALY

Teatime: Mary Anne Ryan pours a cup for JFK.

Before he left, Kennedy made a point of approaching and thanking all those who had helped in the organisation of this special homecoming. In a field behind the homestead, some helicopters landed noisily. There was just enough time for the President to plant a juniper tree behind the house and to shake the hands of some local schoolchildren, who looked up and smiled at this mysterious visitor. That was all they could fit before the "American Kennedy" had to leave.

Accompanied by Frank Aiken, the Minister for External Affairs, and Matt McCloskey, the American Ambassador, the President walked to the gate, and Mary Ryan walked with him. In a most unpresidential moment, Kennedy reached down and kissed his cousin on the cheek, patted her clasped hands and said goodbye. It was the last time he would ever see her; the last time he would ever see home.

A guiding hand: Mrs Ryan brings JFK through the family homestead. Also pictured is Eunice Shriver, the President's sister (left).

CHAPTER NINE

Wexford Harbour

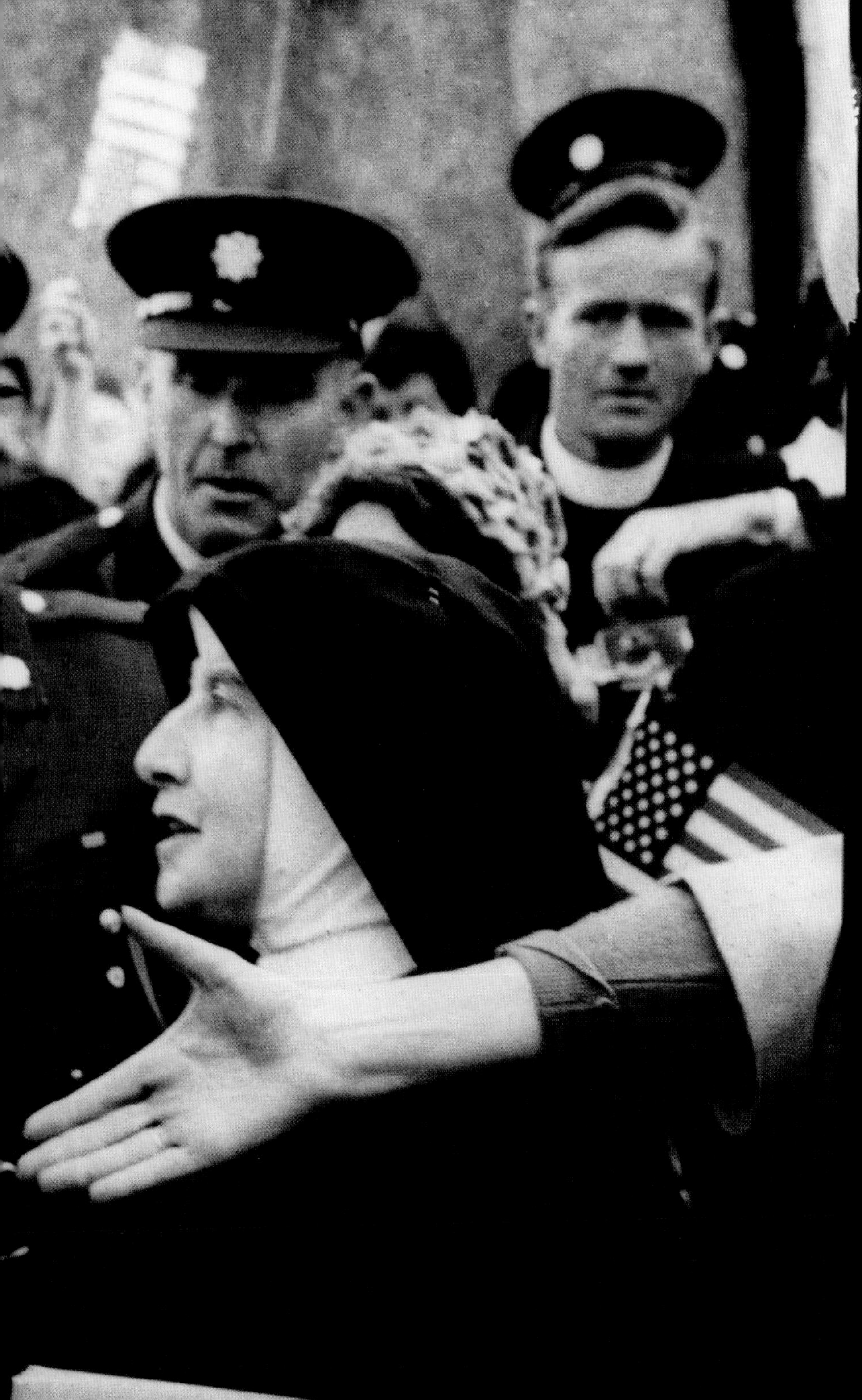

—★—

Less than fifteen minutes later, helicopters were heard above Wexford Gaelic Park, just thirty miles away from New Ross. There was much excitement among the population, which had swelled from the usual 12,000 to 30,000 as people flooded in from surrounding towns and villages.

Beneath the roaring choppers, 5,000 pupils from local primary and secondary schools had gathered to welcome the President. As he descended the steps, a smiling Kennedy acknowledged the crowd before shaking hands with Mayor Thomas F. Byrne and a line of local dignitaries. From there it was into a car, accompanied by Frank Aiken and the Mayor, for the mile-long drive to Crescent Quay. Cheering crowds lined the street as the open-topped vehicle moved slowly and the President stood up and waved constantly at those by the roadside.

The Wexford visit felt more formal, largely because of the contrast with the informality of the previous couple of hours spent with relatives and at the low-key but intimate reception at New Ross. At the quayside, troops stood to attention in neat lines, and there was to be a ceremonial element to the visit. Before any speeches began, the President was to pay tribute to Commodore John Barry, Wexford's favourite son, who was considered by many to be the father of the American Navy. Born in Ballysampson, Barry was celebrated for captaining the first American vessel to record a victory over the British during the War of Independence. Needless to say, such historical moments of anti-British jubilation were popular in Ireland.

The President laid a wreath made of golden cypress branches at the foot of a bronze statue of Commodore Barry that the American people had presented to Wexford in 1956, and then made his way to

JFK meets local dignitaries at Wexford Park, the County GAA Grounds.

Redmond Place, where the Leader of the Free World was given a golden box containing the Freedom of the Town of Wexford. Then, with the formalities over, it was time for Wexford's people to experience that Kennedy magic.

The ceremonial platform was five feet high and faced a monument to the Redmonds, a local family who had contributed much to the community. Ten thousand people had gathered but there was a respectful hush as Wexford's Holy Family Band played the American national anthem. The Mayor made a short speech of welcome then Kennedy rose from his seat and approached the microphone.

As he settled himself at the lectern, a heckler called over the heads

Crowds converge on Loreto Convent in Wexford as JFK visits his cousin, Mother Superior Clement.

Wexford harbour: in a formal ceremony JFK laid a wreath at the foot of the memorial to Commodore John Barry.

of the hushed throng: "Welcome home!" Unfazed by such shenanigans, Kennedy smiled and said "Thank you" before expressing pleasure at being back "from whence I came".

Referring to the fact that he was President, his brother Robert was Attorney General and his other brother Ted was by this stage a Senator, Kennedy quipped that many people back home felt there couldn't be any Kennedys left in Ireland because they were all living in Washington, DC. Addressing the crowd, he asked "I wonder if there are any Kennedys in this audience? Could you hold up your hands so I can see?" Cue a smattering of raised hands, to which the President responded, "Well, I am glad to see a few cousins who didn't catch the boat."

After this light-hearted start to the speech, Kennedy mentioned the ceremony at the Barry memorial and told his audience that he kept the flag Commodore Barry flew and the sword he wore in the Oval Office, such was the historical importance of the Wexford man. Only two months previously, he had visited the site of the Battle of Gettysburg, "the bloodiest battlefield in the American Civil War," where he saw a monument to the Irish Brigade, which had suffered heavy losses. Recalling the words of Irish poet John Boyle O'Reilly and referencing the fact that Irishmen throughout history have fought for virtually every cause but that of Irish freedom, he quoted "War-battered dogs are we, gnawing a naked bone, fighting in every land and clime, for every cause but our own."

Warming to his militaristic theme, the President moved on to contemporary international affairs. He talked about "these dangerous days when the struggle for freedom is worldwide against an armed doctrine" and how Ireland's experience was significant because the Irish people had managed "over hundreds of years of foreign domination and religious persecution [to] maintain their national identity and their strong faith". Sending a message to countries who felt as though "freedom is on the run, or that some nations may be permanently subjugated and eventually wiped out," he said they "would do well to remember Ireland".

Quay moment: a section of the large crowd gathered along the quays in Wexford town.

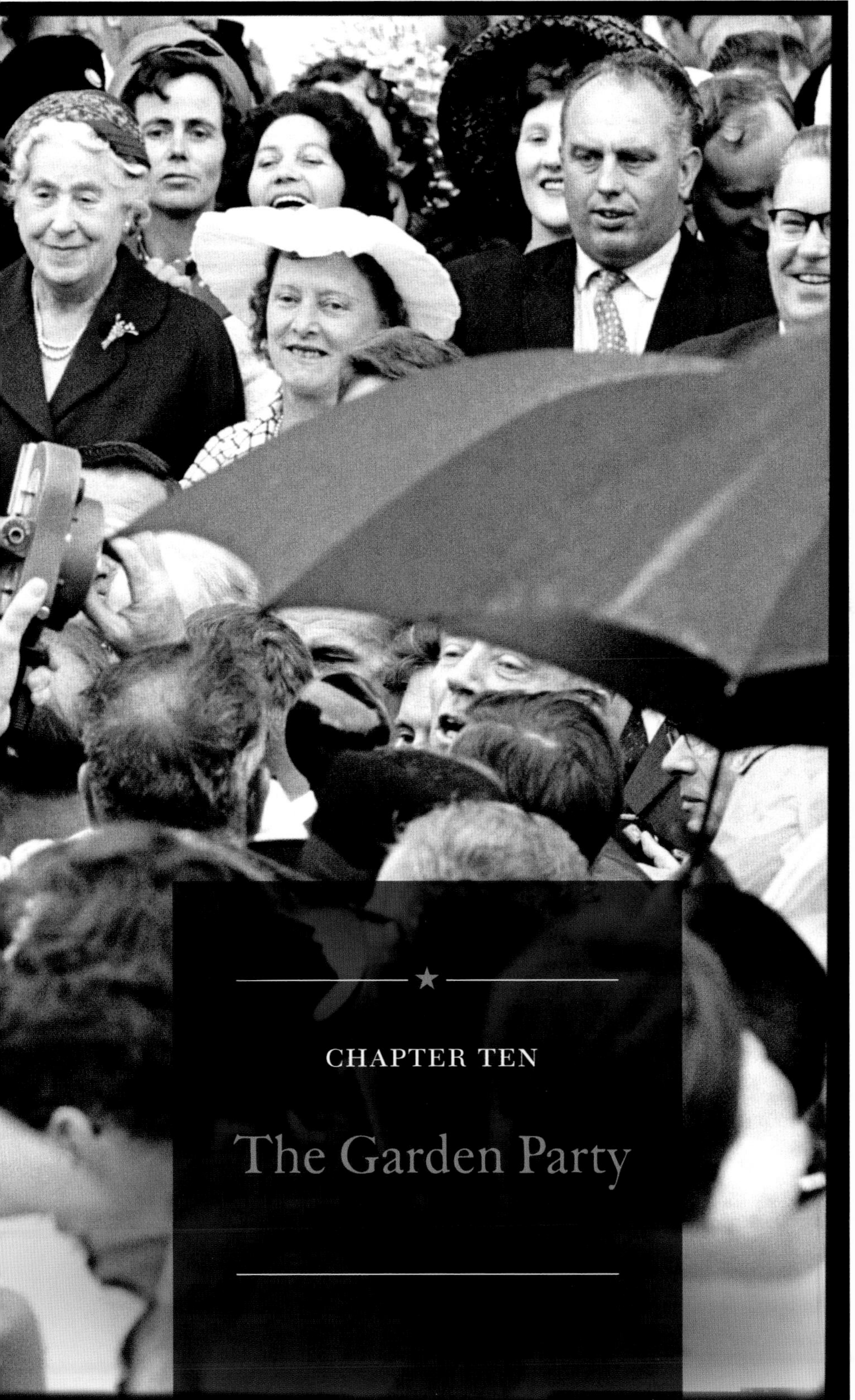

CHAPTER TEN

The Garden Party

★

A VIP approached the counter in a marquee that had been erected to protect heads and hats from the relentless rain. "I'll have a Powers Gold Label," he demanded of the girl in attendance. "Sorry, sir, there is no drink, only tea," she explained politely. "Ah sure, what sort of a garden party is this?" He turned away, disgusted, forced to do without his whiskey.[101]

In what was an extraordinarily busy schedule by any standards, the Irish government and the Kennedy people had packed as much as was physically possible into the brief visit. The trips to Wexford, Cork and Galway would serve some ceremonial purpose. The State dinner and the informal meal at the President's residence made sense for a number of reasons. But there was one event that stands out because it doesn't make much sense on any level. Somebody in one government department or another had decided it would be a good idea to invite 1,500 of the so-called "great and the good" of Irish society to a garden party at the Áras.

Just as they do today, Irish people had a love-hate relationship with such occasions. Some felt they were élitist and lacked meaning or purpose, while others were just envious that they hadn't been invited.

Those deemed worthy of inclusion on the invitation list were several heads of corporations and State bodies, members of the judiciary and assorted government types, along with their wives. In reality, though, this was about which ladies could shine the brightest on the sartorial horizon. The coverage of the garden party is by far the most superficial and unimportant of the Kennedy visit but, intentionally or otherwise, it provides an amusing insight into the people who attended.

While the men were obliged to wear top hats (the one and only dress code rule for men) it was the women who were singled out for attention. In essence, this was Ladies' Day at Ascot for politicos. As it turned out, the event was doomed from the moment the first rains fell from the grey heavens above a dull Dublin in June.

The party was being held in the garden of the de Valeras' residence, and President de Valera's wife Sinéad told Sheila Walsh of the *Irish Press*, "I had planned to wear a lovely silk sheath dress with a huge cartwheel hat"; however, she was forced to amend her plans because of the inclement weather and wear "a black linen coat and dress with a shocking pink hat".

Diplomatic dignitaries: the Pakistan Ambassador and the Australian Chargé d'affaires and their wives enjoy a social conversation at the garden party.

High fashion at the Áras: with 1,500 people attending the garden party at the President's residence, the social pages of the newspapers were filled with details of who wore what.

In her coverage of the party, Sheila Walsh singles out various other luminaries for her attention: "Mrs Hugh McCann, wife of the Secretary of the Department of External Affairs, was elegant in a cream wool coat teamed with a high navy straw hat." There were the wives of several young men whose names would later resonate in Irish history: "Mrs Neil Blaney was nice in an all-cream ensemble … Mrs Eoin Ryan wore a becoming lime yellow straw hat with her black shantung suit … Mrs Hillery, wife of the Minister for Education, wore a petal green hat with a coat in a subtle shade of pale green." Eventually, Sheila Walsh came face to face with President Kennedy and found it all too much: "Now don't ask me what the President said! I was just too overwhelmed to take it in. He's so boyish-looking and so informal, you just wouldn't believe it." Her conclusion? "Yes, it was a good party and the strawberries were lovely, even if the weather wasn't."[102]

The forever po-faced *Irish Times* adopted a bland, neutral tone courtesy of the wonderfully-named Irene Ffrench, whose lengthy report itemises as many outfits as she had space for. "Many of the wives of Government Ministers favoured, I noticed, the always chic navy-and-white ensembles, especially the little navy suit, with the navy and white straw hat." Ms Ffrench singled out the Taoiseach's wife for attention, writing "Mrs Seán Lemass, however, looked especially outstanding, and very colourful with a rich, royal-blue coat, worn over a chiffon sheath dress … and she wore green long gloves and a matching hat of green floral petals." President Kennedy's sister Eunice "was very brave in spite of the weather. She appeared on the terrace wearing a very charming sleeveless silk dress in a rich pink and white design."[103]

Listeners to RTÉ radio heard Maud Liddy do on air what her colleagues were doing in print. Ms Liddy described in clipped tones the outfit worn by Seán Lemass's daughter Maureen, who was married to a future leader of Ireland: "Mrs Charles Haughey is wearing a brown and white silk dress with a seven-eighths length coat." The present author's cousin was mentioned as well: "Mrs Dorothy Tubridy's suit is electric blue, very becoming with her fair hair … the Dior hat is in Bangkok straw."[104]

As for the President himself, according to *The Irish Times* he "found something near to mob hysteria when he finally made his way out of doors. And an afternoon that started out quietly with great dignity and formality ended up on a note suggestive of the adulation of the film or pop star where some guests were concerned."

Irene Ffrench wrote: "What he [President Kennedy] missed of haute couture he certainly received in the warm reception of the women guests, perhaps determined to make up for the lack of feminine charm at the airport on his arrival." And once again, the

President left a strong impression that even the "paper of record" couldn't resist: "Whether it was his infectious smile, his golden suntan, his friendly wave, his well-cut suit, his obvious good humour and delight in what was going on, there was no doubt that President Kennedy appeared to enjoy the occasion as much as the majority of the guests".[105]

But it wasn't all rosy in the Presidential garden. Away from the niceties of straight reporting, word was reaching beyond the garden walls that the behaviour of those attending the party was far from great or good. Such was the President's charm and charisma that the reaction of some of the guests was becoming hysterical and unbecoming as they attempted to get close to him.

The original plan was to let Presidents Kennedy and de Valera stroll around the lawns for an hour, meeting and greeting the well-heeled guests in between sipping cups of tea and dining on delicate punnets of strawberries. As always, the American President was keen to get out and meet the crowd, but on this occasion it wasn't going to be so easy: "The over-exuberant guests, in their eagerness to shake hands with President Kennedy, crowded into an uncontrollable mass: the two statesmen and their guards were borne out onto the lawn, and as the situation deteriorated, struggled back to the haven of the Presidential residence."[106] In the crush that followed, hats fell off elegant heads, cameras dropped to the ground and carefully placed chairs were overturned. Some reports suggest the event was a fiasco that saw the half-blind Irish president elbowed in the ribs and stiletto heels getting stuck in the mud. The walkabout had to be abandoned when the crowd's behaviour was considered to have become a genuine problem for the President's comfort and safety.

Recalling the event three years later, de Valera commented: "The danger there was that there was a mob that was crushing in upon him, and the security men were trying to keep them back, but of course, they were being pressed in with the crowd."[107]

A particularly angry piece appeared in *The Sligo Champion* just days after the President's visit. The anonymous author bemoans the fact that the visit would be remembered for the garden party "when the élite of Ireland's Society behaved like a collection of ignorant Hottentots … I had no idea that they could behave as boorishly as they did."

The article read: "When President Kennedy arrived he drove through the city. The footpaths were lined with the poorest of the poor … who are poor in the world's goods but rich in natural good manners … But in Áras an Uachtarain the men in the top hats … and their women in their expensive finery pushed, scrambled and actually came to blows in their efforts to mob the guest of the nation as if they were a collection of aborigines."

The furious author continues in the same vein, before adding: "Prominent among the ignorant louts and harridans who made this garden party an event of which the entire nation felt ashamed were the higher ups in organisations who by virtue of their office, were invited from many provincial towns. If the invitations had been extended to those people who are now resident in Mountjoy [Prison] there would have been a better show of good manners."[108]

The centrepiece of this ill-fated gathering was to be a tree-planting ceremony. Secret servicemen managed to hold back the crowds as a California Redwood was positioned and the President shovelled a few spadefuls of soil around its roots. He then handed the spade to the groundsman, Patrick Buggy, and remarked: "Now let's see the expert do it." After that it was President de Valera's turn. He shovelled a number of spadefuls into the open ground and Kennedy remarked: "You're making me look awfully old, Mr President."[109] In fact, it was the second tree Kennedy had planted that afternoon and his bad back was starting to feel the strain.

In a final and poignant twist, the willowy sapling that President Kennedy planted would die within months of his bizarre encounter with Ireland's élite that wet and dark afternoon at the Áras.

CHAPTER ELEVEN

Iveagh House

—★—

When they got back to the American Embassy, the President was hoping for a hot bath to ease the pain in his back. What he hadn't counted on was that his sisters had got home first and used up all the hot water. White House staffer Lenny Donnelly was told by her boss, Dave Powers, that members of staff had to carry pots of hot water up stairs to fill the bath.[110] The President had his bath then got dressed for a white-tie dinner being held in his honour at Iveagh House on Dublin's St Stephen's Green, where the Taoiseach Seán Lemass and his wife would be rolling out a green carpet for their guest.

The water situation meant that Kennedy was twenty-five minutes behind schedule. Despite the threatening clouds overhead, 6,000 people lined the few miles that separated the Ambassador's residence from Iveagh House, clutching umbrellas and wearing plastic macs.

In the weeks leading up to this white-tie event there had been much talk in society circles about the sartorial dilemma it threw up. Protocol dictated that the gentlemen attending the event must wear swallow-tailed coats with their white ties, but such coats were considered dated by 1963 and the dress-hire shops didn't have enough of them to go around. The *Evening Herald* reported that "The dearth of full evening dress was first highlighted at the State dinner for Prince Rainier and Princess Grace two years ago when a big number of the guests were attired in dinner jackets. This gave rise to some adverse comment."

Despite the scarcity of swallow-tailed coats and the dilemma this posed for attendees, the Department of External Affairs was not for turning on the issue. A spokesman explained: "White tie is the prescribed dress. To depart from that is entirely up to oneself but

An Taoiseach Seán Lemass arrives at Iveagh House with his wife, Kathleen.

Kennedy-mania: a view of the large crowd that gathered for a glimpse of JFK arriving at Iveagh House.

The caption that accompanied this cartoon in the *Dublin Opinion* read: "And if you get to talk to him, keep your big mouth shut about the evils of emigration."

there is no official encouragement to do so. If one wants to come in dinner jacket, he might by chance, be outstanding."[111]

One man with no such concerns was the Archbishop of Dublin, John Charles McQuaid, who could wear his official robes. In a handwritten RSVP to the Taoiseach's invitation, he explained that "as I leave for Rome on Friday for the coronation of Pope Paul VI, I am very glad to accept your invitation."[112] In fact, the records show that the Archbishop was invited to and showed up at almost every event that the President attended, postponing his trip to Rome so as not to miss a single thing.

At 7.30pm, the Presidential motorcade drew up outside Iveagh House and a dashing-looking Kennedy, correctly dressed in swallow tails and white tie, made his way up the green carpet where he was welcomed by the Taoiseach and Mrs Lemass. Over 2,000 onlookers lined the south and east side of St Stephen's Green. As he made his way up the steps, the President could hear the crowd of screaming girls that had gathered behind specially placed crash barriers. Their chants of "We want Jack, we want Jack!" added to the sense of mania that attended the visit, and which stretched from high society matrons to teenyboppers.

Even as dinner was being served, Kennedy was constantly "switched on", smiling and making sure to have a word with everyone, displaying what Hugh McCann, External Affairs Secretary, described as "the bond or empathy that seemed to exist between him and people on all levels. I mean, he would make a point of going over and speaking to the waitress behind the table."[113] It was this sense of accessibility that so impressed the Irish public. He wasn't just another old man in a suit on a State visit; he was Jack Kennedy, whose "people" were from Wexford and who had done well for himself. He was someone who had no airs and graces – and if he had, the Irish people would have let him know.

The Civil Service Dining Club had sent in suggested menus for the evening – Mayonnaise of Chicken and Pineapple of Baked Clove Ham were among the dishes they considered[114] – but the guests ultimately dined on a very Irish meal of smoked salmon, steak, potatoes and peas, with strawberries and cream to finish.[115]

For dessert, the President was treated to another customised cake. Whereas earlier that day he had eaten a slice of his own image on a cake, this evening he was served a nostalgic slice of a cake that was topped by a sugar model of *PT-109*, the boat Kennedy had famously served on (and whose crew he had saved) in World War II.[116] It was made for him by Chef Pierre Rolland, a celebrated figure from Dublin's Hotel Russell, who had once cooked for the President in the Bahamas when he was attending a summit with British Prime Minister Harold Macmillan.

Such was the demand for "face time" with the President that a second event was held straight after the dinner. Known loosely as a "function", it started at 10pm and allowed those who hadn't made the cut for dinner to shake hands and have their "Kennedy moment".

As all this was going on, the crowd outside was constantly growing and thereby cementing the President's rock star status. Crash barriers were not enough to keep the screaming girls at bay when he finally emerged from the building shortly before midnight.

As happened on nearly every leg of his trip, the President could not resist the opportunity to meet and greet the public. He loved the whole "meeting and charming" routine. He'd been born with a silver rosette on his lapel and brought up in an atmosphere of backroom deals in Boston wards, and some of it had rubbed off. He was a talented networker, good at making personal contact with each person who came within his radar and making them feel special. As Hugh McCann observed that night at Iveagh House: "One gathered the impression that he liked to feel the grip of somebody's hand, actually – the personal contact."[117]

At first Kennedy waved at the crowd and they cheered back, but that wasn't enough for him so he decided, to the horror of his secret servicemen, to go over to them. According to Hugh McCann, "Once he did it, there was a genuine melee. I have a distinct recollection of our Foreign Minister trying to get him back into his [car], having to put both his feet against the side of the car and put his full weight on the door to get it open again. And I must say I never saw his Secret Service agents so worried."

Even at this late hour, the streets were lined with on-lookers as the motorcade drove back to Phoenix Park and a sizeable crowd was waiting for him at the floodlit entrance to the Ambassador's residence. The Irish people in general and their women in particular could not get enough of this man.

Rock star? President? Irish? He had it all.

CHAPTER TWELVE

Cork

—★—

"Down from the hills of Cork they came in their tens of thousands today to cheer the bronzed, busy young man who is President of the United States. Never in its history had the Munster capital been so lavish, so uninhibited, so warm in its welcome to anyone,"[118] according to the *Evening Herald*.

Cork was never meant to be part of the story but by the middle of June, the President took a notion that he would like to visit the Munster capital. During Press Secretary Pierre Salinger's reconnaissance visit to Ireland he told reporters that the President had informed him that Cork was to be included in the itinerary. "He gave no reason," Salinger observed at the time, "but we know that his ancestors on the Fitzgerald side came from near Cork, so that Cork is a direct part of the family heritage."[119] And with that, a ninety-minute visit was arranged that would culminate in Kennedy being made an Honorary Freeman of the City.

First thing in the morning of Friday 28 June, the President flew by helicopter from the Ambassador's residence to Collins' Barracks in Cork city, without his sisters and sister-in-law this time. From the early hours, people from surrounding counties had been swarming into the city to capture the best vantage points on rooftops, in windows, and even along the iron structure of Brian Boru bridge. As soon as the President emerged from his helicopter, it was straight into a relentless schedule with brass bands as mood music and a constant cacophony of cheering from the thousands who lined every stretch of the journey. "The Boys of Wexford" and "Kelly, The Boy From Killane" featured loudly that morning as the motorcade made its way slowly through Cork's main streets. On Grand Parade, one of the banners that adorned the buildings read: "Don't worry Jack, the Iron Curtain will rust in peace."

At the entrance to City Hall, the President was greeted by councillors bedecked in long, crimson robes. Also among the welcoming party were four men who bore a startling resemblance to the esteemed guest, all of them Fitzgeralds from Skibbereen, who had been invited to say hello to their kinsman. As he made his way into the hall, the President paused and smiled at them. "It is great to meet you," he said as he shook hands with each man in turn. "Where are you from?" The answer came in unison: "Skibbereen!" He asked them one by one what they did for a living and one by one they told him they were farmers.[120]

JFK delivers his speech at Cork City Hall on 28 June 1963, where he was welcomed by the City's Lord Mayor Sean Casey as a "truly great Irish man".

R
T
V
RENTALS
PAVILION
Saxone Shoes

The people's President: JFK is met by vast crowds in Cork. Newspapers reported that rose petals, confetti, streamers and ticker tape were thrown in the path of his cavalcade.

The crowd outside City Hall waited for proceedings to start. The speeches would be relayed to them by speakers that had been positioned for the occasion.

The President took his seat on the stage and looked around the hall. There were elaborate floral tributes on display, including some spelling out words of welcome and a large one in front of the lectern that reproduced the American flag in red, white and blue flowers. The ceremony to make him a Freeman of Cork began. As was the custom at meetings of Cork Corporation, a roll was called, a prayer was said in Irish and English and then it was down to the business of the day. The resolution of the Corporation to confer the Freedom of the City on President Kennedy was read out and, by accepting the parchment that confirmed his new status, the President became the 29th person to be so honoured. He wasn't the first American President to receive the honour; Woodrow Wilson was made a Freeman in 1919 but he hadn't shown up to take receipt of his parchment and so it was awarded in absentia.

The Lord Mayor of Cork, Sean Casey, delivered an articulate if lengthy speech in which he praised the President's love of liberty and pursuit of peace, and Kennedy listened intently.

When at last he rose to speak, the President was on fine form. Looking around him with a cheeky grin, he observed that "the Irish have not lost their ability to speak". He then asked some of the Presidential party to stand up while he explained their Irish connections, as he had the day before in New Ross. Dave Powers, Larry O'Brien, Congressman Boland and Monsignor O'Mahoney, "the pastor of a poor, humble flock in Palm Beach, Florida" (the grin reappeared for that one, as his audience must surely have understood the irony that Palm Beach was far from an impoverished place) all stood up when requested. Also on that list was Jim Rowley, head of the United States Secret Service. The President remarked: "Those members of the Secret Service who aren't Irish are embarrassed about it, but we will make them honorary Freemen today."

As if to emphasise the influence of the Irish on the geography of

America, he went on to deliver greetings from the people of the towns of Galway in New York State, Dublin in New Hampshire, Killarney in West Virginia, Kilkenny in Maine, and Shamrock in Texas. Referring to the constant trickle of emigration from Ireland to America, he told his audience: "Most countries send out oil, iron, steel or gold, some others crops, but Ireland has only one export and that is people."

He praised the Irish contribution to the American story and then changed the tone entirely with his next sentence: "We are in a most climactic period, in the most difficult and dangerous struggle in the history of the world, with the most difficult and dangerous weapons which have ever been devised which could annihilate the human race in a few hours." It was an extraordinary statement that was at odds with the jollity of the occasion, and it marked a change in the tone of his speeches, which would get a little more serious in the coming days.

While the contentious topic of Partition was not referred to by name, the President wasn't averse to acknowledging and complimenting the Irish pursuit of independence and liberty: "I come to this island which has been identified with that effort for a thousand years, which was the first country in the 20th century to lead what is the most powerful tide of the century – the desire for national independence, the desire to be free, and I come here in 1963 and find that strong tide still beats, still runs."

In the streets outside, the crowd roared their loud approval, and the noise of their cheers could be heard inside the chambers of the City Hall. They knew his reference to a "desire for national independence" was about their struggle to get free of British rule, and that he was applauding them for achieving it. This is what they wanted to hear. It was music to their ears. Those who were so inclined could read into it support for their campaign to wrest control of the six counties from the British, but Kennedy was careful never to say anything of the sort.

Having entered that Hall a Bostonian, President Kennedy left it a Corkman. He waved to the waiting crowd then his enthusiasm to meet the people once again gave his secret servicemen a security nightmare as he strode over to shake hands with the waiting throng. The crowd surged forwards and pinned the President against a wall in their desire to get a little closer. Eventually, the secret servicemen wrestled their man into a limousine. One well-wisher grabbed Kennedy's hand and refused to let go. The car started moving but the man in the crowd didn't release his grip so the President was pulled around and ended up falling backwards into the car seat.

According to *The Irish Times*, "When the President emerged from the building, his grin was as broad as ever, as he leaned to right and left giving the brush of the fingers. But this gesture was his undoing. A hand clasped his wrist, he pulled, the hand relaxed and he slipped down with a bump on the seat of the car while a security guard who had tried a blocking tackle went head first into the back seat. And through it all the President still smiled."

As the motorcade moved slowly through the streets, they were fêted along the way. "Rose petals, confetti, streamers and ticker tape were strewn along President Kennedy's path as almost 100,000 Leesiders [the River Lee runs through Cork] roared a Céad Mile Fáilte [a hundred thousand welcomes] again and again for the two hours of his visit to Cork,"[121] *The Irish Times* reported.

Thousands crowded the streets back to the field where the helicopters were due to take off but the spectators were standing too close to the aircraft and space had to be cleared before the Presidential party could lift up into the grey and misty Cork skies. The President was in a hurry to get back to Dublin. A formal lunch, a visit to a symbolically important memorial, two degrees, another city's Freedom and an address to the national parliament awaited him, all before dinner.

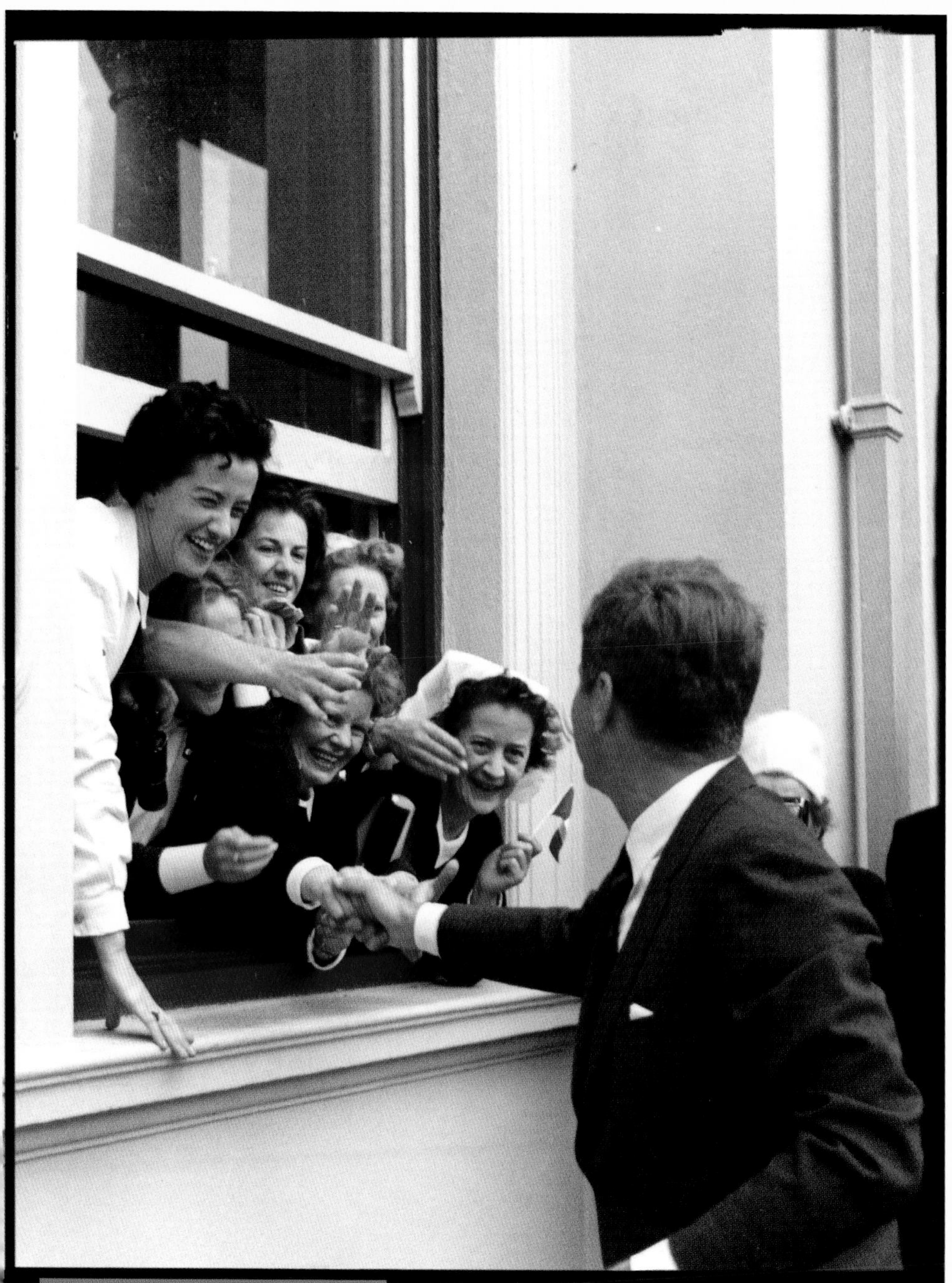

JFK is greeted by well-wishers in Cork.

CHAPTER THIRTEEN

Arbour Hill

JFK lays a wreath at Arbour Hill on 28 June 1963. He was the first head of state to attend the ceremony honouring the leaders of the 1916 Rising.

remembrance services to honour the dead. They carried the Lee Enfield rifle, which they reversed as a mark of respect. The President stood in rapt attention, as if mesmerised, while they marched in neatly choreographed formation, presenting their guns in unison, all of them moving in perfect symmetry. It was a solemn and highly professional display.

When the ceremony concluded, the President took time to walk over and chat to some of the cadets as well as a group of army nurses who were standing nearby. Then, as the rain picked up, he was ushered back to his car.

What Kennedy was trying to say by visiting Arbour Hill Cemetery is unclear but what was read into it by his national hosts was not. The editorial in the *Evening Herald* was certain that this event underlined Kennedy's commitment to the Irish cause, suggesting that he "openly allied himself, and his nation, with the ideals and policies for which these men died". The editorial then takes a leap of considerable proportions (especially given the fact that the subject was never discussed publicly) when it states: "We cannot help thinking that when the President refers to Ireland he means the entire nation and that subconsciously, at least, he would like to see this land united."[125]

Seán Lemass was equally struck by the significance of the Presidential presence at this sacred site. He would later reflect: "This was, itself, an event for us of great emotional significance. He was the first head of state ever to go through the ceremony of honouring the executive leaders of the 1916 Rising. Many heads of state have done it since, but he was the first. The fact that he, as the President of the United States, the greatest nation in the world, [witnessed] the ceremony had to have a tremendously emotional effect on the Irish people."[126]

Kennedy was certainly endorsing the actions the leaders of the Rising had taken, and praising the courage with which the Irish people had achieved independence, but it was going a bit too far to say that he thought the North and the South should be united. That was more than his Special Relationship with the British would allow. Still, it was obvious to all present that he found the whole event at Arbour Hill very emotional and thought-provoking.

Dave Powers and Kenny O'Donnell remembered: "Later, when we were discussing the various memories of our trip to Ireland, the Kennedy sisters … agreed that the President's stirring speech to the Irish parliament later that Friday afternoon was the outstanding highlight of the visit. The President shook his head. 'For me, the highlight was the ceremony at Arbour Hill,' he said. 'Those cadets were terrific. I wish we had a film of that drill so that we could do something like it at the Tomb of the Unknown Soldier.'"[127]

Five months later, the cadets President Kennedy so admired would be performing those same manoeuvres by his graveside at Arlington National Cemetery in Virginia, watched by the eyes of a grieving world.

moment. The bitterness of the Civil war dissolved in this new Ireland, symbolised by John F. Kennedy's visit.

A journalist from the *Sunday Independent* described the moment: "The two white heads, bowed from service to their country, came together in a gesture of reconciliation and brotherhood, significant of the new spirit of the nation. If the visit of President Kennedy was responsible only for this, it was well worth while."[131] The vignette certainly added to the sense of occasion on that June afternoon. It was an historically sweet prelude to the twenty-eight-minute oratorical flourish that was coming their way.

At 4.16, there was silence in the House as the Superintendent stood up and announced, in a clear, purposeful voice, "Uachtarain Stait Aontaithe Mheiricea" [The President of the United States of America]. Those four words in our native tongue meant it was showtime.

Every available seat was occupied that afternoon and several TDs had to perch on stairs. This solemn chamber was normally a closed shop to the public but with the presence of television cameras, everything had changed.

It was 4.18 when the Chamber doors opened and President Kennedy, alongside Seán Lemass, James Dillon and Brendan Corish, entered to a roar of applause and an enthusiastic standing ovation that lasted a full minute. These were unprecedented scenes in Irish politics but, as the previous forty-eight hours had shown, the mould of government was in the process of changing forever. Smiling and with his hand outstretched, the President acknowledged his hosts and walked purposefully across the blue carpet towards the specially made dais where he took his seat alongside the Ceann Comhairle, or Speaker, Padraig Hogan. To *his* right sat the Cathaoirleach of the Seanad (Chairman of the Senate) Liam O'Buachalla.

The Chamber fell silent as Padraig Hogan rose from his seat to address the Dáil. In his brief welcome, the Ceann Comhairle said: "The exiles who landed on the shores of the great Continent of America tasted for the first time the sweet air of freedom and

A view behind the Presidential cavalcade as it passes up Dame Street in Dublin.

ZJ 5000

opportunity as it swept across the great plains of that country."

The theme of exile and emigration hung heavily in the air that afternoon and, to his credit, Hogan kept it brief and was soon wrapping up his words of welcome before asking President Kennedy to "address the eager audience".

Kennedy was listening attentively but one Cabinet Minister with a front row seat noticed that as the Ceann Comhairle was talking, Kennedy's leg was nervously moving up and down. Patrick Hillery, Minister for Education at the time and a future President of Ireland, observed Kennedy's leg "shimmering a bit" from all the shaking, "like a horse, a thoroughbred waiting to go out in a race".[132]

Poetry and prose

The President was anxious to deliver a quality speech in both tone and content. Ted Sorensen had done much of the groundwork and was keen to get the mix right: "A good speech, in addition to the front line, and the bottom line, needs a few side lines. And by side lines I mean quotations, including poetry I should add, and stories, and sometimes humour."[133]

In this respect, Sorensen, helped by creative input from his boss, got it pitch perfect – with just one minor exception.

President Kennedy, dressed in a dark suit, crisp white shirt and a tie of dark blue and green, rose from his chair to yet another ovation. Writing for *The Irish Times*, Tom McCaughrin noted:

"Sitting not more than ten feet from him, I could see tears in his eyes as he looked around the assembly, smiling."[134]

The President gripped his lectern and began with a historical flourish as he remembered the "1,200 men who went into battle wearing a green sprig in their hats" during the American Civil War. This was the Irish Brigade and the battle was at Fredericksburg, Virginia, in 1862. The Brigade was led by Brigadier General Thomas F. Meagher who, Kennedy reminded his audience, "had participated in the unsuccessful Irish uprising of 1848, was captured by the British

OPPOSITE "My great-grandfather might never have left New Ross, and I might, if fortunate, be sitting down there with you," JFK told the 144 deputies and 60 senators in the Dáil chamber.

and sent in a prison ship to Australia from whence he finally came to America". Of the 1,200 men in the Brigade, 280 came out alive. Only a few flags had survived the Fighting 69th's battles and the President presented one such flag to the Irish people, "in recognition of what these gallant Irishmen and what millions of other Irish have done for my country".

Constantly fidgeting with his speech on the lectern, a visibly nervous Kennedy took a little while to relax. As was often the case for him, he calmed down when there was humour or mischief in the air, and that's what happened next. Having acknowledged the historic connection between both countries at a military level, the President came closer to home for his next analogy. Reflecting on one of the great "what if?" questions that historians still like to ponder, he speculated on what might have happened if his relatives had stayed in Ireland in the mid-19th century.

"My great-grandfather might never have left New Ross, and I might, if fortunate, be sitting down there with you." To roars of laughter, he added: "Of course, if your own president had never left Brooklyn, he might be standing up here instead of me."

If they hadn't already been suitably buttered up by their silver-tongued guest, the gathered politicians might not have been so keen on his decision to quote a previous tenant of Leinster House, one Lord Edward FitzGerald. Kennedy read an excerpt from a letter FitzGerald (no relation) had written to his mother, in which he noted: "Leinster House does not inspire the brightest ideas" and suggested another place might be better. Kennedy meant this as a joke, a lighthearted moment in an otherwise serious speech, but not everyone in the House appreciated it, and there was some murmuring and shifting in the seats. Perhaps sensing an uncomfortable change in the mood, the President added swiftly: "That was a long time ago, however."

Éamon de Valera is said to have flinched at the crack, and didn't think it was the slightest bit amusing, according to Seán Lemass, who overheard the two Presidents talking about it later that day at Áras an Uachtarain: "President de Valera said to him [Kennedy] that he had done no service to Irish politicians by this quotation. And I don't know what he did, or how he did it, but it has disappeared completely. It hasn't appeared in any of the records of the speech that have been published. It doesn't even appear in the taped performance of the speech or in the film of the speech which was made simultaneously by Telefis Éireann [the State broadcaster]. How he managed this complete suppression of this sentence, I do not know … But it was the speed with which he acted and the totality of the effect of his whole action in suppressing the statement that surprised me."[135]

Kennedy proceeded to namecheck some of the great Irish leaders of the past, from Daniel O'Connell to Robert Emmet and on to Charles Stewart Parnell, whose 117th birthday would have fallen on the previous day. Kennedy reminded his audience that at the age of thirty-four Parnell had addressed the American Congress on the subject of Irish freedom and he alluded to Parnell's comment that he had received so many tokens of good wishes from Americans to the Irish people: "And today, eighty-three years later, I can say to you that I have seen in this country so many tokens of good wishes of the Irish people towards America."

In a closing argument for the historical part of his speech, Kennedy said: "And so it is that our two nations, divided by distance, have been united by history."

His next line was interpreted by some nationalists as an obtuse reference to Partition: "No people ever believed more deeply in the cause of Irish freedom than the people of the United States." This was the language of de Valera, the New York-born Irish revolutionary who had long ago borrowed the Parnell model of keeping America close to the Irish struggle, financially, politically and emotionally. Those who had hoped for a more politicised visit to Ireland could have wished that this line was more potent than poetic, but that was as far as he would go.

Referring to the emigrants who "came to our shores in a mixture of hope and agony", Kennedy made a literary reference that would have sent shudders down a few conservative spines: "It is no wonder that James Joyce described the Atlantic as a bowl of bitter tears."

Many of those sitting in front of Kennedy would have been virulently opposed to Joyce's name being mentioned in the House. The writer was considered subversive and obscene and his work was still censored in Ireland. Joyce had fled Ireland in 1904 at the age of twenty-two and had always had a love–hate relationship with the country of his birth.

As Seamus Kelly observed in *The Irish Times* the next day, "James Joyce, lovely mummer and considerable fantasist, would not I imagine, in his wildest fantasies have envisaged a day when one of his lines would be quoted by the president of the United States in Leinster House, Dublin, to an assembly of the Oireachtas [Parliament] – and with a full acknowledgement of authorship at that."[136]

Warming to his literary theme, the President went on to quote William Butler Yeats, who urged the Irish not to reduce "that great past to a trouble of fools". He was saying that while it might seem easier to forget the difficulties of the past, we shouldn't be afraid to learn its lessons.

Describing Ireland in 1963, President Kennedy called it "one of the youngest of nations and oldest of civilisations … you have undergone a new and peaceful revolution …This revolution is not yet over, nor will it be, I am sure, until a fully modern Irish economy shares in world prosperity."

This was the language of Seán Lemass, who would have thoroughly enjoyed the combination of revolution and modernity in a political context.

Next Kennedy quoted Irish freedom campaigner Henry Grattan, saying "A country enlightened as Ireland, chartered as Ireland, armed as Ireland, and injured as Ireland, will be satisfied with nothing less than liberty," and he added his own opinion: "Free Ireland will not be satisfied with anything less than liberty." These flattering words formed the headlines in the papers the next morning, and while the President was talking about Ireland's liberty as a young republic, some at the Fianna Fáil-supporting newspapers, *The Irish Press* and

"Free Ireland not satisfied with anything less than liberty"—President Kennedy

"GO BETWEEN" ROLE REJECTED

Historic Address to both houses of Oireachtas

"TODAY, I am certain, free Ireland — a full-fledged member of a world community where some are not yet free, and where some counsel an acceptance of tyranny — free Ireland will not be satisfied with anything less than liberty," said President Kennedy in an address to an historic joint meeting of both Houses of the Oireachtas.

"The central issue of freedom, however, is between those who believe in self-determination and those in the East who would impose on others a harsh and repressive communist system; and here your nation wisely rejects the role of go-between," he said. "Ireland pursues an independent course in foreign policy—but it is not neutral between liberty and tyranny, and I know it never will be."

These excerpts from a major policy speech were greeted with tumultuous applause.

The President's meeting with the special joint session of the Dail and Seanad was the highlight of his visit to this country. A packed house, garish under the TV floodlights, applauded his every sentiment and when he had concluded his speech Deputies, Senators and distinguished visitors cheered him to the echo.

Such scenes of enthusiasm can never have been witnessed in the long life of the ancient home of the Geraldines and certainly never since the foundation of the State.

The Chamber was packed for almost half an hour before the President was timed to arrive. In the Lobby sat distinguished visitors and members of both Houses stood and clapped when Mr. W. T. Cosgrave, first President of the Executive Council entered accompanied by his son, Mr. Liam Cosgrave, T.D.

He bowed to the applause and took his seat in the Lobby. A few minutes later the tribute was renewed when Mr. Sean T. O'Kelly, the former President, entered the Lobby.

As the white-haired former President passed through the Lobby he paused for a moment to place his right arm around the shoulders of Mr. Cosgrave and the two former comrades-in-arms and statesmen shook hands warmly and spoke together for a moment.

'AN HONOUR'

Welcoming President Kennedy, the Ceann Comhairle of the Dail (Mr. P. Hogan) said:—

"It is indeed a great honour to have the privilege as Ceann Comhairle of welcoming you on behalf of my colleagues and myself to the Parliament of Ireland.

"For generations the people of Ireland and the people of the U.S.A. have been closely and intimately associated in times of trial and in times of triumph. The emigrants from our shores have tasted the sweet air of freedom and opportunity sweeping across the broad plains of that hospitable land, and we are proud—very proud indeed—to know that these emigrants were effective and potent factors in the development of that great country—their new homeland.

"Thus in ordinary circumstances it would be an occasion of pride and privilege for any Irishman to welcome the President of the U.S. to an Irish parliament (applause).

"But, Mr. President, this is not an ordinary occasion. Your great personality elevates it far above that level. It is an occasion unique as an event in Irish history—it is an international gesture of kindness and good will of inestimable value. When the citizen who presides over the great American people of the U.S. shares with the people of Ireland the heritage of blood, of name and tradition, then the event is enhanced almost beyond measure.

"May I therefore hasten to extend to you, Mr. President, on behalf of my colleagues and myself a sincere and hearty Cead Mile Failte to the Parliament of Ireland and respectfully request you to address your eager audience."

[illegible] her children — are now investing their capital as well as their vacations here in Ireland. This revolution is not yet over—nor will it be, I am sure, until a fully modern Irish economy fully shares in world prosperity."

"NOTHING LESS . . ."

"But prosperity is not enough. One hundred and eighty-three years ago Henry Grattan, demanding the more independent Irish Parliament that would always bear his name, denounced those who were satisfied by new grants of economic opportunity. A country," he said, "enlightened as Ireland, chartered as Ireland, armed as Ireland and injured as Ireland will be satisfied with nothing less than liberty." And today, I am certain, free Ireland as a full-fledged member of a world community where some are not yet free, and where some counsel an acceptance of tyranny—free Ireland will not be satisfied with anything less than liberty.

"I am glad, therefore, to see Ireland moving into the mainstream of current world events. For I sincerely believe that your future is as promising as your past is proud — and that your destiny lies, not as a peaceful island in a sea of troubles, but as a maker and shaper of world peace.

"WORLD IS SMALL"

"For self-determination can no longer mean isolation; and the achievement of national independence today means withdrawal from the old status only to return to the world scene with a new one. New nations can build with their former governing powers the same kind of fruitful relationship that Ireland has established with Great Britain—a relationship founded on equality and mutual interests. And no nation, large or small, can be indifferent to the fate of others, near or far. Modern economics, weaponry and communications have made us realise more than ever that we are one human family and this one planet is our home.

"'The world is large,' wrote John Boyle O'Reilly. 'The world is large when its weary leagues two loving hearts divide, but the world is small when your enemy is loose on the other side.'

"The world is even smaller today—though the enemy of John Boyle O'Reilly is no longer a hostile power. Indeed, across the gulfs and barriers that now divide us, we must remember that there are no permanent enemies. Hostility today is a fact, but it is not a ruling law. The supreme reality of our time is our indivisibility as children of God and our common vulnerability on this planet.

"Some may say that all this means little to Ireland. In an age when 'history moves with the tramp of earthquake feet'—in an age when a handful of men and nations have the power to devastate mankind — in an age when the needs of the developing nations are so large and staggering that even the richest lands often groan with the burden of assistance — in such an age, it may be asked, how can a nation as small as Ireland play much of a role on the world stage?

SMALL NATIONS

"I would remind those who ask that question, including those in other small countries, of these words of one of the great orators of the English language:

'All the world owes much to the little "five feet high" nations. The greatest art of the world was the work of little nations. The most enduring literature of the world came from little nations. The heroic deeds that thrill humanity through generations were the deeds of little nations fighting for their freedom. And oh, yes, the salvation of mankind came through a little nation.'

"Ireland has already set an example and a standard for other small nations to follow.

"This has never been a rich or powerful country—and yet, since the earliest times, its influence on the world has been both rich and powerful. No larger nation did more to keep Christianity and Western culture alive in their darkest centuries. No larger nation did more to spark the cause of independence in America and around the world. And no larger nation has ever provided the world with more literary and artistic genius.

"This is an extraordinary country, George Bernard Shaw, speaking as an Irishman, summed up your approach to life. Other peoples, he said, see

Continued on Page 16

Symbolise many enduring links

DECLARING that he was proud to be the first American President to visit Ireland during his term of office, proud to be addressing that distinguished assembly and proud of the welcome they had given him, Mr. Kennedy said: "My presence and your welcome, however, only symbolise the many and enduring links which have bound the Irish and the Americans since the earliest days of our history.

"Benjamin Franklin—the envoy of the American Revolution, who was also born in Boston—was received by the Irish Parliament in 1772. It was neither independent nor free from discrimination at that time—but Franklin reported its members disposed to be friends of America.

"'By joining our interests with theirs,' he said, 'a more equitable treatment . . . might be obtained for both nations.'

"INTERESTS JOINED"

"Our interests have been joined ever since. Franklin sent leaflets to Irish freedom-fighters. O'Connell was influenced by Washington and Emmet influenced by Lincoln. Irish volunteers played so predominate a role in the American army that Lord Mountjoy lamented in the British Parliament that 'we have lost America through the Irish.' John Barry, whose statue we honoured yesterday and whose sword is in my office, was only one of those who fought for liberty in America to set an example for liberty in Ireland.

"Yesterday was the 117th anniversary of the birth of Charles Stewart Parnell—whose grandfather fought under Barry and whose mother was born in America—and who, at the age of 34, was invited to address the American Congress on the cause of Irish freedom. 'I have seen since I have been in this country,' he said, 'so many tokens of the good wishes of the American people towards Ireland.'

"And today, 183 years later, I can say to you I have seen since I have been in this country so many tokens of the good wishes of the Irish people towards America.

"So it is that our two nations, divided by distance, have been united by history. No people ever believed more deeply in the cause of Irish freedom than the people of the U.S. and no nation contributed more to the building of the American dream than the sons and daughters of Ireland.

"HOPE AND AGONY"

"They came to our shores with a mixture of hope and agony—for they left behind the broken hearts, blighted fields and a nation yearning to be free. It is no wonder that James Joyce described the Atlantic as a 'bowl of bitter tears.' And an earlier poet wrote:

"They are going, going, going, and we cannot bid them stay."

But today Ireland was no longer the country of hunger and famine those emigrants left behind, he said.

Ireland was not rich, its progress was not yet complete but it was, according to international statistics, one of the best-fed nations in the world. Nor was it any longer a country of persecution, political or religious. It was a free country and that, too, was why he felt at home here.

"There are those who regard this history of past strife and exile as better forgotten. But, to use the phrase of Yeats, 'let us not casually reduce that great past to a trouble of fools.' For we need not renew the bitterness of the past to discover its meaning for the present and future. And it is in the present and future of Ireland that today holds so much promise to my nation as well as yours, and indeed to all mankind.

PEACEFUL REVOLUTION

"For the Ireland of 1963—one of the youngest of nations and oldest of civilisations — has discovered that the achievement of nationhood is not an end but a beginning. In the years since full independence, you have undergone a new and peaceful revolution — an economic and industrial revolution, transforming the face of this land while still holding fast to your spiritual and cultural values.

"You have modernised your economy, harnessed your rivers, diversified your industry, liberalised your trade, electrified your farms, accelerated your rate of growth and improved the living standards of all your people. The other nations of the world—in whom Ireland has long invested

President Kennedy acknowledges the cheers from spectators as he leaves Arbour Hill, where he laid a wreath on the graves of the 1916 leaders yesterday. Included in the picture are the Taoiseach, Mr. Lemass, and Lt.-General Sean McKeown, Chief of Staff.

BIG OVATION FOR PRESIDENT IN LEINSTER HOUSE

"IRISH INDEPENDENT" POLITICAL CORRESPONDENT

"THIS is an extraordinary country," remarked President Kennedy yesterday, as he looked across row upon row of the country's leaders and chief citizens in Leinster House.

An American President was addressing, for the first time in our history, the joint session of the Dail and Seanad called together to pay him our highest civil honour. He got a tumultuous welcome from all sides.

Never before in the history of the State had there been such a gathering, from the venerable former Seneschal Domhnall O Buchalla, the former President of the Executive Council, Mr. W. T. Cosgrave, and the former President Mr. Sean T. O'Kelly, to today's leaders in the front benches, Mr. Lemass, Taoiseach, Mr. Dillon and Mr. Corish.

The scene was unusual

The scene in the Dail Chamber, thrown into sharp relief by the television floodlighting, was memorable. Contrasting with the wealth of aged, polished mahogany around the benches and walls were the cameras, cables and lights and microphones, and the rush and bustle of technicians so alien to the normal Oireachtas atmosphere.

Yet the quiet dignity of the assembly and of the Chamber itself triumphed over all the trappings of modern communication, and the world saw for the first time a spectacle unfamiliar even to the majority of Irish people — our deliberative assembly in solemn session.

Indeed, many Irishmen who have never been near Leinster House but who may have had a rather distorted idea of its working were surprised and pleased, and not a little proud of the extraordinary dignity of the simple ceremony.

All polished and shining

Everything about Leinster House seemed different yesterday. The magnificent main marble staircase wore a new carpet and was bedecked with flowers. The main reception room from the the Merrion St. entrance was renovated for President Kennedy's entrance. All woodwork was newly polished and gleaming, and the last speck of dust had been removed from all floor coverings.

Apart from members, the first distinguished stranger to arrive was Mr. Cahir Healy, M.P., and he was later joined by a number of his Nationalist colleagues from Stormont, including Mr. E. McAteer and Mr. Joseph Stewart.

Soon the Division lobbies filled with members of the Diplomatic Corps headed by the doyen, Most Rev. Dr. Sensi, Apostolic Nuncio, and other dignitaries including the Chief of Staff, General McKeown, General R. Mulcahy, Mr. Justice Davitt and Garda Commissioner Costigan.

Two standing ovations were given during this seat-taking period. The first was for Mr. W. T. Cosgrave, who was shown to his seat with the Diplomatic Corps by his son, Mr. Liam Cosgrave, T.D. Until Mr. Kennedy's arrival, Mr. Cosgrave talked animatedly with diplomats on either side of him. The second ovation was for Mr. Sean T. O'Kelly, who had a seat close to former Chief Justice Conor Maguire and the former Seneschal, Domhnall O Buachalla.

Applause for President

Perhaps the most impressive part of the ceremony was President Kennedy's arrival in the Chamber, escorted by Mr. Lemass, Mr. Dillon and Mr. Corish. All present stood and applauded as he came down the main steps on to the floor of the House and over to the dais beside the Ceann Comhairle's Chair.

Along the front benches were the members of the Government on one side and the Opposition "shadow" Ministers on the other. In the Labour front benches were Mr. Corish and Mr. Norton, and between them the "Father" of the Dail, Mr. James Everett, who has unbroken service since 1918. Prominent on the Opposition side was the former Taoiseach, Mr. John A. Costello.

The seats nearest to the floor of the House were occupied on both sides by Deputies, and the Senators occupied the back benches. The Cathaoirleach of the Seanad, Professor Liam O Buachalla, the Leas Cathaoirleach, Mr. P. J. Lindsay S.C., and the Leader of the Seanad, Mr. T. L. Mullins, had special seats.

In front of the Ceann Comhairle were seated the Clerk of the Dail, Mr. Peter O'Connell and his assistant, and in front of them the Clerk of the Seanad Mr. John Smyth and his assistant. At a specially provided table the official note of the proceedings was taken on this occasion by the editor of the Dail Debates, Mr. Robert P. Kelly.

A flag with a history

President Kennedy's valuable gift to the Houses of the Oireachtas, which he presented early in his address, was a flag famous in American history and which commemorates the part Irishmen played in the American Civil War. Framed in gilt, it was taken into the House covered in blue velvet, which was removed only for the actual presentation.

In one corner of the green flag is a harp and the inscription:

"69th Regiment, N.Y.S.V. (1st Regiment of the Irish Brigade) Brigadier-General Thomas Francis Meagher commanding. In grateful appreciation of their gallant and brilliant conduct on the battlefields of Virginia and Maryland in the war to maintain the national domain and the American Union, November, 1862."

Was shot to tatters

Apparently the regiment's colours had been shot to tatters in previous battles, and 11 standard-bearers went down while carrying them. The new colours had not arrived as the Regiment fell into battle line at Fredericksburg, although big preparations had been made to receive them with due honour.

In this dilemma, Meagher decided that his Regiment would go into battle under the colours of their native country, and he ordered each man to stick a sprig of boxwood in his hat-band.

A sprig was also pinned on a green flag, which came right through the battle.

In fact, it is not the only flag of the regiment commanded by Meagher of the Sword in safe keeping in this country. Waterford Corporation has one also, presented to Meagher's native place by his widow together with his sword, and journals. Indeed, it is on this flag that the sprig of evergreen mentioned by President Kennedy is pinned.

Waterford Deputy Ald. T. Lynch told me at Leinster House last night that this sprig was really a sprig of boxwood, the only plant of this nature readily available on the Fredericksburg battlefield in December, 1862. Mr. Lynch said that Captain Michael Cavanagh, an officer of the 69th, has written in his memoirs how the sprig of boxwood came to be used.

It is this historic flag which is now in Waterford—and to this day the sprig of boxwood is firmly pinned to it, although no longer green. Mr. Lynch said that Waterford, always intensely proud of its treasure, would have even greater pride now in view of Mr. Kennedy's gift to the Oireachtas.

Apart from the fact that it was the most important function of a ceremonial nature in the history of the State, the Dail ceremony was also outstanding as the vehicle for President Kennedy's most important and impressive speech of his visit.

The President's emphasis on the idea that Ireland's destiny lay as a maker and shaper of world peace, and that self-determination could no longer mean isolation, made a particularly strong impact on all his listeners inside and outside the House. During delivery, his speech was frequently interrupted by prolonged applause obviously entirely spontaneous.

President's programme for today

10.30 a.m.—President Kennedy leaves the United States Embassy, Phoenix Park, accompanied by Taoiseach, Mr. Lemass.

11.30—Arrives Sports Ground, College Road, Galway. Receives greetings of Mayor of Galway and dignitaries.

11.40—Motor procession to Eyre Square. President is received by members of Borough Council and dignitaries.

11.55—Addresses and presentation of Honorary Freedom of Galway and reply by President Kennedy. Motor procession to Salthill.

12.30—President departs for Limerick.

1 p.m.—Arrives at Green Park Race Court, Limerick. Address and presentation of Honorary Freedom of Limerick and reply by President.

1.45 — Arrives Shannon Airport. Address and presentation of gift from Clare Co. Council. Leave taking ceremonies.

2.0 — President Kennedy departs.

Exhibition visit cancelled

A visit by members of President Kennedy's party to the Berlin Exhibition in the Mansion House arranged for yesterday, was cancelled.

A spokesman for the Irish Council of the European Movement, which organised the exhibition, said that due to a mix-up in the arrangements the visit had to be put off.

ANSWER TIME

(Questions on opposite page)

1—[illegible] (1892-1955). 2—A member of Parliament responsible in his party for the organisation of the voting M.P.s. 3—The official residence at Washington of the President of the United States. 4—In 1932.

An Irish American 'Hibernia'

The July "Hibernia" will be a special Irish-American issue and will be on sale from July 12. The annual subscription is 10/- (U.S. $1.50).

Hibernia, 90 Lower Leeson St., Dublin 2.

Tribute by Cathaoirleach of Seanad

PROF. L. O BUACHALLA, Cathaoirleach of the Seanad, thanking President Kennedy for his address said:

"[illegible] [illegible] dúinn."

"It is my privilege to convey to President Kennedy the profound thanks of this joint assembly of the Houses of Oireachtas Eireann. President Kennedy has done us a high honour by accepting our invitation to visit and to address us here today. We assure him of our deep appreciation of the sentiments and of the high ideals enshrined in that address.

"HISTORIC OCCASION"

"This, indeed, is truly an historic occasion and, in addition, unprecedented in the annals of our parliamentary institutions. This is the first time, since the foundation of the State, a visitor has been accorded the distinction of addressing us in joint session from the floor of the House.

"Today, Mr. President, your responsibilities are many and they are heavy. The great cause of truth and liberty is being assailed. The battle for the rights of man, for his economic, social and political uplift, is being waged in every land and in every clime, regardless of creed or colour. To you has fallen the task of leadership in this desperate struggle. The members of Dail Eireann and of Seanad Eireann are proud of you.

"In common with true lovers of freedom and progress everywhere, we repose, fully, our confidence in you. We assure you of our steadfast support in your task and we pray that God will sustain you and that He will crown your efforts with success.

"In conclusion, may I once again assure you how deeply we have been honoured by your coming and how deeply we are inspired by your address which we shall be privileged to record in our official proceedings. As you leave us, you carry with you the warm affection of the members of this Parliament and, indeed, of Irishmen and Irishwomen all over the world. Go dtéidh tú slán."

The Taoiseach, Mr. Lemass; Mr. Dillon, Leader of the Opposition, and Mr. Corish, Leader of the Labour Party then left their seats and conducted President Kennedy through standing, cheering Deputies and Senators and out of the Dail Chamber.

When the President had left, the Ceann Comhairle adjourned the House until 3 p.m. [illegible].

Poem in Irish for President

When President Kennedy leaves Ireland today he will have among the many gifts he has received here a poem in Irish welcoming him to this country. Written by the well-known Irish poet and scholar, Liam Gogan, the poem was presented to the President by the Ireland-America Society to mark his visit.

The poem, hand-set and printed on vellum for the Society by the Dolmen Press, was given to the President by the American Ambassador, Mr. M. McCloskey, Patron of the Society at President Kennedy's luncheon for the Government in the U.S. Embassy yesterday.

The Cork Examiner

NO. 45,063 SATURDAY MORNING, JUNE 29, 1963 PRICE THREEPENCE

Stirring Address To Historic Joint Session Of The Oireachtas

IRELAND'S DESTINY

"Maker And Shaper Of World Peace" Says President Kennedy

"I AM glad to see Ireland moving into the mainstream of world events, for I sincerely believe that your future is as promising as your past is proud, and that your destiny lies, not as a peaceful island in a sea of troubles but as a maker and shaper of world peace," said President Kennedy when he addressed a joint session of both Houses of the Oireachtas yesterday.

"Ireland's hour has come. You have something to give to the world more glorious than even your past and that is a future of lasting peace with freedom," he declared, in a stirring address, which made Irish parliamentary history.

It was the first time that a visitor had ever addressed the Parliament from the floor of the Dail.

President Kennedy was given a tumultuous reception when he entered the Chamber and was conducted to the Ceann Comhairle's dais by the Taoiseach, Mr. Lemass, Mr. Dillon, Leader of the Fine Gael Party, and Mr. Corish, Leader of the Labour Party. Deputies and Senators and others who crowded the lobbies and galleries of the Chamber, rose and clapped enthusiastically for several minutes, then broke into loud prolonged cheering.

(CONTINUED ON PAGE 11)

LAST DAY OF U.S. PRESIDENT'S VISIT

The programme for President Kennedy's last day in Ireland is as follows:—

10.30 a.m.—Leave Dublin by helicopter for Galway.
11.30 a.m.—Arrive Sports Ground, Galway.
11.40 a.m.—Motor to Eyre Square.
11.55 a.m.—Conferring of Freedom of Galway.
12.30 p.m.—Leave Galway by helicopter for Limerick.
1.00 p.m.—Arrives Greenpark Racecourse, Limerick. Address and conferring of Freedom of City.
1.45 p.m.—Arrive Shannon Airport. Presentation of gift from Clare Co. Council.
2.00 p.m.—President Kennedy leaves Ireland.

A general view of the joint session of both Houses of the Oireachtas as President Kennedy (centre) delivers his address. The Government members are seated on the right of the picture headed by An Taoiseach, Mr. Sean Lemass (1st of front bench), An Tanaiste, Mr. Sean MacEntee; Dr. J. Ryan, Minister for Finance; Mr. Frank Aiken, Minister for External Affairs; Mr. Patrick Smith, Minister for Agriculture; Mr. Erskine Childers, Minister for Transport and Power; Mr. Jack Lynch, Minister for Industry and Commerce. On the left are members of the Opposition, headed by Mr. James Dillon, T.D.

Cheers All The Way

President Kennedy waves in acknowledgment of the cheers and applause as he is driven to Cork City Hall and an enthusiastic crowd breaks the barriers.

Reception In Cork Was Greatest Of The Tour

THE flags have been furled, the barriers have been taken away, the crowds have gone home. The final curtain has gone down on the biggest spectacle historic Cork has ever seen—the visit of John Fitzgerald Kennedy, President of the United States of America yesterday.

But this exciting day will linger in the memory of every man, woman and child who had become part of it. Cork yesterday, through its people, gave President Kennedy the greatest reception in his tour of Ireland — a tour in which every place he visited surpassed even the most optimistic expectation in the magnitude of their welcomes.

Cork, indeed, did President Kennedy proud and its people put on a welcome that is likely to be never surpassed for any great man or woman again.

Cork, indeed will remember. And President Kennedy will never forget.

(CONTINUED ON PAGE 11)

Special Word Of Thanks For Cork

PRESIDENT KENNEDY had a special word of thanks for the people of Cork yesterday. In conversation with the chief reporter of this newspaper at the reception which followed the conferring of the freedom of the city the President asked that it should be conveyed.

"I was most impressed," he said, "by the welcome I received as we drove through the streets and by the ceremony in your beautiful City Hall. I am most grateful for it all."

Members of the Presidential party from Washington said the reception given by the Cork people excelled anything they had experienced on the tour and they were loud in their praise of what they termed the wonderful setting provided by the City Hall for the freedom ceremony. They recalled, too, the President's particular pleasure at the manner in which the American national anthem was rendered by the band of the Southern Command.

Hopes To Lead Again

16 BRITISH MAY BE FREED

Man Killed, Eight Injured As Cars Crash

LOST IN PASSAGE

BICYCLE BOMBS KILL 11

Moon Tests This Year

Helicopters Snatch 15 From Blaze

THRESHER "CLUE" SPOTTED

POPE PAUL RECEIVES NIXON

TWO NEW CASES IN TYPHOID TOWN

THE WEATHER

THE TIDES

K. Denounces Kennedy's Berlin Visit

MR. KHRUSHCHEV flew into East Berlin yesterday and joined Herr Ulbright, East German Communist leader, in denouncing Wednesday's West Berlin visit by President Kennedy as a move in cold war politics.

"FRIENDSHIP VISIT"

Mr. Khrushchev was greeted at the airport by a band playing the "Prussian Presentation Anthem"—the same as was played when President Kennedy landed in Bonn last Sunday and by cheering crowds who had earlier been rehearsed in the chant of "Hoch, hoch, hoch" (Hurrah).

SWEDISH OFFICER FOR TRIAL

CONTENTS

Preparations For Pope's Coronation

Pope Paul will be crowned with a three-tiered silver and gold crown, made by craftsmen from his former archbishopric of Milan, as the climax to a three-hour ceremony beginning with Pontifical High Mass at 6 a.m. (I.S.T.)

PRESIDENT LEAVES TO-DAY

POPE THANKS TAOISEACH

CITY SPECIAL

Irish Independent

VOL. 72. No. 154 (INCORPORATING THE "FREEMAN'S JOURNAL") SATURDAY, JUNE 29, 1963 PRICE 3d.

'A country enlightened as Ireland, chartered as Ireland, armed as Ireland, and injured as Ireland, will be satisfied with nothing less than liberty'

Members of the Dail and the Seanad applaud as President Kennedy rises to address the joint session of the Oireachtas. In the front line of the members of the Dail (facing camera) are An Taoiseach, Mr. Lemass; An Tanaiste, Mr. MacEntee; Dr. Ryan, Minister for Finance; Mr. Aiken, Minister for External Affairs; Mr. Smith, Minister for Agriculture, and Mr. Childers, Minister for Transport and Power. On the extreme left (seated) is the Ceann Comhairle, Mr. P. Hogan.

HISTORIC DAIL SESSION

Mr. Kennedy presents battle flag to nation

HISTORY was made yesterday when President John F. Kennedy addressed the assembled members of the Dail and Seanad from the floor of Leinster House. The proceedings were broadcast and televised and photographers took the first pictures of a meeting of the legislature.

This first joint session of the Oireachtas was made memorable by the stirring message delivered by the President of the U.S., who in his opening remarks recalled the deeds of the Irish Brigade under Thomas Francis Meagher and then presented to Ireland the battle-flag of the Fighting 69th Regiment.

"A country," he declared, quoting Henry Grattan, "enlightened as Ireland, chartered as Ireland, armed as Ireland and injured as Ireland will be satisfied with nothing less than liberty.

"And today, I am certain, free Ireland as a full-fledged member of a world community where some are not yet free, and where some counsel an acceptance of tyranny—free Ireland will not be satisfied with anything less than liberty."

President Kennedy made it clear once again that this small country had a vital part to play in the world of today. "It matters not how small a nation is that seeks world peace and freedom," he said, emphasising every word.

"Ireland pursues an independent course in foreign policy," Mr. Kennedy continued, "but it is not neutral between liberty and tyranny, and I know it never will be."

'IRELAND HAS LESSON FOR ALL'

In Ireland's endurance through oppression from foreign domination, he saw a lesson for other peoples.

"Those who suffer beyond that wall I saw in Berlin on Wednesday must not despair for the future," he said. "Let them instead remember the constancy, the faith, the endurance and the ultimate success of the Irish."

And when he added: "Let them remember, as I did yesterday, the boys of Wexford, who fought with heart and hand to burst in twain the galling chain and free our native land," there was a thunderous roar of approval from all sides of the House.

In the magnificent setting of St. Patrick's Hall in Dublin Castle later, President Kennedy was the recipient of academic honours from the universities and he was made a Freeman of the City.

Now, the U.S. Chief Executive, who is a scholar in his own right, recalled the honoured place this country holds as the educator of Europe in the Dark Ages.

Its great monastic schools were, he said, "the core of the foundation of what became the enlightened religious revival in Europe."

In the forenoon President Kennedy went by helicopter to Cork where he was given a tumultuous reception. Thousands had come from all the southern counties to join the citizens in a joyful demonstration of affection and esteem.

In the City Hall, where the Freedom of the City was conferred on him, the Lord Mayor, Ald. Sean Casey, T.D., told him that no one had received such a welcome there before.

He delighted his audience by his friendly introduction of members of his party who were Irish, including Monsignor Michael O'Mahony, a native of Skibbereen, who is Pastor of the President's own church in Palm Beach, Florida.

"Pastor of a poor and humble flock," said the President with an engaging grin.

Then something of the harsh reality of the outside world obtruded itself for a moment. "We are in the most difficult and dangerous struggle in the history of the world," he said, "with the most dangerous weapons ever devised which could annihilate the human race in a few hours."

In this world he felt Ireland had a role to play. "Ireland is still the old Ireland," he declared, "but it has found a new mission in the 1960s to lead the Free World and join with other countries of the Free World, to do what she has done for the past 800 years when she had been intimately associated with independence and freedom."

The U.S. President paid his tribute to the 1916 patriots when he laid a wreath on the graves of the executed leaders in Arbour Hill before he went to Leinster House.

He read with interest the words of the Proclamation which are engraved on the wall behind the graves and spoke with several of the army officers before departing for Dail Eireann.

The final engagement for Mr. Kennedy yesterday was a private dinner given in his [illegible]

Continued on Page 14

Soldiers escape as Khrushchev arrives

THREE East German soldiers fled into the Federal German Republic in an armoured car yesterday as Russian Premier, Mr. Nikita Khrushchev, arrived in East Berlin.

They were Lance Corporals and they drove across a barbed-wire border fence at the River Werra, reaching the Federal German side unharmed. They asked for political asylum.

"Foreigners have often come to Berlin in the recent past—both to East and West Berlin," Mr. Khrushchev said. "But what have these visitors in their baggage? Some come to the west and say they want to improve and normalise relations but the negotiations prove otherwise.

"As far as we are concerned, we have come to Berlin to celebrate the 70th birthday of our friend, Walter Ulbricht."

NO BREACH

Perhaps to scotch rumours of a divergence of opinion between Herr Ulbricht and himself, Mr. Khrushchev said: "We are in full agreement with our good friend and comrade, Ulbricht, as we have always been before."

The entire diplomatic corps in East Berlin, including the Chinese Ambassador, was at the airport to welcome Mr. and Mrs. Khrushchev to Berlin, where the Soviet leader will have talks with the party chiefs of other East European Communist states.

He and Herr Ulbricht drove to East Berlin's town hall along bannered, crowded streets, amid the cheers of hundreds.

LATE NEWS

BIG EARTHQUAKE OFF JAPAN

The University of California Seismology Station yesterday recorded a strong earthquake, believed to be centred somewhere in the Kurile Islands north of Japan.

The tremors were first picked up at about 11.00 a.m. and were still being recorded nearly an hour later.

EIGHT DIE IN RAIL CRASH

Eight Czech soldiers were killed and 11 injured in a collision between an army truck and a goods train at a railway crossing in Northern Bohemia, Radio Prague reported yesterday.

The Evening Press, read into his words tacit support for Ireland's struggle against the British.

Next the President told the attentive Chamber: "Your destiny lies not as a peaceful island in a sea of troubles, but as a maker and shaper of world peace" and in a line that might have caused de Valera, the battler for Irish neutrality during World War II, to shift uncomfortably in his seat, Kennedy added, "Self-determination can no longer mean isolation … And no nation, large or small can be indifferent to the fate of others, near or far."

There followed a quote from Irish-American poet John Boyle O'Reilly, which Ted Sorensen explained was "a very short verse that had some application to the Cold War as well as to the struggle for independence."[137]

The world is large when its weary
leagues two loving hearts divide,
But the world is small when your enemy
Is loose on the other side.

Continuing with the "martial versus peaceful" theme, Kennedy asked the question that de Valera had asked in his speech about Irish neutrality in the war, concerning small nations and their role in a big and increasingly belligerent world order: "In an age when a handful of men and nations have the power literally to devastate mankind – in such an age … how can a nation as small as Ireland play much of a role on the world stage?"

In answer to this rhetorical question, Ted Sorensen wanted to quote ex-British Prime Minister Lloyd George. He recollects: "The best quotation on that subject, about little five-foot nations, was too good to leave out of the speech, but I journeyed down with my final draft to New Ross … and rode back to Dublin on the plane [*sic*] with Kennedy … And he saw that quotation, and then he saw who was being quoted and he said, 'Better take this out' – not the quotation but the name of who said it."[138]

Lloyd George had famously said that dealing with de Valera was like trying to pick up mercury with a fork. You could say that they had "previous". No wonder Kennedy decided not to mention his name in the speech to the Dáil. Instead the final text credited the words to "one of the great orators of the English language", thereby side-stepping a potential oratorical and political landmine.

The quote itself read: "All the world owes much to the little 'five feet high' nations. The greatest art of the world was the work of little nations. The most enduring literature of the world came from little nations. The heroic deeds that thrill humanity through generations were the deeds of little nations fighting for their freedom. And, oh yes, the salvation of mankind came through a little nation."

Continuing with the "small nations" theme, Kennedy delivered a powerful few lines that mixed facts and flattery: "This has never been a rich and powerful country, and yet, since earliest times, its influence on the world has been rich and powerful. No larger nation did more to keep Christianity and Western culture alive in the darkest centuries. No larger nation did more to spark the cause of independence in America, indeed, around the world. And no larger nation has ever provided the world with more literary and artistic genius."

As if to back up his point, Kennedy reached into Irish literature once more: "This is an extraordinary country. George Bernard Shaw, speaking as an Irishman, summed up an approach to life. Other people, he said, see things and … say 'Why?' … But I dream things that never were – and I say: 'Why not?'"

After some talk of Europe and developing nations, Kennedy briefly took on his role as Cold Warrior and political evangelist, preaching against "the harsh and oppressive Communist system". Knowing his audience and the Chamber he was standing in, Kennedy appealed to the Irish underdog mentality: "For knowing the meaning of foreign domination, Ireland is the example and inspiration to those enduring endless years of oppression."

He touched on some of his experiences earlier in the week: "Those who suffer beyond that wall I saw on Wednesday in Berlin must not despair of their future. Let them remember the constancy, the faith, the endurance, and the final success of the Irish. And let them remember, as I heard sung by your sons and daughters yesterday in Wexford, the words, 'the boys of Wexford, who fought with heart and hand, to burst in twain the galling chain and free our native land'."

Towards the end of his speech Kennedy the pacifist appeared, commending Ireland for its role on the world stage: "The major forum for your nation's greater role in world affairs is that of protector of the weak and voice of the small, the United Nations. From Cork to Congo, from Galway to the Gaza Strip, from this legislative assembly to the United Nations, Ireland is sending its most talented men to do the world's most important work – the work of peace."

At 4.46, just shy of half an hour since beginning his speech, the President concluded with one last quote, from George William Russell: "A great Irish poet once wrote: 'I believe profoundly … in the future of Ireland … that this is an isle of destiny, that that destiny will be glorious … and that when our hour is come, we will have something to give to the world.'"

And with that, the leader of the Free World concluded: "My friends: Ireland's hour has come. You have something to give to the world – and that is a future of peace with freedom."

To thunderous applause, the President left the Dáil Chamber. As he was making his way through the throng, an observer in the visitor's gallery pointed out to a Kennedy aide that "All of us love your President Kennedy, and that's the only thing that all of the people in Ireland have completely agreed upon since the British passed the Conscription Bill in 1918."[139]

The newspapers were unanimous in their approval of the speech, with its mixture of historical and cultural flattery, and its message about Ireland's importance on the world stage. It was a major shot of confidence for a fledgling nation from the most powerful man in the world, and one they were happy to celebrate.

Kennedy himself was pleased with his reception in the Dáil. When he met up with his advisors later on, he turned to Dave Powers and asked, "Of those you've met, who do you think are the best politicians in America?" Powers replied "Daley and Mansfield." (He was referring to Richard Daley, Mayor of Chicago, and Mike Mansfield, Senate Majority Leader, both of them Irish-American.) The President nodded. "I agree with you. The Irish do seem to have an art for government." He paused a moment, then smiled: "Perhaps we are both prejudiced."[140]

Waving up to some staff members who appeared at the windows of their offices around Leinster House, the President, accompanied by Seán Lemass and Frank Aiken climbed into his car for a brief journey that would bring him a long way towards being a fully fledged Irishman.

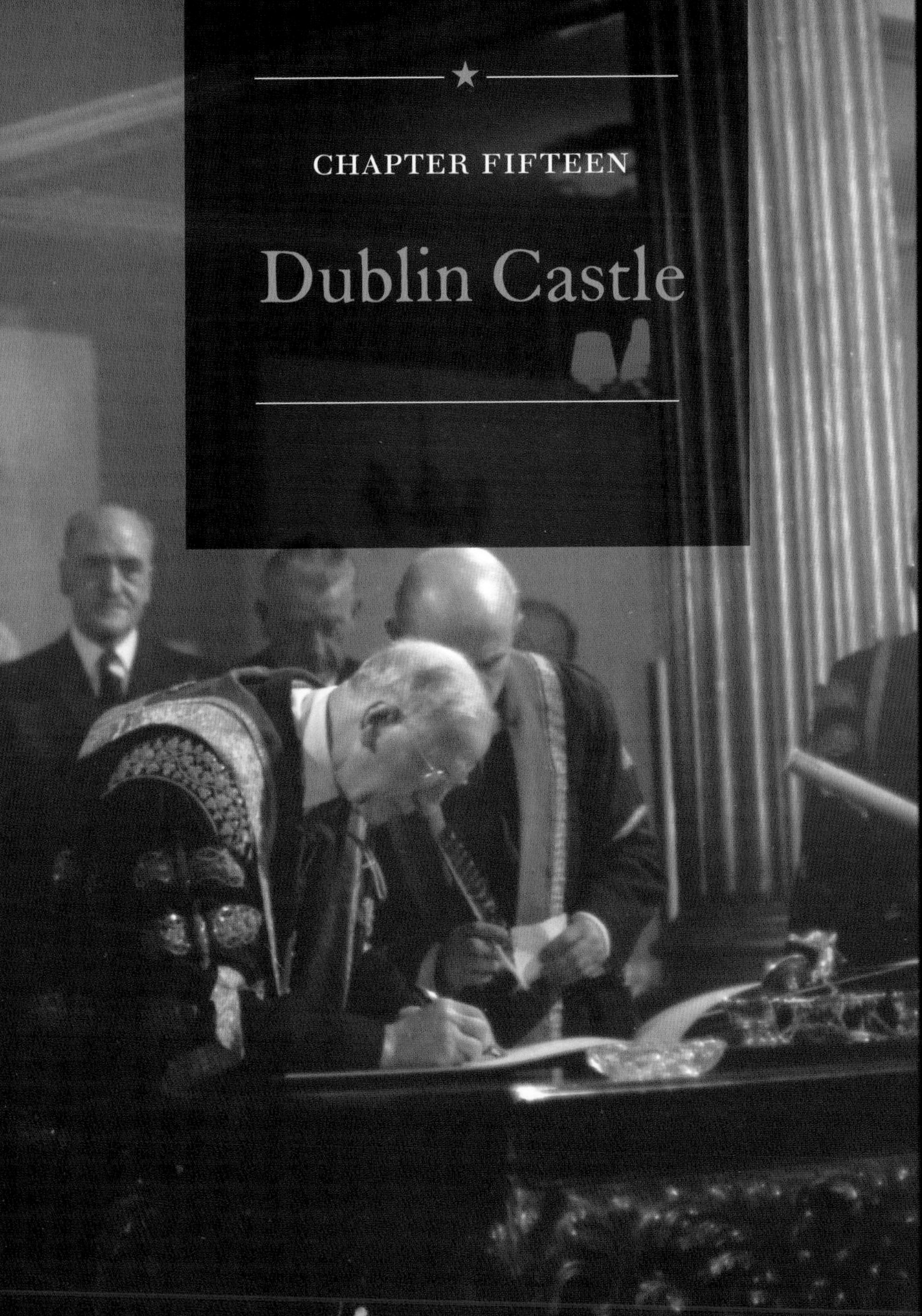

CHAPTER FIFTEEN

Dublin Castle

—★—

A short drive from Leinster House to Dublin Castle brought the President to what *The Irish Times* called "a smooth, neat package of pageantry".[141] In the course of an hour, Kennedy would receive two honorary degrees and the Freedom of the City of Dublin during three ceremonies that were organised and run with military precision. This was going to be everything the Áras garden party was not.

Ceremony One saw history repeat itself. On his way from one august institution to the other, the President must have been mindful that he was about to receive the very same honour that his father had been awarded by the very same man back in 1938, a quarter of a century earlier. Joseph P. Kennedy had never professed any great interest in his Irishness and it has even been suggested that he resented his ethnic background. His son had no such hang-ups and he wasn't just an Ambassador but Leader of the Free World. This was different.

As always on this visit, President de Valera was early and arrived at Dublin Castle before Kennedy, accompanied by an aide holding his arm. The crowd that had gathered outside the Castle gates gave their own President a rousing ovation before settling back to wait patiently for America's leader. It wasn't long before the Presidential motorcade turned into Dame Street. Seán Lemass, Frank Aiken and various other government ministers were accompanying their guest and a stream of shiny black cars swept into the cobblestoned courtyard. At the door of the regal Throne Room, de Valera welcomed Kennedy in his capacity as Chancellor of the National University of Ireland.

The doors of the Throne Room opened and a hush descended in St Patrick's Hall. Lemass and the assorted dignitaries made their way down the centre aisle and took their seats. Moments later, the two

Presidents entered the room and, despite the solemnity of the occasion, there was a spontaneous burst of applause as they sat down close to the dais. Kennedy wasn't a fan of pomp, and we can confidently guess that he didn't enjoy donning the ornate purple, green and scarlet ceremonial robes of the National University. *Irish Times* journalist Michael Viney noticed his discomfiture straight away. After noting the President's elaborate robes, he wrote: "He also wore, with somewhat less aplomb, the large and floppy black cap, which he doffed at the first permissable moment. There was the suspicion of a blush beneath his tan."[142]

The University Registrar, Seamus Wilmot, stood up and announced the beginning of proceedings. Next up was the Vice Chancellor, Dr Michael Tierney, who gave a concise history of the Kennedy clan that went all the way back to the Normans, serving to bolster any Hibernian credentials the President may have felt he was

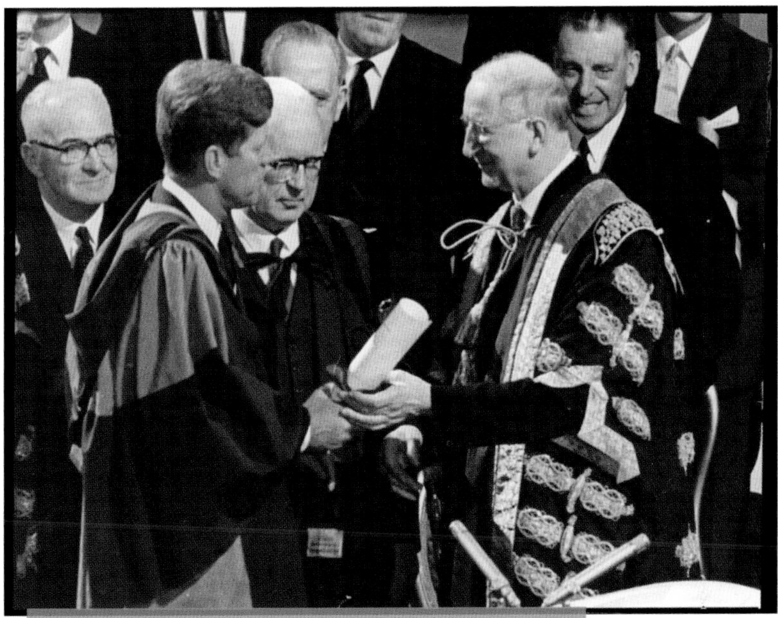

Following in his father's footsteps: JFK accepts his honorary degree from Éamon de Valera, Chancellor of the NUI, as Ambassador Kennedy had done in 1938.

Cheering for Trinity, praying for National: the scene at Dublin Castle where JFK was awarded honorary degrees from Dublin's two rival universities.

lacking. When he'd finished, President de Valera stood up and shook hands with Kennedy, who picked up a quill, dipped it in a gold ink pot and proceeded to sign the official roll. He was now an honorary law graduate of the National University of Ireland. The Presidents left the Hall, as did all the National University officials, who were swiftly replaced by those representing Dublin University. It was an academic changing of the dons.

Behind the scenes, Kennedy was swapping one set of robes for another and was soon entering the Hall again, this time in the scarlet and rose colours of Trinity and hatless, no doubt to his relief. Introduced in Latin to the assembled dignitaries as Johannes Fitzgerald Kennedy, Praesses Civitatum Foederatarum Americanarum, the President's doctor of law degree was conferred by the Vice Chancellor, the Earl of Rosse. The newest graduate of Trinity signed the roll in front of him and received his second honorary degree in the space of twenty minutes.

With that, he disappeared once more (as did the Dublin University officals). By the time Kennedy entered the Hall for the third time, the robes were gone and he must have felt a little more at ease dressed in his grey lounge suit. Looking out at a new set of faces, mostly Dublin politicians, the President was about to be awarded the Freedom of the city that had given him such an extraordinary welcome.

The Lord Mayor of Dublin, Alderman Sean Moore, now sat in the chair beside Kennedy. In his speech, the Mayor described the President as "the personification of that earliest dedication of your illustrious predecessor [Thomas Jefferson], who held certain truths to be self-evident, the principle of which was that all men are created equal in their right to the pursuit of happiness."

He told Kennedy: "We think kindly, sir, of the American people … and we would like them to think kindly of us. We would like them – very many of them – to come and judge us personally and not take us as we are too often depicted on stage, screen and in script."

It was time for the thrice-honoured guest to stand and speak for the first time since arriving in Dublin Castle. It was a short but clever little speech that neatly addressed all three institutions that had honoured him in less than an hour.

To the Mayor, Kennedy explained: "I can imagine nothing more pleasant than continuing day after day to drive through the streets of Dublin and wave, and I may come back and do it."

To the university heads and dons, he offered a historical compliment: "For so many hundreds of years this country had colleges and universities of 2,000, 3,000 and 4,000 students in the darkest ages of Europe, which served as the core, as the foundation, for what became the enlightenment and the religious revival of Europe."

And as always with Kennedy in Ireland, there was time for some knowing humour. Acknowledging the difference between the very Protestant Trinity College and the distinctly Catholic National University of Ireland, he proclaimed: "I now feel equally part of both, and if they ever have a game of Gaelic football or hurling, I shall cheer for Trinity and pray for National."

As he left the Hall and climbed into his car once more, he heard cries of "Good ould Jack"[143] before his motorcade drove out through the Castle gates.

Laden down with degrees and citizenships, having made history as the first head of State to address the Irish parliament and paid his respects to fallen heroes of the 1916 Rising at Arbour Hill, the President ended his second full day in Ireland.

He returned to the American Embassy to freshen up before dinner with President and Mrs de Valera at the Áras. It would be a casual, informal affair, insofar as such occasions can be when you are dealing with one of the most charismatic American presidents of all time and a huge roomful of people dying to meet him. Within twenty-four hours, President Kennedy would be ferried away to another country, leaving Ireland for the last time.

CHAPTER SIXTEEN

The Last Supper

CHAPTER SEVENTEEN

Galway

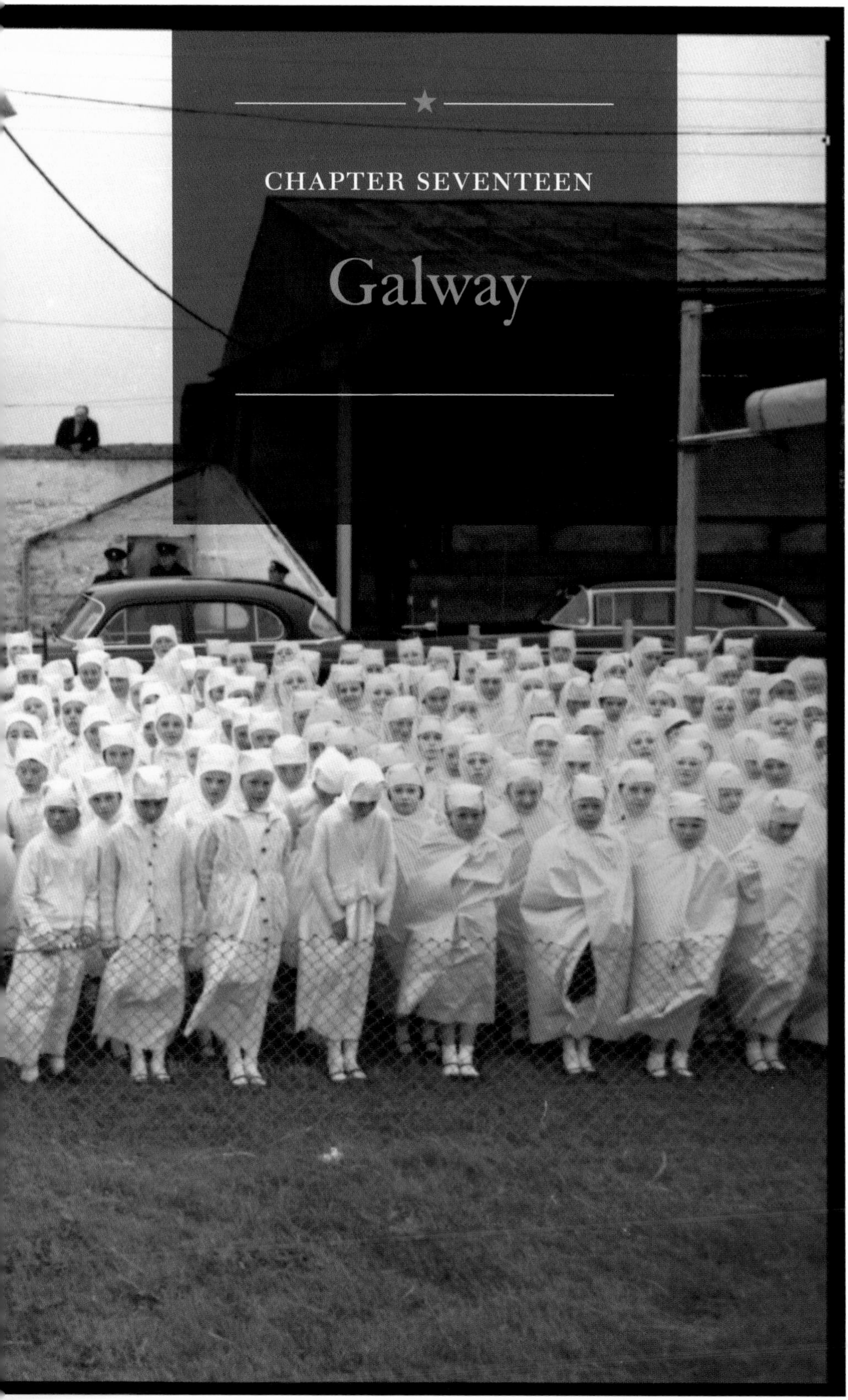

—★—

As if reflecting the mood of its people, the weather was grim and grey over the whole island of Ireland on the last day that President Kennedy would spend there. In contrast to the previous few days of anticipation and welcome, this was a day for farewells and instant nostalgia.

The doorbell of the Embassy rang early. Upstairs, Kennedy knew that President de Valera, his neighbour for the last three nights, was coming to say his goodbyes. When the two men met for the last time, the American President asked his Irish counterpart to say a few words. In a speech that was as emotional as it was brief, de Valera thanked his host for coming but regretted that the visit had to be so short.

For his part, Kennedy was equally regretful and wistful when he told the assembled group: "I will be back again; I do hope to be back again."

Before leaving the Embassy, Kennedy took a characteristic detour to thank the staff who had looked after the Kennedy party since they arrived earlier in the week. He told them: "You did a great job for us and did much to make our stay so pleasant and comfortable."

Outside, the familiar chopping sound of the helicopters could be heard and the President knew it was time to go. When asked by a journalist what the highlight of the trip had been for him, Kennedy replied straight away: "The highlight? That was the memorial service at Arbour Hill yesterday. It was very impressive." He added: "I must say, too, that the people everywhere have been wonderful. We had a tremendous welcome."

At the door of the Embassy, President de Valera stood waiting. John F. Kennedy walked briskly towards him and took his arm. There was a cheer as the two men made their way towards the waiting

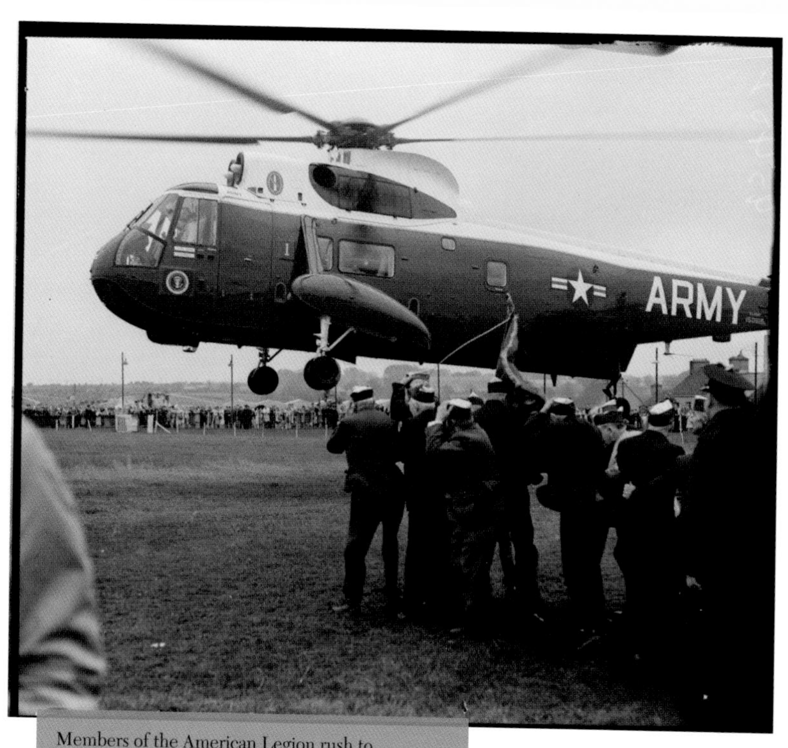

Members of the American Legion rush to meet JFK as his helicopter lands in Galway.

helicopter. Kennedy was halfway up the carpeted steps when he stopped suddenly and ran back down to find Sinéad de Valera. He didn't want to leave without saying one last goodbye. The President hurried over towards the vivacious old lady, kissed her on the cheek and held onto her arms. It was a moment of genuine affection between two people who had "clicked". The President turned on his heels and hopped back up the helicopter steps, pausing only to wave one last time.[148] He had a broad grin on his face when he gazed into the crowd and beyond. The President looked happy as he took his last few breaths of Dublin air.

Dr Thomas Kiernan, the Irish Ambassador to Washington, was among the party in the Presidential helicopter that morning and he noticed how closely Kennedy was observing the towns, fields and houses that lay beneath: "He was constantly asking about places. We were low enough to see large-sized houses. He was costing houses. How much would a place like that cost with a certain amount of land attatched? I assumed he was wondering just what it would be like to live in Ireland or to have a pied à terre where he could come or send the children … One could almost see an affection for Ireland deepening during that visit."[149]

As the two Presidents were saying their goodbyes in Dublin, there was mounting excitement on the other side of the country. In Galway, 600 Gardaí were up early, lining the streets ahead of the crowds that began to arrive from 7am. The Great Southern Hotel was abuzz with the comings and goings of over 150 journalists from around the world. *The Connacht Tribune* reported that the Galway and Salthill tourist board had set up an information bureau at the hotel. Hostesses representing Aer Lingus (of whom one was a lady named Kennedy) and CIÉ (Ireland's national train and bus company) were on duty to provide all necessary travel information.[150]

As his helicopter circled the skies above Galway Bay, the President will have caught sight of a massive Irish flag on the sports field beneath him. A closer look saw the flag shimmering strangely. It was composed of 320 children from the Convent of Mercy, who had been dressed in waterproof capes and hoods that were either green, white, gold or brown: green, white and gold for the Irish flag, while the children in brown formed the flagpole.

Coming down the steps of the helicopter, Kennedy spotted the guard of honour of thirty members of the American Legion, veterans of the US military, some of whom had seen action in both World Wars. He turned to Kenny O'Donnell and shook his head, remarking: "You can't get away from the American Legion no matter where you go. I'll bet they have a post at the South Pole."

According to O'Donnell, Kennedy had a hard time trying to keep a straight face when one Irish Legionnaire broke away from the line, handed the President an envelope and said, "It's about my pension.

Would you use your influence and see if you can get me an increase?"

A bemused Kennedy assured the man that he would do what he could and handed the letter to Dave Powers. It transpires that many weeks later, back in the White House, the President remembered this man and asked Powers, "Did you take care of that fellow in Galway?"

Powers had already looked into the matter and the Galwegian Legionnaire was the richer for it.[151] It was a wonderful illustration of small town politics with a global nudge and it was all very Irish indeed.

The President was introduced by Seán Lemass to the Mayor of Galway, Alderman Patrick Ryan, who in turn introduced their guest to various other local dignitaries.

As he made his way to the waiting motorcade, Kennedy waded into the crowd so that he could shake hands with and thank the children from the Convent of Mercy school. All initial nervousness quickly disappeared when the youngsters saw how friendly this visiting President was. He even asked them to sing for him and they duly obliged with a rendition of "Galway Bay".

The journey from the sports field to Eyre Square in the city centre was interrupted by a stop outside the Mayor's house. Members of Mayor Ryan's family had gathered outside their residence to wave along with everyone else but when the Mayor pointed them out to his guest, the President insisted on stopping his car and getting out to meet them. He shook hands with Mrs Catherine Ryan, the Mayor's mother, and with the five Ryan children, the oldest of whom was eight years old. Clearly a resourceful lady, Mrs Ryan grabbed a copy of an old American history book off the shelf and asked the President to sign it, which he duly did!

As the motorcade drove on to Eyre Square, it was watched by a massive turnout of around 100,000 people waving and cheering the President from every available vantage point. Stars and Stripes and Irish Tricolours flew from every nook and cranny and the bells were ringing out in St Nicholas' Collegiate Church where, legend has it, Christopher Columbus stopped to pray in 1477. A few hundred metres away was the Atlantic Ocean, which linked the West coast

Visit to Galway of

John F. Kennedy

President, United States of America.

Ceremonies at Eyre Square, June 29, 1963.

Invitations must be shown to Gardai, on demand, and to Stewards at Eyre Square.

All guests are requested to be in their places by 11.15 a.m.

Entrance will be via the Browne Doorway.

From 9 a.m. on June 29, all vehicular traffic will be diverted by the Gardai from the processional route, including the environs of Eyre Square.

N.B. To facilitate arrangements, please reply by return, stating if you will attend.

Town Clerk,
Galway Corporation,
22, Dominick Street,
Galway.

June 19th, 1963.

Presidential protocol: the Town Clerk issues guidelines to guests attending the Galway leg of the visit.

of Ireland with the East coast of President Kennedy's homeland, on the continent Columbus would discover in the course of his voyages.

Eyre Square

The crowd at Eyre Square came alive when the black limousines hummed into sight. They roared their appreciation while Kennedy inspected two lines of troops presenting arms. He was then greeted by Council members in their robes, who formed a guard of honour. After shaking hands with each member, the President took his seat on the podium. The ninth Freeman-elect of Galway (he followed in the footsteps of three presidents of Ireland – Douglas Hyde, Sean T. O'Kelly and de Valera) then had some gifts to receive. An Irish linen banquet cloth and some linen napkins were added to the long list of gifts received by the President, which by now was heaving under the weight of beautiful Irish linen of every description.

It took a while for the cheers to subside and when they did, the Town Clerk stood up and read the decision of the Council to make Kennedy a Freeman of Galway, which led to more cheering.

It was 11.30 when Mayor Ryan got to his feet and delivered a speech that proved controversial because of his decision to speak only in the Irish language. The President sat through it patiently, reading the words of an English translation that had been handed to him. Mayor Ryan extolled the ties that bound Galway with America. Reference was made to St Brendan the Navigator (who died at Annaghdown near Galway city) and how he had reached America in the 6th century, long before Columbus. The Mayor spoke of a sailor on Columbus's ship, the *Santa Maria,* who came from Galway, and of course there was talk of the Great Famine. Mayor Ryan reminded the President of the thousands who fled the shores of Galway and their subsequent arrival in the President's home city of Boston. The Claddagh district of that city was named after the Claddagh district in Galway. Mayor Ryan ended his speech by urging the President to return some day and maybe take a trip out to see "the beauty of Connemara" with Mrs Kennedy and the family. He concluded:

A troupe of Irish dancers perform in front of JFK at Eyre Square in Galway City.

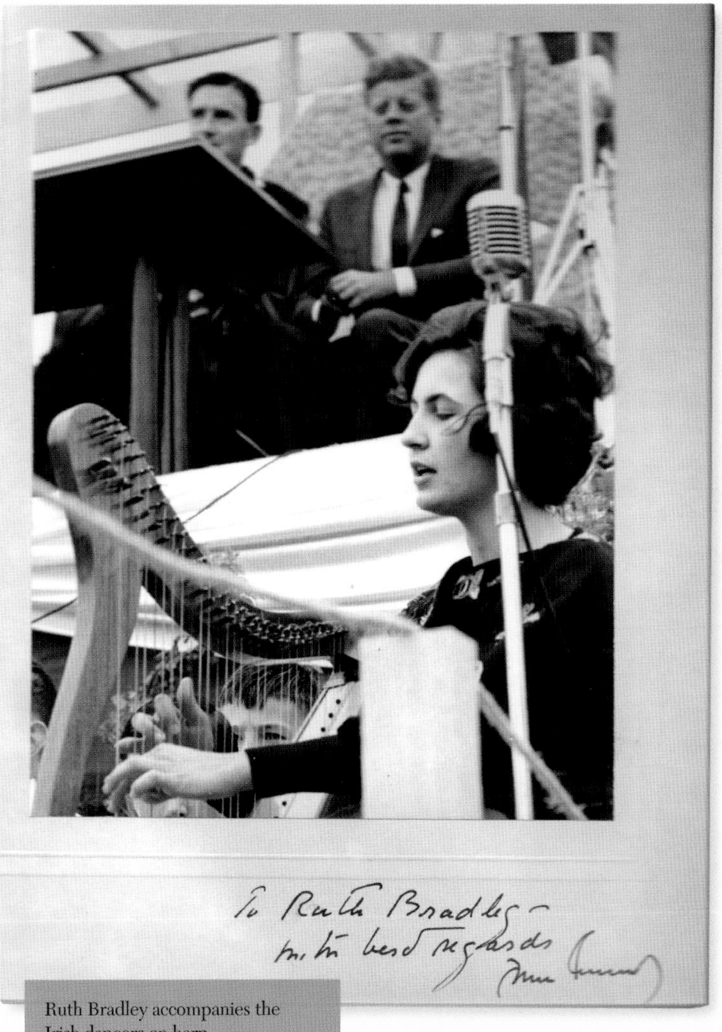
To Ruth Bradley—
with best regards

Ruth Bradley accompanies the Irish dancers on harp.

The winning smile: JFK is caught by surprise by rookie photographer Stan Shields who evaded security to capture this moment. Shields was sent to cover the Presidential visit on his first day at work for the *Connacht Tribune*.

Lemass decided not to pass on Kennedy's "Spartans" comment. "I never reported this down in Salthill because it would damage their publicity as a tourist resort."[153]

He did speak warmly of the President's capacity for putting people at ease, whether it was a crusty old dignitary, a pretty waitress at a State function or a young schoolchild waving a flag: "It was this type of spontaneous response to a situation, the constant asking questions, certainly lighthearted and occasionally humorous, would lighten … any situation in general, which was certainly characteristic."

There was obviously a degree of mutual respect, as Kennedy would demonstrate when Lemass went to Washington four months later. Theirs was a practical relationship between two heads of state with the power to make deals and influence events. They understood each other and felt they could work together productively.

Meanwhile, the rumbling of helicopters could be heard across Galway Bay as the President's car drove into the field in Salthill from which he would depart. Minutes later, he was up in the air and making the short trip to Limerick where he was dropping by for a visit that was never meant to happen. The Lord Mayor of Limerick, however, had other plans. There was no way she was letting the US President come to the West Coast without visiting her town.

LT COL
SEAL OF THE PRESIDENT OF THE UNITED STATES

CHAPTER EIGHTEEN

Limerick

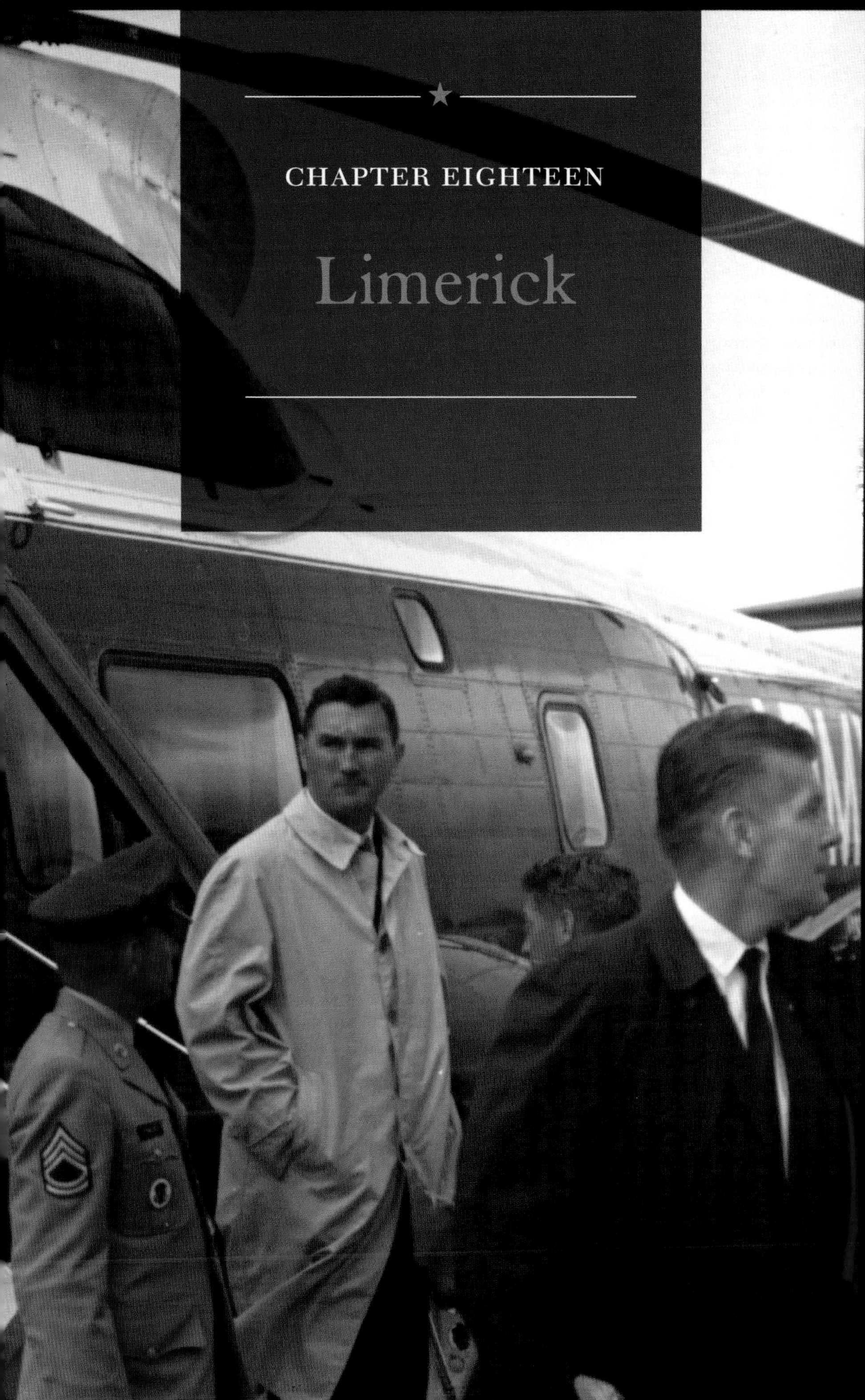

—★—

It was originally meant to be a straightforward leap from Galway to nearby Shannon airport and on to England but nobody had counted on the persistence and charm of Frances Condell.

Limerick city was over 98 per cent Catholic in 1963 but that did not stop Mrs Condell, a Protestant, standing for and becoming the first woman to hold the office of Lord Mayor. A determined, astute and feisty woman in her forties, with a grown-up family and grandchildren, Condell was determined that the President would visit her town while he was on the West Coast. The problem was that the President had no time to visit Limerick and his handlers had no intention of making room. But Frances Condell had five older brothers and she knew how to handle men. She had a challenge on her hands and she was going to rise to it.

On first hearing that Kennedy was coming to Ireland, Condell was adamant that he should visit Limerick: "On the distaff side I felt that we had some claim on President Kennedy because his mother's people, you see, came from County Limerick … We women of Limerick decided that we must have him visit the city. But, unfortunately, by this time his schedule had been arranged, and according to the Ambassador, there wasn't a hope of getting him to come."

Such pessimism was grist to Condell's mill and she took it upon herself to lobby the usually brusque Ambassador to Ireland, Matt McCloskey, but he was having none of it despite three separate requests. When Pierre Salinger, the President's Press Secretary, came to Ireland on his reconaissance visit, Condell made sure she was seated next to him on the bus: "And I pleaded with him, you know, to try and arrange this visit, and he said, 'No, you haven't a chance'."

Undeterred, the Mayor made her fourth call to Ambassador McCloskey and bent his ear yet again. She'd done all she could. Now it was just a case of waiting to see. Exactly a week before the President was due in Ireland, Mayor Condell was woken at 1am by the sound of her phone ringing. It was Ambassador McCloskey and his words would change Frances Condell's life: "You've got your wish, now will you get off my back?"

Her persistence had paid off and President Kennedy was coming to town. The Mayor had one week to put the arrangements in place. A city centre visit was out of the question for logistical reasons so alternatives were looked at. City, field, back garden, it didn't matter to Mrs Condell so long as he set foot on Limerick soil. The soil that was chosen was Greenpark Racecourse, a few minutes from the city. As it turns out, the space was perfect for such a visit and allowed some of the most efficient crowd management of the entire visit.

The day before the Limerick visit Mayor Condell came across to Cork to watch the President being made a Freeman of the City and she was introduced to Kennedy by Ambassador McCloskey as "Your hostess on Saturday, Mr President." To which the President commented: "Oh yes, you're the Mayoress of Limerick." The Ambassador corrected Kennedy by interjecting, "No, this is the Mayor of Limerick."

Condell described the scene later: "He looked at me for a moment and suddenly it registered with him, apparently, that he had made a mistake. And he said, 'Are you Frances Condell?' I said, 'I'm afraid I am, sir.' So then he paid me a lovely compliment: he said, 'But they told me you were a grandmother.' He came back quickly like that and recovered himself!"

While standing in Cork's City Hall that morning, admiring the beautiful floral decorations, the Mayor came up with a clever plan: recycling. "I went to all the people who mattered in Cork, to the Lord Mayor, of course, and I said, 'Look, please may we beg, borrow, or steal some of these beautiful flowers for Limerick?' And the City Manager looked me in the eye and he said, 'Provided you can arrange transport for them.' So then I suddenly saw out of the corner of my eye, a colonel,

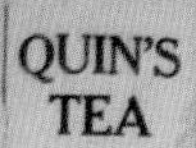

Limerick Leader

Vol. 75. No. 13975. SATURDAY, JUNE 29, 1963. PRICE FIVEPENCE

CÉAD MÍLE FÁILTE

A GREAT DAY FOR LIMERICK

Big welcome for Mr. Kennedy

A TYPICALLY Irish welcome, wholehearted in its sincerity, will be given to America's first citizen, 46-year-old President John Fitzgerald Kennedy, when he arrives by helicopter from Galway at Greenpark racecourse, Limerick, at about 1 p.m. to-morrow.

A racecourse bedecked with flags and bunting, with the Stars and Stripes of the great United States flying side by side with the Tricolour, will give enthusiastic colour to a voluminous, vociferous greeting from thousands of citizens and visitors. This will be Limerick's day to remember: the first time a U.S. President walked on Limerick soil and spoke to its people.

In the minds and hearts of our people, President Kennedy will find a truly affectionate place. With ancestral links in the city and county, we have come to regard him as our own.

With a very hearty CEAD MILE FAILTE we greet this great man of democracy, an outstanding champion of liberty and universal peace, whose character mirrors the true concept of the American nation's love of freedom. He is one of the great personalities of our time.

BUSINESS HOUSES ASKED TO CLOSE

IT was requested at a special meeting of the City Council in the Circuit Court house, finalising arrangements for President Kennedy's visit to the Limerick racecourse on Saturday next at 1 p.m., that business houses and other establishments close between the hours of 12 noon and 3 p.m. to give everybody an opportunity of welcoming the President and party to Limerick.

It was mentioned that 300 Gardai would be drafted from Dublin to augment the local police force. They will be on duty at the racecourse and to guard the approaches leading to it.

Greenpark racecourse will be extensively decorated with a large flag dropping in the direction and all public buildings will be suitably decorated.

All people not going to the Greenpark by care. The main gates will be open from 9.30 a.m. and cars may be parked in the areas as early as possible.

All the strip lands are being by clad to attend The American National Anthem will be sung by the advice of President Kennedy. The proceedings will conclude with the Irish National Anthem.

TRAFFIC AND CROWD ARRANGEMENTS

THE following are the traffic and control arrangements: 1—Entry to racecourse will be via Ballinacurra; 2—One way street, from Gerard St./Henry St. junction to McDonnell's Cross, in easterly direction, 11 a.m. to 3 p.m.; 3—No cars to be parked on main road, particularly from Mallowmell's Cross to Gerard Street/Henry Street junction; 4—Motorists will be directed to their places in the car park by Gardai and their cooperation is requested; 5—Gates to the racecourse will open at 10.30 a.m.; 6—The general public will be accommodated in enclosure at the racecourse; 7—No person, other than those in possession of official invitation cards, and accredited representatives and photographers of the Press, will be admitted to racetrack. Invitations must be produced to Gardai at admission point; 8—No hawkers will be permitted under any circumstances in the enclosure; 9—No person will be permitted to racecourse except by main gate; 10—For their own safety, children under 14 should not attend at racecourse; parents are advised to insist on this.

OUR GUEST

WHY NO LIVE TV ?

LATE this afternoon Mr. D. B. O'Malley, Parliamentary Secretary to the Minister for Finance, was in contact with Mr. Kevin McCourt, Director-General, Telefis Eireann, in a last-minute bid to try and have to-morrow's ceremonies at Greenpark televised "live."

Telefis Eireann are reported to have stated that all their cameras are in use in Galway and at the Irish Sweeps Derby at the Curragh, but, surely, if they wanted to, an additional camera could be borrowed from one of the many British networks.

Failing that, it must be remembered that it is only a five-hour flight across the Atlantic and, surely, N.B.C. of America would be only too willing to assist another country that is desirous of bringing their own President into the homes of thousands.

Telefis Eireann are said to have also stated that they did not receive sufficient notification of of "J.F.K.'s" plan to visit here.

32 Pages to-day

This week's issue contains full details of President Kennedy's visit to Limerick as well as a splendid feature on the well-known Limerick firm of Cannocks.

Next Week

Order your copy now of next week's "Limerick Leader" which will give full news and pictorial coverage to the historic visit of President Kennedy to Limerick. It will also contain a big number of news items, such as Co. Council reports, which were held over due to extreme pressure on space.

OFFICIAL PROGRAMME

At 1 p.m. the President of the United States arrives.

President Kennedy is greeted at helicopter by Her Worship the Mayor (Mrs. Condell) and the City Manager (Mr. T. F. McDermott).

President Kennedy and party escorted to dais.

Receives greetings of dignitaries.

American National Anthem played by Boherbuoy Brass and Reed Band.

The meeting opens with a silent prayer, all standing.

Roll Call.

Her Worship the Mayor calls on City Manager to read report.

City Manager reads report covering resolution adopted by City Council.

Address by Her Worship the Mayor.

City Manager reads Certificate of Freedom.

Mayor presents Certificate of Freedom to President Kennedy and declares him elected a Freeman of Limerick.

President Kennedy signs the Roll of Freemen and replies.

Her Worship the Mayor presents her personal gift and brings meeting to a conclusion.

Irish National Anthem played by St. John's Brass and Reed Band.

1.30 p.m. President departs for Shannon.

THE FIRST FREEDOM CERTIFICATE

The first certificate conferring the Freedom of Limerick on Richard O'Shaughnessy, M.P., on January 1, 1875, is hung in the City Museum, Pery Square, and though 88 years old is in a very good state of preservation.

It is headed "City of Limerick," and contains the following in hand-writing: "Be it remembered, that at a special meeting of the Corporation of the City of Limerick held on Monday the first day of January one thousand eight hundred and seventy four, the Right Worshipful, James Spaight, Mayor, in the chair, it was unanimously resolved that the Freedom of this city be and is hereby presented to Richard O'Shaughnessy, M.P., in recognition of the valuable services rendered by him to our city and who has been mainly instrumental in having the recent amendment of the Poor Law Rating system improved and which has so reduced taxation in the city.

"Given at the Town Hall in the City of Limerick under the seal of said city. This twenty-second day of May, one thousand eight hundred and seventy four.

(Signed):

JAMES SPAIGHT,

Mayor."

Redemptorist Retreat House Old Debt

	PENNIES
NEEDED	2,369,839
Received last week	5,637
DEBT NOW	2,364,202

Have You Subscribed This Week?

SOCIAL and PERSONAL

Dr. Spellman will be away from Limerick on July ... till D. P. a. Jones will be absent from July 1 to July 15.

DIOCESE OF LIMERICK

To mark the occasion of the Coronation of His Holiness Pope Paul VI, there will be a Solemn Pontifical High Mass at St. John's Cathedral ... The faithful are cordially invited to attend.

Aerial view of Limerick Racecourse, where the President will receive the Freedom of the City. Legend: (1) President's "chopper" will land here; (2) Presidential stand on which the conferring will take place; (3) TV and Cine Camera stand; (4 & 5) Press, Radio, V.F.S. relatives, etc.; (6) V.I.P.'s special car park; (7) & 8) public car park.

the army colonel. I said, 'Here's my man.' So I went up to him and I said, 'Do you think you could afford to give me transport for these flowers?'"[154]

The colonel duly obliged and the floral depictions of the American flag and words of welcome in Irish made their way across the country from Cork City Hall to Greenpark Racecourse in Limerick.

As the crowds waved their hats in the air around the streets of Galway on the morning of Saturday 28 June, excitement was already brewing in Limerick. Kennedy's connection was genuine, in that ten miles outside the city lay the village of Lough Gur, from whence the President's maternal great-grandparents are said to have hailed. Among those making their way to Limerick city that morning were forty-six Fitzgerald cousins. Amongst the audience at the racecourse were Jim Hogan, a ninety-year-old retired victualler from Glin, and his eighty-year-old sister, Celia Morgan from Adare, both second cousins of the President. Their sister-in-law, eighty-year-old Ann Hogan, representing her late husband Richard, explained the family's kinship with the President: "Catherine Fitzgerald, a sister of President Kennedy's great-grandfather, Tom Fitzgerald, married Patrick Sheehan. They had a daughter, Margaret Sheehan, who married David Hogan of Adare who was our father."

In fact, in 1938, the very year when the President's father, Joseph P. Kennedy, was visiting Dublin as Ambassador to London, his grandfather, John "Honey Fitz" Fitzgerald, was back in Limerick, tracing his ancestors. When Honey Fitz got to the remote township of Lough Gur, near Bruff, County Limerick, he was driven around by local taxi-driver Denis Conway. Conway recalled how the former Mayor of Boston asked him to pull over so that he could gaze out at the patch of land on which the Fitzgerald homestead once stood. It was from here that Honey Fitz's father, Thomas Fitzgerald, fled the Famine. When the President was elected to the White House, Denis Conway wrote him a note explaining the connection and received a reply from the White House in May 1961.[155] On the morning of 29 June 1963, the sixty-seven-year-old Denis was among those making his way to Greenpark Racecourse.

Limerick's First Lady

The gates to the racecourse were opened at 9am and over the next two hours up to 40,000 people crowded into it. According to local papers, women outnumbered men and spontaneous tea parties and picnics were taking place all around the outlying fields. By 1pm, as grey clouds made way for a splash of sunshine, the numbers had swelled to some 50,000 souls. *The Limerick Chronicle* captured the atmosphere: "The great moment of expectancy had arrived when two small specks appeared over the Clare Hills, one of them carrying the President and the other carried his security guards. And what a tremendous cheer went up from the crowd ... when the President's helicopter eventually came in sight and Mr Kennedy alighted smilingly."[156]

For most, this was their only chance to get that much-sought-after glimpse and the people of Limerick and the surrounding counties did not want to miss their moment.

The President came straight out of the helicopter and walked over to meet a cluster of officials. Politicians in archaic robes, bishops in black, and excited citizens with genealogical connections to the Kennedys lined up for the First Handshake.

From here, the distinguished guest was led to a platform that had been erected on the racecourse in front of the judge's box. Here, more church dignitaries were introduced to the guest of honour.

As the Mayor and the President passed by the floral display depicting the American flag, Kennedy paused for a moment, turned to Mayor Condell and asked, "Haven't I seen this somewhere before?" Amid much laughter, the Mayor confessed, "Yes sir, we borrowed it. We knew you liked it so well."

After a silent prayer, the Assistant Town Clerk called the roll and the City Manager read out the resolution that would make the President a Freeman of Limerick.

Taking her cue, Mayor Condell stood up to deliver her speech. Unlike most other speeches the President had had to sit through when he reached each new city or venue, this one had enough humour and lyricism to keep him interested and smiling throughout.

Frances Condell, the Mayor of Limerick, stands for a photograph alongside JFK and An Taoiseach Seán Lemass. In a speech that owed much to Kennedy's oratorical style, Condell encouraged American industrial investment in Limerick City and the Shannon region.

The Mayor first paid tribute to the American Ambassador to Ireland: "I am well aware that His Excellency, your Ambassador, Mr McCloskey, played a very important and effective part in your granting us this honour. I wish to thank him for his understanding and patient bearing with me in allowing me to use him as an Ambassadorial pin cushion whom I kept on prodding ... Is it any wonder that the dear man eventually said in exasperation: 'Heaven protect me from persistent women.'"

In a speech that aped the Kennedy style to perfection, Mayor Condell touched on the recurring theme of emigration, talking about the exodus from Limerick docks back in the 1840s before adding that such days were gone "and I am sure you will agree with me that you have enough of us over there to keep you happy and to assure you of our faithful support at all times."

Having dealt with the past, the Mayor moved on to the present and the future, using words that echoed the language of Lemass. Referring to the recent inauguration of five major businesses on a nearby industrial estate at Shannon, she looked pointedly at Kennedy and said: "We trust that you will use your influence to send many more industrialists like them, not alone to Shannon but to our city of Limerick. I assure you that we shall be very pleased to see a concentration of American industry in Limerick."

Having bamboozled the President with her wonderfully Irish mix of compliments and demands, Mayor Condell seized her moment to bring a feminine touch to proceedings, as the only woman to make a speech during the Presidential visit. "You see, Mr President, we, the women of Limerick city and county, feel that we have a special claim on you. We claim the Fitzgerald in you, and are extremely proud of your heritage." Pointing out into the crowd, the Mayor singled out all the Fitzgeralds who had come to see their cousin, while paying tribute to the President's mother, Rose, and his grandfather, Honey Fitz.

Moving on to more recent and important women in the President's life, Mayor Condell added a little glamour to the day by mentioning the First Lady: "We must not forget ... another woman, who is dear to our hearts – your lovely wife, Jacqueline … whose gracious motherhood, and wifely devotion and help to you has endeared her to us all. We mothers especially, sir, only excuse your not bringing your charming Jackie with you to Ireland for the excellent reason that she has for staying at home."

During this introduction, the President leant towards one of his advisors and remarked: "These introductions would seem awfully long if they weren't such good speakers."[157]

By now, the Mayor was wrapping up her speech and urged the President to accept the honorary Freedom of the City of Limerick while offering him godspeed for his onward journey.

Following in the footsteps of politicians such as Charles Stewart Parnell and philantropists such as Andrew Carnegie, John Fitzgerald Kennedy rose from his seat as a Freeman of Limerick.

Casting a glance towards Mayor Condell, the President paid her a particularly gracious compliment when he said: "I want to express my thanks and also my admiration for the best speech that I have heard since I came to Europe."

What followed was an uncharacteristically clumsy speech that suggested the President was either tired, emotional or overwhelmed. There was a striking incoherence and disorder in the three-paragraph address that was totally out of place among his previous speeches.

By way of example, Kennedy said: "I asked your distinguished Ambassador to the United States, Dr Kiernan – where is he? I said, 'What is this country noted for?', and he said, 'It is noted for its beautiful women and its fast horses.' And I said, 'You say that about every country,' and he said, 'No, this is true about this country.'"

Laughing and clearly in a good mood, the President followed this with an unlikely non sequitur about how happy he was to see the Fitzgeralds in the crowd, adding, "One of them looks just like Grandpa – and that's a compliment."

Maybe it was exhaustion at the end of a relentless trip but the President stumbled into an unnecessarily awkward moment: "I wonder, this is the last place, I go to another country, and then

I am going to Italy." He was trying to be tactful by not mentioning England directly, despite the fact that everyone present knew that within an hour he would be on a plane bound for London.

The crowd roared with laughter, dispelling any potential embarrassment. Then the President moved onto more familiar territory as he asked the people of Limerick if any of them had relations in America. If so, he said, they should be as proud of them as they are of their family members in Ireland.

There was also talk about the importance of the words "freedom" and "independence" to the Irish, leading him once again to talk about his visit to Arbour Hill: "I don't think that I have passed through a more impressive ceremony than the one I experienced in Dublin when I went with the Prime Minister to put a wreath on the graves of the men who died in 1916."

There were words of praise for President de Valera "who has played such a distinguished part, whose life is so tied up with the life of this island in this century – all this has made the past very real and has made the present very hopeful."

It was the closing moments of this brief speech that made up for what went before when President Kennedy quoted from a song he had heard the previous evening at Áras an Uachtarain:

Come back to Erin Mavourneen, Mavourneen.
Come back aroun' to the land of your birth.
Come with the shamrock in the springtime, Mavourneen.

These lines struck a chord with President Kennedy, whose visit to Ireland, initially meant as a sentimental diversion, had become a kind of personal awakening for him. The Harvard-educated anglophile had been transformed in the course of a heady and hectic few days in Ireland. His final two sentences would have been extraordinary ones for anyone to utter but coming from the mouth of the First Citizen of the United States of America, the sentiment was profound: "This is not the land of my birth but it is the land for which I hold the most affection and I certainly will come back in the springtime."

Éamon de Valera, the New York-born President of Ireland, mulling over this bipartite patriotism, later commented: "Now look here, a man can love his wife and love her best in the world, but that doesn't prevent him at all from having a very deep love for his mother. And for us, as for a lot of our people, this was the mother country."[158]

The President descended from the platform and made straight for the outstretched hands that beckoned. According to *The Limerick Leader*, "Cries of 'Please shake my hand, Mr President' were the order of the day and few along the barrier were disappointed."[159]

The secret service, who by now must have been wishing the whole visit was well and truly over, tried to keep up with the President and restrain the enthusiastic crowds. They sighed with relief when Kennedy hopped up the steps of his helicopter for the last time in Ireland.

Waving and smiling, the crowd lapped up every final moment. Within minutes, the newest Freeman of Limerick was circling the skies above the racecourse as though on a victory lap before moving slowly out of view and into the grey June sky, bound for Shannon and his last minutes on Irish soil.

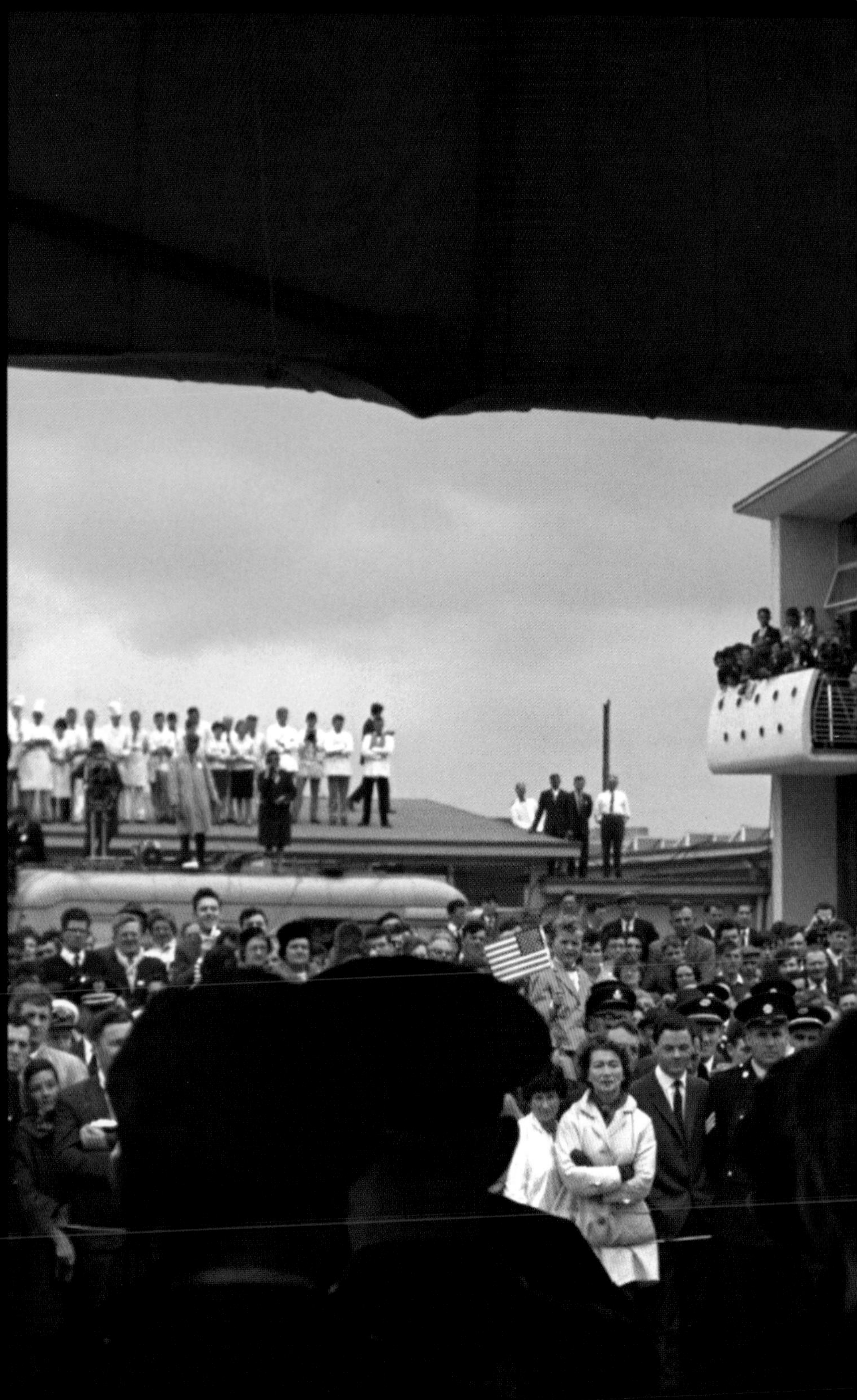

This random observation was followed by a reference to the only woman other than Frances Condell who appears to have made an impact on him during the visit: "Last night, I sat next to the wife of your President, who knows more about Ireland and Irish history [than anyone], so I told her I was coming to Shannon, and she immediately quoted this poem and I wrote down her words because I thought they were beautiful."

He pulled from his pocket the scrap of paper on which he had written down the Gerald Griffin poem. Seemingly he had perused the place card from the previous evening's dinner in the helicopter a few minutes before and had trouble deciphering his handwriting so his advisors had been busy trying to recreate the poem from memory as they started their descent towards Shannon airport. Years later, Éamon de Valera chuckled to himself as he remembered that Kennedy "wasn't able to read his own handwriting when he was going down in the helicopter … and they all put their heads together, with the result they turned out something which wasn't the real poem at all."[162]

Kennedy's makeshift version came out as follows:

Tis it is the Shannon's brightly glancing stream,
Brightly gleaming, silent in the morning beam,
Oh, the sight entrancing,
Thus returns from travels long,
Years of exile, years of pain,
To see old Shannon's face again,
O'er the waters dancing.

What Gerald Griffin actually wrote in the early part of the 19th century was quite different:

Tis, it is the Shannon Stream
Brightly glancing, brightly glancing,
See, oh see the ruddy beam
Upon its waters dancing
Thus returned from travel vain,

With the military guard of honour in the background, JFK, his family and aides bid farewell to the Bunratty Castle Singers.

Years of exile, years of pain,
To see old Shannon's face again,
Oh, the bliss entrancing
Hail, our own majestic stream,
Flowing ever, flowing ever,
Silent in the morning beam
Our own beloved river!

The sentiment was well-intended and served its purpose when the President uttered his final official words in Ireland: "Well, I am going to come back and see old Shannon's face again and I am taking, as I go back to America, all of you with me. Thank you."

The crowd roared its approval as President Kennedy descended from the platform.

In his pocket, the President carried a telegram that had made its way to Shannon from President de Valera, who wrote:

"Your visit has been a source of joy and pride to all the people of Ireland and to all their kin throughout the world. We wish you long life, health and happiness, and pray God's blessing upon you and upon the people of the United States. Beannacht Leat. [Blessings be with you.]"

A twenty-one gun salute could be heard for miles around as the President did the obligatory military inspection.

Alongside Air Force One, the Bunratty Castle singers, who had been at the Thursday night banquet in Dublin, sang one of the President's favourites, "Danny Boy". After that, the army band played the tune "Come Back to Erin", of which the President had earlier recited the lyrics when he stood on the racecourse in Limerick.

Shannon airport was heaving with enthusiastic well-wishers who pushed their noses against any available stretch of window that might afford them a last glimpse of President Kennedy in Ireland.

On his way towards the plane, he broke away one last time from his security men to shake hands with the crowds at the security barrier. Kennedy was characteristically keen to greet journalists,

Frances Condell, Mayor of Limerick, welcomes JFK to her home city. Condell was also to attend his departure from Shannon airport a short time later.

The parting: JFK waves goodbye to Ireland as he boards Air Force One in Shannon.

airport staff, gardaí and St John Ambulance officials, all of whom reached out for a press of the famous flesh.

Making his way slowly towards the plane that would take him to England, the President was amused to see Francis Condell, Mayor of Limerick, smiling up at him with outstretched hand. After bidding farewell to Kennedy at Limerick racecourse, the doughty Mayor had been driven the seventeen-mile journey in a police car at breakneck speed, often reaching eighty miles per hour on the road below as the President's helicopter flew in the sky above her.

Recognising Mrs Condell immediately, Kennedy asked: "Did you have your own helicopter? How nice of you to go to all this trouble."[163]

The President's advisors were already boarding the plane as their boss made his way through the adoring crowd. Dave Powers looked out from his window seat and saw a sign being held up with five words hastily painted on it. He later wrote: "When we were bringing President Kennedy's body back from Dallas, I thought of that sign at Shannon airport and I think of it often now. It said, 'Johnny, I Hardly Knew Ye.'"[164] Powers and Kenny O'Donnell would later borrow this phrase when they wrote a book about Kennedy with the title *Johnny, We Hardly Knew You*.

When he got to the bottom of the steps that would take him up to the plane and away forever, President Kennedy paused one last time to listen to the Southern Command Band. God knows what he was thinking as he turned to ascend those few steps with the tune of "Come Back To Erin" being carried in the wind behind him.

And then Ireland's favourite son disappeared. He would not be coming back.

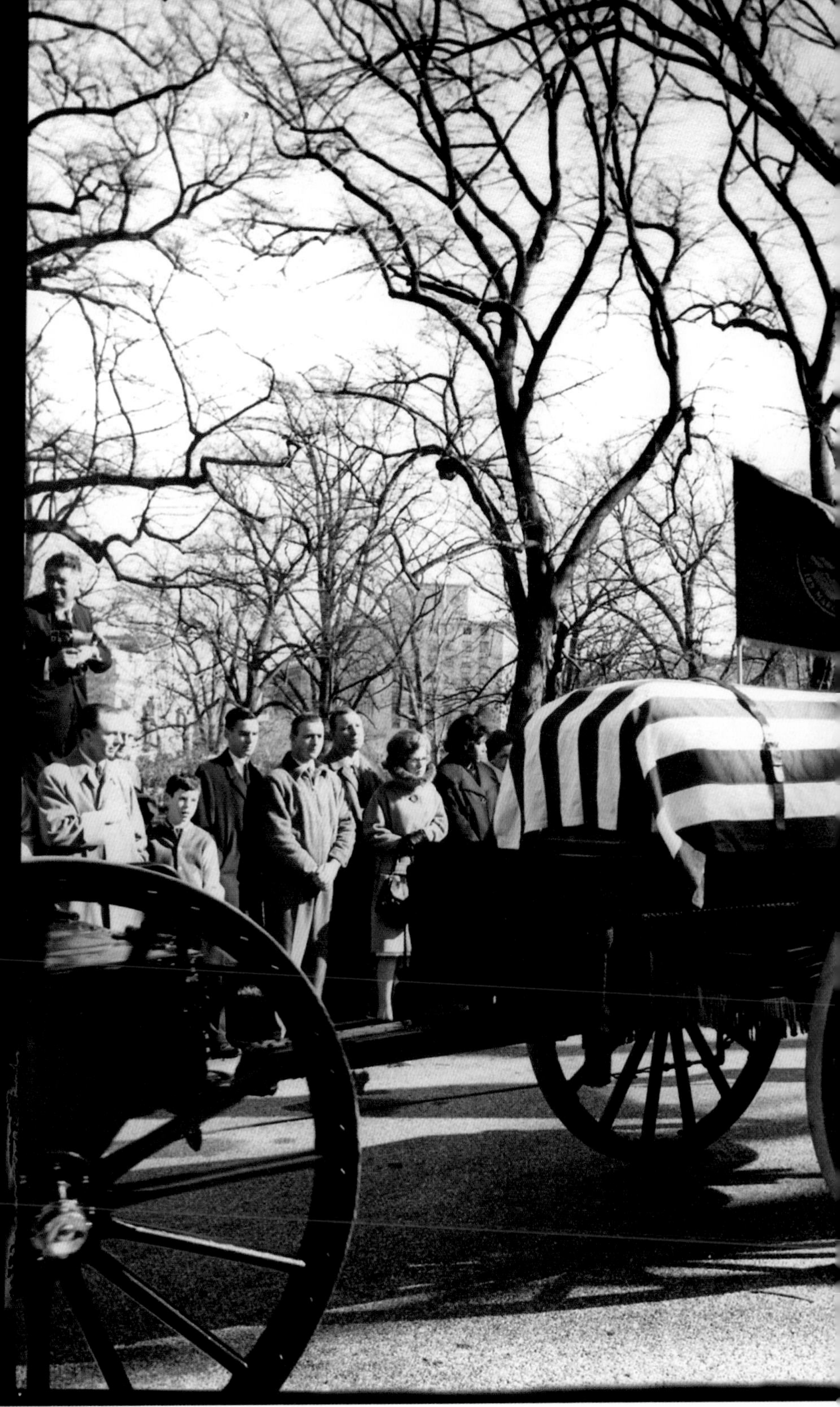

CHAPTER TWENTY

The Road to Dallas

—★—

The next stop in President Kennedy's whirlwind tour of Europe was Great Britain, where reaction to the President's Irish homecoming had been mixed. An unnamed Irish civil servant based in London gave a pithy but concise assessment of the British newspaper coverage of the visit. *The Observer* described it as Ireland's "first wholly satisfactory act of nationhood" while the *Evening Standard* provided a "mean editorial". *The Guardian* came across as "peevish" and the tabloid reporting was a "cause of concern", as illustrated by the *Daily Mail* whose "disparagement is calculated" and the *Daily Sketch*, in which "no avoidable reference to pubs, rain, dirt, chaos was omitted". The civil servant goes on to note: "The editorial policy of the mass circulation papers in regard to the visit was greatly determined by the age-old British conviction of the deficiency of the Irish and their incapacity for civilised action." He added: "Where the correspondent sent to Ireland did not come up with the expected material, the editorial staff moved in with headlines, cartoons and selected photographs to strip the visit of dignity and significance."[165]

Kennedy's election to the post of President of America may have done a lot to boost the image of the Irish in his home country, but in Britain the old stereotypes persisted. Still, no one wanted to cause offence by taking issue with him over anything that had happened during his Irish visit.

Air Force One landed at Gatwick airport outside London, where the President was greeted by Harold Macmillan, and he made a brief speech in which he pointed out that it was his seventh meeting with the prime minister, but each time they returned in their discussions

The President asked the State Department to track down the lyrics to one of his favourite songs of the trip, "The Boys of Wexford".[172] Having clearly lost the lyric sheet that the nun handed him in New Ross after the Artane Boys' Band sang it for him.

A measure of just how much Kennedy appreciated the reception he was afforded in Ireland can be seen in the way he reciprocated the generosity when Seán Lemass travelled to Washington four months later. The Taoiseach landed at Andrews Air Force base on 15 October and was flown by helicopter to the White House lawn, where he was met by Kennedy himself. The President gave Lemass a motorcade tour through the streets of Washington and told him that for him and his companions, the visit to Ireland was "among the warmest memories of our lives".[173]

Lemass recalls: "It was this continuous flow of comment from him as he was driven along which I particularly remember. He was, I think, a little bit worried that I wouldn't get in Washington anything like the same turnout of people along the street for the ceremony there that he got in Dublin, and no doubt that this would have been so. But he apparently gave orders that all the Civil Service staffs in Washington were to take the morning off on condition that they be there. [Laughter] And there was quite a considerable turnout along the main thoroughfares. But this, I gathered, was contrived for me."[174]

That evening the President hosted a black-tie dinner at the White House which featured a Who's Who of Irish America, as well as a number of Senators, the Secretary of State Dean Rusk and the Chief Justice Earl Warren (whose name would later be associated with President Kennedy for all the wrong reasons after he chaired the commission formed to investigate his assassination). An extra splash of colour was added to the affair when Hollywood superstar Gene Kelly joined the party.

In the course of his visit to America Lemass, as Kennedy had in Ireland, became an honorary citizen of three cities: Philadelphia, Chicago and Washington. The Taoiseach also received honours in New York and Boston as well as securing some important business investments for his country. As he was leaving the United States, there was a sense that the Irish-American story was entering a new phase and that Ireland had cemented their own "special relationship" with that powerful nation. As he sat in his plane on the runway at Washington airport, Lemass dictated a telegram to be sent to the White House that read: "I share your convictions that we do good work together and have demonstrated once more the close and enduring ties and real understanding that exists between our countries."

Within thirty-two days, the President to whom he was writing would be dead.

THE WHITE HOUSE

WASHINGTON

July 22, 1963

Dear Mr. Prime Minister:

The week-end following my European trip I went to Hyannis Port where my family is staying for the summer, and I took with me the lovely Carrickmacross lace tablecloth and napkins that you and Mrs. Lemass gave me. Needless to say, Mrs. Kennedy was delighted with this very beautiful gift and she asked that I express her warm sincere thanks, along with my own, for your thoughtfulness.

I shall never forget the wonderful reception given to me in Ireland -- it will always be one of my most pleasant memories.

Mrs. Kennedy joins me in extending every good wish to you and your family.

Sincerely,

His Excellency
Sean F. Lemass
Prime Minister of Ireland
Dublin

In the months between his visit to Ireland and his assassination in Dallas, JFK found time to write a series of letters to Taoiseach Seán Lemass.

THE WHITE HOUSE

WASHINGTON

July 23, 1963

Dear Prime Minister:

I am very grateful to you and the members of your government for making my trip to Ireland the enjoyable and unforgettable experience that it was. I know of the efforts made to insure its success and appreciate the care that was given to every detail.

I was particularly pleased to have the opportunity to talk with you at length about problems we both face and found our discussions extremely useful.

Since our meeting, as you know, there have been important new developments in our effort to reach a workable agreement in the area of nuclear testing. Governor Harriman's visit to Moscow, so far, is going forward in a way which gives us some real hope that a limited agreement may be possible, and this meeting and the steps which come after it may give us a better understanding of Soviet intentions.

I hope you will give my warm thanks also to Mrs. Lemass -- she was very kind to us all, and I shall not forget the generous hospitality you both extended. Mrs. Kennedy and I look forward with great pleasure to your return visit here at your convenience, especially now that TIME has made you properly famous in this country.

Sincerely,

[signature]

His Excellency
Sean Lemass
Prime Minister
Ireland

THE WHITE HOUSE

WASHINGTON

October 22, 1963

Dear Mr. Prime Minister:

I want to take this opportunity to tell you again how delighted I was to welcome you and Mrs. Lemass at the White House recently, and to thank you for the handsome gifts you so graciously brought with you.

That you should choose to have especially printed and bound the Report of the Joint Sitting of the Houses of the Irish Legislature, which I addressed last June, touched me deeply. This, along with your photograph and the fine set of 18th Century Malton prints of Dublin, will be lasting mementos of both my wonderful visit to Ireland and yours to the United States. I truly am grateful for the friendship that exists between our two countries.

With warm personal regards to you and your family, and with every good wish to the people of Ireland,

Sincerely,

His Excellency
Sean F. Lemass
Prime Minister of Ireland
Dublin

The event that shocked the world

Anyone of a certain vintage in Ireland can tell you where they were and what they were doing on 22 November 1963, the day President Kennedy was killed in Dallas. It was early evening when the first reports came through on the radio and television stations in Ireland. Other programmes were suspended as commentators talked endlessly about the President's recent visit, watched the tragic pictures of Jackie Kennedy, utterly shocked and still wearing her blood-stained suit, and covered the news that Lyndon B. Johnson had been sworn in as President on board Air Force One. According to *The Irish Press*, "Cinemas, theatres and all places of entertainment rapidly emptied as the chilling facts of his death spread like wildfire among an unbelieving and bewildered populace. The rain-washed streets of Dublin were filled with hurrying people who made their way to the Pro-Cathedral and other churches to pray."[175]

A shocked Éamon de Valera made a radio broadcast, in which he said:

"You will all have heard of the tragic death of President Kennedy. I am here simply to give public expression to our common sorrow. We sympathise with all the people of the United States, but in particular with his grief-stricken wife and other members of his family. During his recent visit here we came to regard the President as one of ourselves, though always aware that he was the head of the greatest nation in the world today. We were proud of him as being of our race and we were convinced that through his fearless leadership the United States would continue increasing its stature amongst the nations of the world and its power of maintaining world peace. Our consolation is that he died in a noble cause, and we pray that God will give to the United States another such leader."[176]

Seán Lemass wrote to Jackie Kennedy: "The world has today lost a great statesman and leader and the U.S. of America its finest citizen. During his visit to Ireland last June and my recent visit with him in Washington I had the privilege of getting to know personally his great qualities, his courage, his integrity and his sense of high purpose. My

Mourners gather at Ballykelly Church, New Ross, following JFK's assassination.

colleagues in the Irish Government and I extend to you and to your family our most heartfelt sympathy on your tragic bereavement."[177]

The following day, word came through the State Department that Jackie Kennedy had asked whether Irish army cadets could attend her husband's funeral and perform the drill the President had admired so much. It was decided that President de Valera should lead the offical Irish party, which would also include New Ross Mayor Andrew Minihan and the President's closest Irish relative, Mary Ann Ryan, who only months previously was laughing with the President over cups of tea and freshly cut sandwiches at her home in Dunganstown. Arrangements had to be made quickly. The President was killed on a Friday and the funeral was being held on the Monday, just three days later.

By the time the Irish delegation landed in what would soon be renamed JFK International Airport, the assassin, Lee Harvey Oswald,

A Memorial Mass for JFK at Ballykelly Church.

was already dead, shot while the police were taking him from one jail to another. In Washington, de Valera and Frank Aiken paid their respects under the vast dome of the Capitol where the late President lay in state. Huge queues of people waited right through the night for the chance of one last look at their charismatic head of state. De Valera was quoted in *The Irish Times* as saying "The great grief of the American people is just as deep among the people of Ireland. … When the terrible news of his death came over, every house in Ireland felt that not only had a great leader been lost but they had lost a personal friend."[178]

The funeral procession, viewed by thousands on the streets of Washington and millions around the world on television, led from the Capitol to the White House and then on to St Matthew's Cathedral, where a mass was heard in front of a huge audience, including 220 Presidents, Prime Ministers, dignitaries and members of the royal family from ninety-two different countries. After that they made their way across the Potomac River, accompanied by a sombre drum beat, to Arlington National Cemetery where rows of elderly statesmen who had fought and survived two world wars gathered to pay their respects.

In the skies above them, fifty fighter aircraft executed a fly-past, followed by Air Force One, and then a silent pause filled the air. Twenty-six young Irish Army cadets like the ones whom the President had been so taken with had been standing beside his freshly dug grave for three hours, waiting for the cortège to arrive. For some of them, aged only eighteen or nineteen, it was their first trip abroad. As they began the Queen Anne drill, the quiet was broken only by the metallic clicks of rifles against brass buttons, the shuffling sound of their uniforms and the occasional clipped order in the Irish national tongue. They were the first foreign army ever to form a guard of honour at the graveside of an American president.

The drill was executed with immaculate precision and military dignity then the cadets took up their positions with the rest of the military escort as the coffin bearing the thirty-fifth President of the United States of America was lowered into the ground.

President Kennedy is laid to rest at Arlington National Cemetery, Virginia. At his widow's request, twenty-six Irish cadets participated in the military ceremony at the graveside.

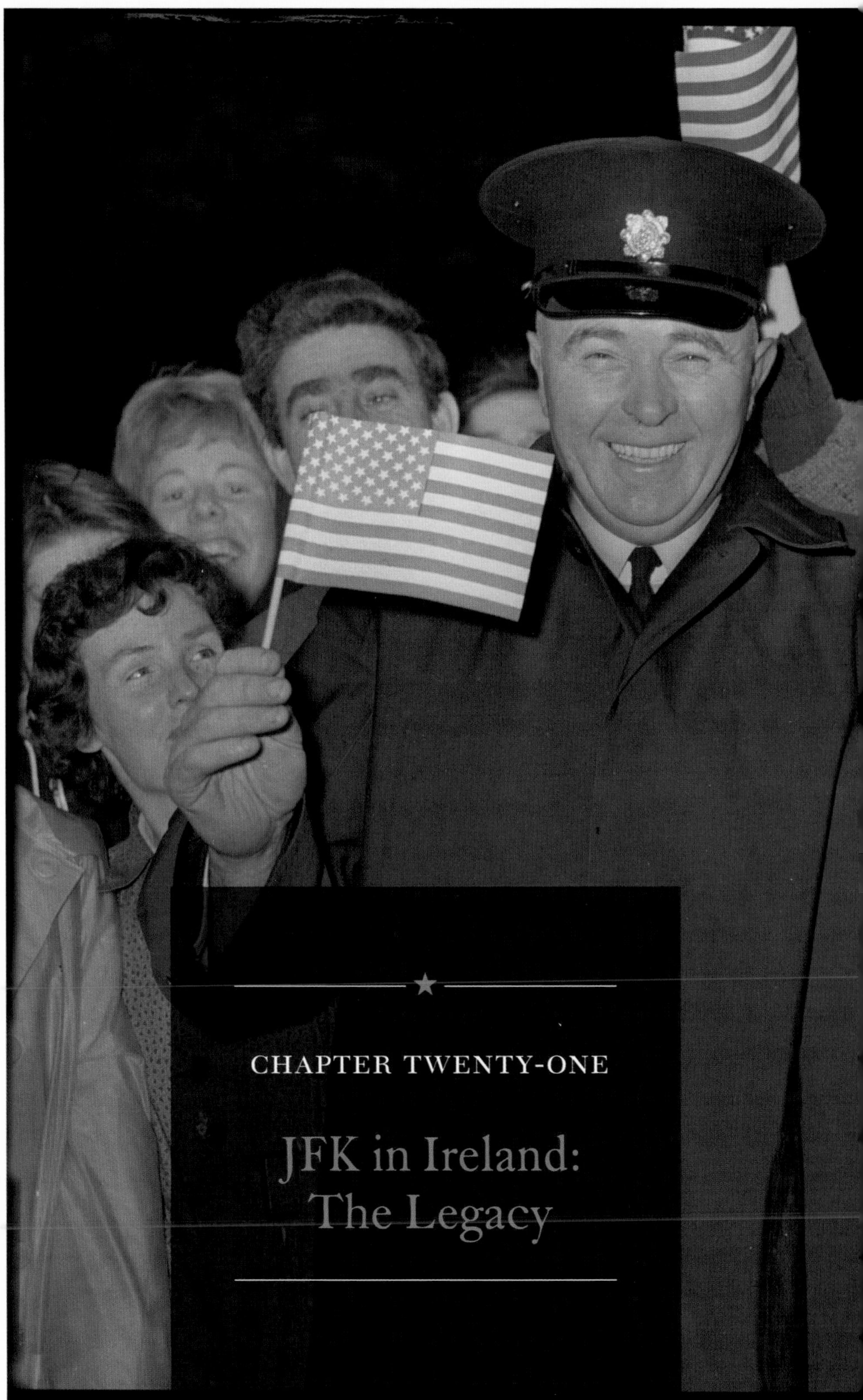

CHAPTER TWENTY-ONE

JFK in Ireland: The Legacy

—★—

Those who encountered John F. Kennedy when he came to Ireland in June 1963 are unanimous in pointing out his physical attributes. Everyone the present author interviewed and all the accounts read in the course of researching this book describe the President's tanned face, thick hair, exceptionally white teeth and piercing blue eyes. Why is this?

Perhaps it is because the Irish hadn't come across anyone quite as colourful him before. While Norman Mailer was hailing Kennedy's arrival at the White House as a chance for America to become "at last again… adventurous"[179], Irish writers such as Sean O'Faolain were bemoaning the fact that after a hard-fought battle, Ireland's hopes to become an independent idyll were replaced by what he called "a dreary Eden".[180]

That dreary Eden manifested itself in the dour Ireland of the 1950s. John F. Kennedy descended from the skies like a splash of colour in a monochrome world and the Irish people were mesmerised. It was one thing looking at black and white photographs in the newspapers but to see him in the flesh changed everything. He was no longer some sort of fairytale prince from another land; he was very real and very Irish, with a sense of humour to match their own. To a whole generation, here was hope, a ticket out of a dull and dreary place or, at the very least, a signpost towards what could be achieved if you put your mind to it.

John Kennedy was more Irish than he is given credit for. We can see this from his early interest as a journalist in 1945 and from the number of books about Ireland that he read as part of his research, listed in a barely legible scrawl in his diaries. He did the Irish

American "thing", walking in the St Patrick's Day parade as a young Senator and delivering eloquent speeches about the home country on several occasions as he ascended the political ladder. He came to Ireland three times before the State visit in 1963. He was a curious boy and an interested adult but it would be some time before passing curiosity would be replaced by visceral interest and then a profound emotional attachment.

On the flip side, John F. Kennedy was probably not as Irish as he could have been. Given the purity of his ancestral lineage, he should have been immersed in the Irish story – but he wasn't. His East Coast upbringing was predominant. He was a Kennedy to the core, the boy born with a silver rosette on his lapel. A combination of charisma and capital helped to sweep him from House to Senate to Pennsylvania Avenue despite his Irish Catholic background rather than because of it.

By the time Kennedy got to Ireland in 1963, he was a man very comfortable in his own skin dealing with a country that was just getting used to its own, relatively new identity. There are a few hints that his sense of his own Irishness was growing stronger by the year. A country house in Virginia that Jackie designed for them in early 1963 was given the name of Wexford, after the county where the Kennedy ancestral home was situated in Ireland. In June 1963, not long before he set off on his European tour, the President played a game with his little daughter, Caroline. At just six years old, she could name all fifty states in America, but now the President told her he had added a fifty-first state – Ireland. From then on, every time she got to the fiftieth state, her Dad would always ask for the last one, to which she would respond "Ireland".

Sweet anecdotes like this provide evidence to suggest that Kennedy had a growing fondness for the old country, but at the same time it's clear he had no interest in getting his hands dirty with complicated issues like Partition. Britain and the United States had fought together against Nazi Germany less than twenty years earlier, and the Special Relationship remained as strong as ever. Kennedy was never going to risk alienating one of his closest allies over such an emotive issue as Partition while he was busy dealing with Russia, Cuba and an increasingly problematic Vietnam. No, Ireland was about thatched cottages and a fun excursion for his Irish-American entourage, the so-called Murphia. JFK was too smart to upset the British so he walked a tightrope, praising the Irish love of freedom but never mentioning the North in public.

Speaking three years after the visit, Minister for External Affairs Frank Aiken expressed disappointment that Kennedy hadn't been more assertive on this issue: "I would like to have seen him be a bit more active in getting a solution for Partition. We urged him to do it." He knew it would have been too much to ask though. "An American President has a long list of problems and over the years, the relations between Great Britain and the United States have been very close, and they felt a great need to keep together so, in those circumstances great powers don't take any public action that might upset that relationship."[181]

Hugh McCann, Secretary of the Department of External Affairs at the time, admitted that "we had always the hope that privately perhaps he [Kennedy] might do something to, you know, bring nearer the day when there would be unification" but said there was a question over his real commitment. "Naturally, we wouldn't put him in the position of asking him."[182]

The visit to Arbour Hill was an important symbolic gesture on President Kennedy's part, acknowledging what had happened to those men from whose blood a nation was eventually formed, but that was as far as he would go. If he hadn't been assassinated, had served a second term as President and then perhaps become American Ambassador to Ireland, would he have done more? It's another of those unanswerable "what if?" questions that history is full of but it's hard to imagine that he wouldn't have tried to use his influence to bring an end to the Troubles.

After Kennedy's death, his siblings would maintain and develop the links that his visit had created. Ted Kennedy in particular was a very important friend of Ireland during the years of the Troubles, flying the flag for Irish nationalism in a significant and heartfelt manner. He was always a staunch opponent of violence committed by either side, but led the parties firmly towards the negotiating table and gave them a voice in Washington, DC, as far back as 1971. It is said that his office door was always open to Irish politicians of any persuasion who wanted to talk, and many private negotiations began there that would be crucial in bringing about the end of armed struggle.

Perhaps the most important single thing Ted Kennedy did over the years was to persuade President Clinton to let Sinn Féin leader Gerry Adams visit the United States in 1994, a trip that was instrumental in the declaration of an IRA ceasefire just a few months later. When Ian Paisley, head of the Democratic Unionist Party, finally stood alongside Sinn Féin's Martin McGuinness, as Northern Ireland's first and deputy first ministers in 2007, Ted Kennedy was deservedly standing right beside them.

In 1993, Ted Kennedy persuaded President Clinton to appoint Jean Kennedy Smith to be the US Ambassador to Ireland, following in the footsteps of her father, who had, of course, been US Ambassador to Britain, and she would also play a small but significant role in moving the peace process forward. During the five years she spent in that post she worked hard to increase communication between the factions, in particular helping to make Sinn Féin renounce violence and take part in the political process, and this work was recognised in 2007 when she was awarded a gold medal by the Éire Society of Boston. At the end of her tenure as ambassador she accepted honorary Irish citizenship – something her brother John hadn't been allowed to accept while President due to constitutional difficulties.

All this was part of John F. Kennedy's legacy. On the one hand, he had opened the door that allowed the Kennedys to gain trust from those at the heart of the Irish political system, and on the other he had ignited his family's interest in their heritage. This would be one of the most important legacies of his 1963 visit: that it helped to bring to an end a violent and bloody era in Ireland's history.

It wasn't just his own family who President Kennedy inspired to get closer to their ethnic background. In his wake, Irish blood became positively desirable in American society, in stark contrast with the old days when it was hard for those of Irish descent to get into the best schools and clubs, to find decent housing or a good job. Travelling back to the "old country" to look up your relatives became a rite of passage for Irish-Americans, and the American-Irish Foundation set up by John F. Kennedy along with Éamon de Valera provided a first port of call.

As a country, Ireland was very young when Kennedy came to visit, having only officially claimed its status as a Republic in 1949. History had cast a particularly long shadow in the previous hundred years. The mental scars caused by the Great Famine of the 1840s endured to the present day, while the bloodstained years between 1916 and 1922 both north and south as well as elements within the nationalist community. A visit from the glamorous young leader of the Free World gave credibility and confidence to the fledgling Irish nation, making the rest of the world sit up and take notice. If President Kennedy was proud to be Irish, then surely the Irish people living on the island should be proud as well?

If, as has been said, the 1963 Kennedy visit to Ireland was just about light relief, then it was light relief that Ireland needed as much as the president of America did. This may go some way to explaining the near-hysteria that marked his trip. But it wasn't just fun and tourism. The trip was also the physical embodiment of an historical cycle being completed. Kennedy's great-grandparents had been forced to leave Ireland during the Famine and Ambassador Thomas Kiernan for one believed his visit delivered a profound message to the Irish people: "I think that his coming back to Ireland was a closing of a chapter that began with the Famine. It was triumphant in that way ... At the back of people's minds was a feeling of failure. Famine spelled failure. And the entire government of the country since the Famine had been a government of non-Irish. This again indicates failure. And here was a success come at top level. Here was a fellow

The Kennedy Connection: JFK's brother, Ted, maintained the family's ongoing interest in Ireland, playing a key role at crucial times in the Northern Ireland peace process. He is pictured here alongside Northern Ireland leaders Ian Paisley (DUP) and Martin McGuinness (Sinn Féin) in December 2007 on Capitol Hill in Washington, DC.

who came from Famine stock on both paternal and maternal sides and who had reached the very top in the United States. That was felt throughout the country."[183]

All of Kennedy's ancestors made America their home and started off at the bottom rung of the ladder. Swiftly, from one generation to the next, they worked extraordinarily hard to climb higher in a social, economic and political context until that November evening in 1960 when it was announced that Senator John Fitzgerald Kennedy was the 35th President of the United States of America. There are dozens of clichés that could be used here but the most accurate, if hackneyed, is that of rags to riches. The Kennedy forebears would have been in rags when they left Ireland, with no idea of the financial, social and political riches that one of their own would ultimately achieve. By the time John F. Kennedy visited Ireland, there was a sense that this very "ethnic" president was more than just the symbol of American power; he also represented the closure of a painful chapter in modern Irish history.

There are a number of parallels with the rise of President Barack Obama. Kennedy was the first successful Catholic to run for President, and Obama was the first successful black man. They were both urged by their aides to take it slowly, to give the electorate time to get used to the idea. As Ted Sorensen points out: "Some of those local Irish politicians would urge Kennedy to take it slow. Maybe Vice-President for eight years, just as they urged that on Obama, a black man."[184] But neither of them took that advice. Kennedy went head to head with those who were opposed to having a Catholic in the White House in the speech in which he declared: "I am not the Catholic candidate for President. I am the Democratic Party's candidate for President who happens to be a Catholic." Obama did the same thing by confronting the race issue head on in a speech entitled "A More Perfect Union", pointing out that some people had called him "too black" while others said he was "not black enough".

They were both comparatively young when they won the Presidential race: Obama was forty-eight, Kennedy just forty-three. They were both charismatic, with the power to electrify a crowd as well as to charm at any face-to-face meeting. And the election of both caused a huge upsurge in national pride and international adulation. In a society becoming increasingly obsessed by fame, these were two men who were truly at the top of the tree. If Barack Obama went searching for his family's roots in Kenya or Indonesia, or indeed in Ireland where his roots have been found, he would undoubtedly receive a hero's welcome. But when John F. Kennedy went to Ireland in 1963, the story was more than just a personal family one.

What happened to the Kennedys between 1848 when Patrick Kennedy got on the boat to Boston and 1963 when his great-grandson John flew in to Dublin on Air Force One is not just the story of one family but of an entire nation. It is the story of a country on its knees, a country that was defined by death and departure. It is the story of a clutch of people who were spat out onto the shores of America. It is the story of their insatiable appetite to better themselves and how that hunger led them not only to the top of the ladder but also back to Ireland and, ultimately, back home.

FOLLOWING PAGES At home while away: a clearly relaxed JFK raises a smile in Cork.

NOTES

Prologue

1 Kenneth P. O'Donnell and David F. Powers, with Joe McCarthy, *Johnny, We Hardly Knew Ye: Memories of John Fitzgerald Kennedy,* Little Brown & Company, NY, 1970.

2 "Kennedy Tour Despite Critics", *The Irish Press*, 17 June 1963.

3 "U.S. Press Attacks Kennedy's Trip", *The Evening Herald*, 19 June 1963.

The Kennedys: From Poverty to Power

4 Peter Collier and David Horowitz, *The Kennedys: An American Drama*, Encounter Books, 1984, p.9.

5 Doug Wead, *The Raising of a President: The Mothers and Fathers of Our Nation's Leaders*, Atria, NY, 2005, p.201.

6 Nigel Hamilton, *JFK: Reckless Youth,* Random House, London, 1992, p.201.

7 Lord Longford, *Kennedy*, Weidenfeld & Nicolson, 1976, p.2.

8 *Ibid.* p.54

9 Peter Collier and David Horowitz, *op.cit.*, p.21.

The Kennedys Come Home, 1930s–1950s

10 "Mr J. Kennedy to Arrive at Baldonnel To-morrow" *The Irish Press*, 6 July 1938.

11 "Reason for Secrecy", *The Irish Times*, 8 July 1938.

12 University College Dublin Archives, Papers of Éamon de Valera (1882–1975) IE UCDA P150/2844.

13 "You Have Done Honour to Our Race", *The Irish Press*, 9 July 1938.

14 University College Dublin Archive Archives, Papers of Éamon de Valera (1882–1975) IE UCDA P150/2849.

15 "Eire Honours U.S. Ambassador", *The Irish Times*, 8 July 1938.

16 "Mr. Kennedy's Visit: A Future King" *The Irish Times*, 8 July 1938.

17 Joan and Clay Blair Jr, *The Search for JFK*, NY, Berkeley, 1974, p.356.

18 *Prelude to Leadership: The Post-war Diary of John F. Kennedy*, Regency Publishing Inc., NY, 1995.

19 Arthur Mitchell, *JFK and his Irish Heritage*, Moytura Press, 1993.

20 "De Valera Aims to Unite Ireland", article by JFK. *New York Journal American*, 29 July 1945.

21 *Prelude to Leadership, op.cit.*, p. 81.

22 Robert Dallek, *John F. Kennedy: An Unfinished Life*, NY, 2003, p.126.

23 James MacGregor Burns, *John Kennedy: A Political Profile*, NY, 1959, p.57.

24 Robert Dallek, author interview, Washington, DC, 2010.

25 *Prelude to Leadership, op.cit.*, p. 81.

26 James Robert O'Carroll, *One of Ourselves: Robert Fitzgerald Kennedy in*

Ireland, Images from the Past, NY, 2003.

27 Kenneth P. O'Donnell and David F. Powers, *op.cit*.

28 Doug Wead, *op. cit.* p.249.

29 "U.S. Senator Visits Dublin", *The Irish Independent*, 1 October 1955.

30 Liam Cosgrave, Oral History Interview, 8 May 1966, John F. Kennedy Presidential Library and Museum.

31 Liam Cosgrave, letter to author, 13 February 2009.

32 Ted Sorensen, author interview, New York, 16 March 2009.

33 Robert Dallek, author interview, Washington, DC, 17 March 2009.

Wooing the President

34 M.E. Collins, *Ireland 1868-1966: History in the Making*, The Educational Company, 1993.

35 Brian Girvin and Gary Murphy, eds., *The Lemass Era: Politics and Society in the Ireland of Seán Lemass*, University College of Dublin Press, 2005.

36 Tim Pat Coogan, *Ireland Since the Rising*, Pall Mall Press, 1966.

37 *Dictionary of Irish Biography*, Cambridge University Press, 2010.

38 Thomas J. Kiernan, Oral History Interview, 8 May 1966, John F. Kennedy Presidential Library and Museum.

39 Irish National Archives, (Cremin to Kiernan, 11 April 1961).

40 This poem was written by D.L. Kelleher for Dr Kiernan's son.

41 Irish National Archives, Taois s/17401 k/63 (Kiernan to Cremin, 5 June 1963).

42 Irish National Archive, DFA/p345 (Kiernan to Cremin, 27 April 1962).

43 Irish National Archives, Taois s/17401 A/63 (Kiernan to McCann).

44 Irish National Archive Taois s/17401 A/63 (Kiernan to McCann 19 March 1963).

45 Irish National Archive Taois s/17401 A63 (JFK to de Valera).

46 Irish National Archive, Taois/s17432/63 (Kiernan to McCann, 2 May 1963).

47 "A Mess But Wonderful", *Time* magazine, 7 June 1963.

Planning the Visit

48 Irish National Archive, Taois/s17432/63 (Kiernan to McCann, 14 May 1963).

49 Irish National Archive, Taois/s17432/63 (Lemass to Dillon/Corish).

50 Article by Alan Cowell, *The New York Times*, 29 December 2006.

51 Éamon de Valera, Oral History Interview, 15 September 1966, John F. Kennedy Presidential Library and Museum.

52 Thomas J. Kiernan, Oral History Interview, 8 May 1966, John F. Kennedy Presidential Library and Museum.

53 National Archives of Ireland, P 262/1 (Kiernan to McCann, 5 June 1963).

54 Thomas J. Kiernan, Oral History Interview, 8 May 1966, John F. Kennedy Presidential Library and Museum.

55 *Ibid.*

The European Tour Begins

56 "Kennedy Stand Dims U.S. Hopes", *The New York Times*, 17 June 1963.

57 "Text of the President's Message to Congress Calling for Civil Rights Legislation", *The New York Times*, 20 June 1963.

58 "Adenauer Lauds U.S., Awaits Kennedy Visit", *The Washington Post*, 23 June 1963.

59 "JFK's Trip Coincides with Europe's Upsets", *The Washington Post*, 9 June 1963.

60 "Nixon Hopes Kennedy Trip Will Provide 'Lift' to U.S.", *The New York Times*, 20 June 1963.

61 "Kennedy Hailed by British Press", *The Washington Post*, 21 June 1963.

62 "President Delays Rights Message", *The New York Times*, 4 June 1963.

63 "President's Order Prepared Early", *The New York Times,* 12 June 1963.

64 "Policy Gain Seen in Kennedy's Trip", *The New York Times*, 21 June 1963.

65 "Kennedy, in Bonn, Pledges to Keep Forces in Europe", *The New York Times*, 24 June 1963.

66 *Ibid.*

67 "Communists: The Place is Berlin, The Problem is Peking", *Time* magazine, 5 July 1963.

68 Robert Schlesinger, *White House Ghosts: Presidents and their Speechwriters*, Simon & Schuster, NY, 2008, pp.139-40.

Arriving in Dublin

69 Ted Sorensen, author interview, New York, 16 March 2009.

70 O'Donnell and Powers, *op. cit.*, p.362.

71 O'Carroll, *op. cit.*, p.173.

72 "Papal Visit Seen As Embarrassing", *The Washington Post*, 2 July 1963.

73 O'Carroll, *op. cit.*, p.173.

74 O'Carroll, *op. cit.*, p.16.

75 *JFK in Ireland*, DVD, 1996.

76 Éamon de Valera, Oral History Interview, 15 September 1966, John F. Kennedy Presidential Library and Museum.

77 "President Kennedy in Ireland", programme on RTÉ Radio, 27 June 1963.

78 Angier Biddle Duke, Oral History Interview, 29 July 1964, John F. Kennedy Presidential Library and Museum.

79 Seán Lemass, Oral History Interview, 8 August 1966, John F. Kennedy Presidential Library and Museum.

80 Powers and O'Donnell, *op. cit.*, p.362.

81 Angier Biddle Duke, Oral History Interview, 29 July 1964, John F. Kennedy Presidential Library and Museum, p.363.

New Ross

82 Seán Lemass, Oral History Interview, 8 August 1966, John F. Kennedy Presidential Library and Museum.

83 Hugh McCann, Oral History Interview, 8 August 1966, John F. Kennedy Presidential Library and Museum.
84 "J.F.K.'s Happy Co. Wexford Tour", *The Evening Herald*, Thursday 27 June 1963.
85 "Kennedy Stay Too Short", *New Ross Standard*, Friday 24 May 1963.
86 O'Donnell and Powers, *op. cit.*, p.363.
87 Andrew Minihan, Oral History Interview, 7 August 1966, John F. Kennedy Presidential Library and Museum.
88 "Handshakes From a Relaxed Returner", *The Irish Times*, Friday 28 June 1963, p.7.
89 *JFK in Ireland*, DVD, 1996.
90 Minihan, *op. cit.*
91 Angier Biddle Duke, Oral History Interview, 29 July 1964, John F. Kennedy Presidential Library and Museum.
92 Minihan, *op. cit.*

Danganstown

93 Dave Powers, *JFK in Ireland*, DVD, 1996.
94 "President Kennedy in Ireland", programme on RTÉ Radio, 27 June 1963.
95 Josephine Grennan (nee Ryan), Oral History Interview, 8 July 1966, John F. Kennedy Presidential Library and Museum.
96 *New Ross Standard*, Friday 28 June 1963.
97 Dave Powers *JFK in Ireland*, DVD, 1996.
98 "Not Necessary, But Nice", *Time* magazine, 5 July 1963.
99 "Kennedy Has Tea, Cake With 13 Irish Cousins", *Los Angeles Times*, 28 June 1963.

Wexford Harbour

100 "Cousin Jack Comes to See the Folks", *The Irish Times*, Friday 28 June 1963.

The Garden Party

101 "Strawberries, tea and rain", *Evening Press*, 28 June 1963.
102 "Meeting the great man", *Irish Press*, 28 June 1963.
103 "Tears are near as rain ruins fashion highlight for 1,000", *The Irish Times*, 28 June 1963.
104 "President Kennedy in Ireland", programme on RTE Radio, 27 June 1963.
105 "Tears are near as rain ruins fashion highlight for 1,000", *The Irish Times*, 28 June 1963.
106 "President 'Mobbed' At Party", *The Irish Independent*, Friday 28 June 1963.
107 Éamon de Valera, rec. int. by Joseph O'Connor. Oral History Interview, 8 July 1966, John F. Kennedy Presidential Library and Museum.
108 *Sligo Champion*.

109 "Crowd Mobs Kennedy at Garden Party", *The Irish Times*, Friday 28 June 1963.

Iveagh House

110 O'Carroll, *op. cit.*, p.96.

111 "State Dinner for JFK Poses Dress Problem", *Evening Herald*, 20 June 1963.

112 Irish National Archive S/17401/63 Schedule of Suggested Dress for Iveagh House Dinner.

113 Hugh McCann, Oral History Interview, 8 August 1966, John F. Kennedy Presidential Library and Museum.

114 Irish National Archive DFA 434/682/20 Annex B.

115 Irish National Archive S/17401/63 Iveagh House Dinner Menu Card.

116 "Made sugar JFK boat", *Evening Press*, Friday June 28 1963.

117 Hugh McCann, Oral History Interview, 8 August 1966, John F. Kennedy Presidential Library and Museum.

Cork

118 "From the hills of Cork they came", *Evening Herald*, Friday 28 June 1963.

119 "President puts Cork on visiting list", *Evening Herald*, Friday 14 June 1963.

120 "Cousins showed him Sunday Independent", *Evening Herald*, Friday 28 June 1963.

121 "Rose Petal Showers", *The Irish Times*, Saturday 29 June 1963.

Arbour Hill

122 "Enjoying my visit very much", *Evening Press*, Friday June 28 1963, p.1. The journalist is not named.

123 O'Donnell and Powers, *op. cit.*, p.365.

124 "8 Girls Sing at Embassy luncheon", *Irish Press*, Saturday 29 June 1963, p.7.

125 "Today at Arbour Hill", *Evening Herald*, Friday 28 June 1963.

126 Seán Lemass, Oral History Interview, 8 August 1966, John F. Kennedy Presidential Library and Museum.

127 O'Donnell and Powers, *op. cit.*, p.366.

Leinster House

128 Ted Sorensen, author interview, New York, 16 March 2009.

129 Seán Lemass, Oral History Interview, 8 August 1966, John F. Kennedy Presidential Library and Museum.

130 "Cold, wet and windy – but they love him", *The Irish Times*, Saturday 29 June 1963.

131 "The Scene TV Cameras Missed", *Sunday Independent*, Sunday 30 June 1963.

132 O'Carroll, *op. cit.*, p.117.

133 Ted Sorensen, author interview, New York, 16 March 2009.

134 "A Speech to Wring", *The Irish Times,* Saturday 29 June, 1963.

135 Seán Lemass, Oral History Interview, 8 August 1966, John F. Kennedy Presidential Library and Museum.

136 "President's Pride in his Literary Inheritance", *The Irish Times*, Saturday 29 June 1963.

137 Ted Sorensen, author interview, New York, 16 March 2009.

138 *Ibid.*

139 O'Donnell and Powers, *op. cit.*, p.367.

140 *Ibid.*

Dublin Castle

141 "A Smooth, Neat Package", *The Irish Times*, Saturday 29 June 1963.

142 *Ibid.*

143 "Pageantry in Dublin Castle", *The Irish Times*, Saturday 29 June, 1963.

The Last Supper

144 Angier Biddle Duke, Oral History Interview, 29 July 1964, John F. Kennedy Presidential Library and Museum.

145 O'Donnell and Powers, *op. cit.*, p.368.

146 *Ibid.*

147 *Ibid.*

Galway

148 "Last words from Jack…", *Evening Herald*, Saturday 29 June, 1963.

149 Thomas J. Kiernan, Oral History Interview, 5 August 1966, John F. Kennedy Presidential Library and Museum.

150 "Great Welcome for US President", *Connacht Tribune*, Saturday 29 June, 1963.

151 O'Donnell and Powers, *op. cit.*, p.369.

152 "President Kennedy", *Connacht Sentinel*, Tuesday 2 July 1963.

153 Seán Lemass, Oral History Interview, 8 August 1966, John F. Kennedy Presidential Library and Museum.

Limerick

154 Frances Condell, Oral History Interview, 31 July 1966, John F. Kennedy Presidential Library and Museum.

155 "Céad Míle Fáilte – A Great Day for Limerick", *Limerick Leader*, Saturday 29 June 1963.

156 "Historic Visit", *Limerick Chronicle*, Saturday 29 June, 1963.

157 O'Donnell and Powers, *op. cit.*, p.370.

158 Éamon de Valera, Oral History Interview, 15 September 1966, John F. Kennedy Presidential Library and Museum.

159 "J.F. Kennedy is Freeman", *Limerick Leader*, Saturday 6 July 1963.

Shannon Airport

160 O'Donnell and Powers, *op. cit.*, p.370.

161 "Ireland is an Unusual –Very Special – Place", *The Irish Times*, Monday 1 July 1963.

162 O'Donnell and Powers, *op. cit.*, p.371.

163 "Barriers Bend in Big Crush…", *The Irish Times*, Monday 1 July 1963.

164 O'Donnell and Powers, *op. cit.*, p.371.

The Road to Dallas

165 Irish National Archive DFA 434/682/32.

166 "Not Necessary, But Nice", *Time* magazine, 5 July 1963.

167 White House Central Subject File #6.1, Box 985, TR 56/CO 125 Ireland (General, 6-26-63).

168 Presidential Office Files, Subject Files, Box 108, Ireland, Kennedy to de Valera, 11 July 1963.

169 "The Presidency: A Moving Experience", *Time* magazine, 12 July 1963.

170 President's Office Files #3, Subject Files, Box 108, Ireland, Kennedy to Lemass, 23 July 1963.

171 President's Office Files #3, Subject Files, Box 108, Ireland, Kennedy to Aiken, 23 July 1963.

172 President's Office Files #3, Countries Files, Box 119a, Ireland (General 1/63-8/63).

173 Presidential Office Files, Speech Files, Box 47, Lemass visit, Exchange of Remarks, 15 October 1963.

174 Seán Lemass, Oral History Interview, 8 August 1966, John F. Kennedy Presidential Library and Museum.

175 "Ireland Numbed by Shock", *The Irish Press*, 23 November 1963.

176 Éamon de Valera's tribute on radio Telefis Eireann, 22 November 1963.

177 "Our nation grieves, says Mr. de Valera", *The Irish Press*, 23 November 1963.

178 "Grief as Deep in Ireland as in U.S.", *The Irish Times*, 25 November 1963.

JFK in Ireland: The Legacy

179 Harris Woffard, *Of Kennedys and Kings: Making Sense of the Sixties*, Farrar Straus Giroux, NY, 1982.

180 J.C. Beckett, *A Short History of Ireland*, Hutchinson and Co., 1952.

181 Frank Aiken, Oral History Interview, 15 September 1966, John F. Kennedy Presidential Library and Museum.

182 Hugh McCann, Oral History Interview, 8 August 1966, John F. Kennedy Presidential Library and Museum.

183 Thomas J. Kiernan, Oral History Interview, 5 August 1966, John F. Kennedy Presidential Library and Museum.

184 Ted Sorensen, author interview, New York, 16 March 2009.

INDEX

Page numbers in *italics* indicate images

ACKNOWLEDGEMENTS

In many ways, this is the hard part …

When the idea was mooted that I might write a book, I thought that's what it would remain, an idea. As a book lover I'd always felt I'd be a reader, not a writer, and so it was critical to live by Grandfather's credo, "Always surround yourself with people who are better than you," which I've done all my life. I will name-check a selection of them here but to the ones whose names are not listed, I apologise but please know that I'm grateful for the guidance and friendship that kept this show on the road.

Let's start at the beginning by thanking Jenny Heller at HarperCollins who provided the "Yes We Can" spirit that got the book going. To her, the irrepressible Moira Reilly in Dublin and all the HarperCollins people, I offer my thanks.

To my colleagues on both the radio show (what was *The Tubridy Show*) and the *Late Late Show*, I'm sorry for being an absentee presenter but I had to steal every hour I could. For your patience, generosity and support, I am so grateful.

I've spent a lot of time in libraries in the past eighteen months. They are vital places, staffed by dedicated and important people who feed the minds of a nation. The beautiful National Library of Ireland, my local library in Dalkey and the reference library at RTE were part-time homes. I should also like to thank Kate Boylan and Laurie Austin at the John F. Kennedy Presidential Library in Boston. To the staff in all these wonderful places, I appreciate what you do.

Even on holidays, I stole time in quiet rooms with a pot of tea and a sandwich for company. Some chapters were written in my favourite bolthole, the Abbeyglen Castle Hotel in my beloved Clifden. To Brian Hughes and staff, cheers!

For the gusts of confidence blown into my weary sails, I salute the history boys, a wily triumvirate of Mark Duncan, Paul Rouse and Sean Kearns. I love your love of the past.

One of the pleasures I discovered was the treasure trove that lies with Catríona Crowe and her helpful staff at the National Archives of Ireland. It was my Indiana Jones moment to sit there rummaging through yellowed files until a sparkling diamond appeared – a wonderful feeling. Thanks too to Sara Smyth at the National Photographic Archive, Sandra McDermott at the National Library of Ireland, Seamus Helferty at the UCD School of History & Archives, and Stan Shields who photographed JFK in Galway, thanks for the scones. Photographer Michael O'Reilly, your work is much appreciated. I was blessed by the cooperation of so many people in the search for appropriate photographs: Susan Kennedy at Lensmen; Denise O'Connor Murphy at the Denis O'Connor Photographic Archive, Wexford; Darren Loughnane at Getty Images; and Anne Kearney at the *Irish Examiner*.

I was inundated with envelopes stuffed with memorabilia from the time that were sent to me by listeners and viewers who heard about the book, and I'd like to thank them so much for taking the time to help out.

Kate Collins and Niamh Kirwan kept the ship afloat in a low-key but important way. Also, they listened while I talked. Grazie!

To the man who makes things happen, a constant support and a close friend, my consiglieri and agent, Noel Kelly, I'm glad I'm in your gang…

I lost someone dear to me in the past year who would have enjoyed this book, as we shared an interest in American politics and history in general and the Kennedy story in particular. He was a mentor and he was my friend. To Gerry Ryan, I miss you as much as I thank you.

To my cousin, Dorothy Tubridy, an unsung heroine in the efforts to bring President Kennedy to Ireland, thank you for the stories. At the Kennedy Homestead in Dunganstown, Patrick Grennan and his family were always welcoming hosts and helpful with Kennedy lore.

James Robert Carroll's *One of Ourselves* proved a most helpful guide to the story of the 1963 visit, while Diarmaid Ferriter's *Judging Dev* inspired the illustrated nature of this book.

Closer to home, I want to thank my friends who sat there as I mutated into a Kennedy pub bore. I would be lost without my friends. Michael and Kirsty, Neil and Suzanne, Mark and Tara, Nialler, and Sinead in NYC, thank you and let's keep it dark.

To Ann-Marie, for being such a good mother and important role model to the little dotes, thank you so much.

Even closer to home, I want to put it in print that I love my family and what they have meant and continue to mean to me. Dad brought me to museums when I was young and opened my eyes to the past and all its possibilities for the future. Mum had the radio on in every room in the house, and so a career was born. The mix of politics, history and family has always interested me, and my parents allowed that to happen.

Judith, Niall, Rachel and Garrett have been my constants in an incredibly shifting world. They also put up with lots of Kennedy stories but weren't shy when it came to telling me to shut up.

To the next generation: Eloise, Molly, Christopher and Sean-Felipe, read lots please.

To Aoibhinn, the patient and elegant lady who held my hand throughout an extraordinary eighteen months, I don't know how you did it but I will always be grateful for such generosity.

And finally, to the girls for whom my heart has unlimited love, Ella and Julia, who became fun-size experts on the Kennedy presidency. The first word I saw Julia write was "Kennedy" which she saw on the pencil she was writing with. Ella can name all the presidents from FDR to Obama, thanks to a presidential souvenir tea towel in the kitchen. Girls, you're up next and if you and your friends are to carry the torch for the next generation, then the future is safe.

RT, Dublin, August 2010

PICTURE CREDITS

pp. vi–ix: UCD Archives, P150/2841; pp. x–xi, 106–7, 128–9, 140-1, 166–7, 170–1, 204–5, 234–5, 246–7, 250, 252–3: Robert Knudsen/John F. Kennedy Presidential Library and Museum, Boston; pp. xiv–xv: NLI, IND 95327 R; pp. xviii–1, 13: Getty Images; pp. 4–5, 6, 17, 82–3: John F. Kennedy Presidential Library and Museum, Boston; p. 9: © John F. Kennedy Library Foundation; pp. 14–15, 31: NLI, LROY 03624; pp. 20–1: UCD Archives, P150/2179; p. 22: UCD Archives, P150/2842; p. 25: Hy Peskin for *Look* magazine/John F. Kennedy Presidential Library and Museum, Boston; p. 32: Patrick Grennan; p. 37: Carl Mydans/Time & Life Pictures/Getty Images; pp. 40, 60–1: Abbie Rowe, 1 National Park Service/John F. Kennedy Presidential Library and Museum, Boston; pp. 42–3, 51, 68: Abbie Rowe/ White House/John F. Kennedy Presidential Library and Museum, Boston; p. 45: UCD Archives, P150/3497; p. 57: NAI, D/Taoiseach S1740 a63; p. 59: NAI, DFA, Washington Embassy D27; p. 64: Cecil Stoughton, 1 White House/John Fitzgerald Kennedy Presidential Library and Museum, Boston; p. 67: Robert Knudsen, 1 White House/John Fitzgerald Kennedy Library; pp. 76–7, 274–5: Time & Life Pictures/Getty Images; pp. 86–7: NLI, IND 95145; pp. 89, 103, 148–9: Michael O'Reilly; pp. 90–1: NLI, IND 95162; p. 92: NLI, IND 95456; p. 94, 184–5, 212–13, 216: Lensmen; pp. 100–1: NLI, IND 95180; p. 114: NLI, IND JFK 95201; p. 118: NLI, IND 95241; pp. 136-7 from the private collection of Mrs Mary Cullinan; pp. 125, 132–3: John Dominis/Time & Life Pictures/Getty Images; p. 130, 139, 140, 144–5: The Denis O'Connor Archive, Wexford; p. 135, 175, 218–19: Cecil Stoughton/John F. Kennedy Presidential Library and Museum, Boston; p. 151: NLI, IND 95299; p. 152: NLI, IND 95291; pp. 156–7: NLI, IND 95335; p. 159: NLI, IND 95329; pp. 160–1: NLI, IND 95336; p. 169: courtesy of *Irish Examiner*, ref. 892M; pp. 176–7: NLI, IND 95410; p. 176–7: NLI, IND 9538a; p. 181: NLI, IND 95454; pp. 190–1: NLI, 95216; p. 192: Bettman/Corbis; p. 207: UCD Archives, LA30-PH-065; pp. 208–9: NLI, IND 95432; p. 221: NLI, IND 95482; pp. 226–7, 232: Stan Shields; p. 241: *Limerick Leader*; pp. 255, 256: Irish Press plc; pp. 258–9: Abbie Rowe/ John Fitzgerald Kennedy Library, Boston; p. 267, 268: NAI, D/Taoiseach S 17401 d 63; p. 269: NAI, D/Taoiseach S 17400 d 63; pp. 271, 272: Terrence Spencer/Time & Life Pictures/Getty Images; pp. 276–7: NLI, IND 95412; p. 283: Tim Sloan/AFP/Getty Images; pp. 286–7: Keystone/Getty Images.

While every effort has been made to trace the owners of copyright material reproduced herein and secure permissions, the publishers would like to apologise for any omissions and will be pleased to incorporate missing acknowledgements in any future edition of this book.